ARIES ☆ SAGITTARIUS

What would it be like if Superman hooked up with Hercules? Cosmic love, cosmic fights, cosmic rescues in the skies over Metropolis. So what if a building gets leveled—neither of these guys *meant* any harm. It takes the embarrassment of putting their super feet in their super mouths to bring them back to earth.

GEMINI ☆ LEO

Each member of this pair will always think the other is a little ditzy. To Gemini, Leo's single-mindedness and sincerity seem supremely unsavvy. Leo thinks that all of that Gemini flitting and manipulation are distractions from what really matters. So why would a Gemini and Leo come together? It is because they fulfill deep needs for each other.
And because ditzy can be cute.

SCORPIO ☆ AQUARIUS

This is a nervous romance. Two men, with little in common other than a mile-wide streak of stubborness and an inability to color inside the lines, come together to frighten the bejesus out of each other between sudden, uncontrollable attacks of sexual passion. If that isn't love . . .

gay
astrology

THE COMPLETE
RELATIONSHIP GUIDE
FOR GAY MEN

By Michael Yawney

GRAND CENTRAL
PUBLISHING

NEW YORK   BOSTON

Grand Central Publishing
Hachette Book Group USA
237 Park Avenue
New York, NY 10017

Visit our Web site at www.HachetteBookGroupUSA.com.

Printed in the United States of America

First Edition: June 2001
10 9 8 7 6 5

Grand Central Publishing is a division of Hachette Book Group USA, Inc.
The Grand Central Publishing name and logo is a trademark of Hachette
Book Group USA, Inc.

Library of Congress Cataloging-in-Publication Data
Yawney, Michael.
    Gay astrology : the complete relationship guide for gay
men / Michael Yawney.
        p.   cm.
    ISBN 978-0-446-67739-4
    1. Astrology and homosexuality. 2. Gay male couples—
Miscellanea. 3. Love—Miscellanea. I. Title

BF1729.H66 Y38 2001
133.5'086'642—dc21
                                                    2001017540

Cover design by Michael Storrings
Book design and text composition by Ellen Gleeson

*This book is dedicated to a group of people without whom
neither it, nor its author, would exist:
Katharine Bitler
Robert L. Johnson
Christopher Renstrom,
and most of all
Henry Hample, the best husband a boy could ever have*

CONTENTS

The Signs
LOVING YOUR MAN AND THE FIVE FACES

The Relationships

CONTENTS

CONTENTS

CONTENTS

INTRODUCTION

What makes a gay astrology book different from a straight one?

The question is a good one. After all, an astrological sign is what it is. Should it not be the same for anyone, gay or straight?

The answer is that the basic qualities of a sun sign are the same for everyone. However, these qualities do express themselves differently depending on the specifics of someone's life. A Capricorn in boot camp behaves differently from one working in a hair salon. In each case the behavior will be Capricorn, but the particulars will be different.

And gay lives are different from straight ones in many ways. Straight people do not need to worry about coming out, relationships with competing male egos, parenting without society's support, and a whole pile of issues that every gay man faces every day of his life. A gay astrology book should deal with the particulars of gay life and how each sun sign deals with these concerns.

But gay lives are also different from each other. As are the lives of various people with the same sun sign.

Each sun sign represents an energy that has to be acted out by someone of that sign in order for that person to be happy. A Leo leather daddy and a girly-girl Leo might act out their sun sign's energy in ways that are very far apart—but still unmistakably Leo. A gay astrology book should recognize the diversity of the gay community and show how there are many different ways to be a sun sign. Just like there are many different ways of being gay.

(Quick explanation: If you do not know what a sun sign is, it is the astrological sign that you look up when you check your horoscope. Each person has many signs in his or her astrological chart—one for each celestial body and other indicators in the sky when the person was born. This book will not get technical and will only deal with sun signs. The other signs do affect behavior and the psychological makeup of an individual, but the sun sign is the most important factor in a chart.)

Now, on to a bigger question: Does astrology work? In my experience, yes. *Why* does astrology work? I have absolutely no idea.

Yet it does work. Most people have noticed that their best friends tend to be of one sign and that persons of another sign will make their skin crawl. Workplaces are usually dominated by one or two signs. The reason is that most people have signdar. It kind of works like gaydar. And, like gaydar, you might be using it without realizing that you are. Here is a good example. I worked for a Libra who hated astrology and purposely avoided looking at applicants' birthdates. She also avoided asking about sexual orientation. She made six to ten hires a year. A full 50 percent were Libras! Nearly half the women hired were lesbians! This boss had fully operational signdar and gaydar.

If you have never done it, it is a good exercise to make a list of all your ex-boyfriends. Even the ones you had the most casual, short-lived relationships with. (For some of you this may take a few hours.)

Next to their names, write their astrological signs. (Come on. You probably know it for most of them.) Chances are that one or two signs will dominate the list. Flip to the part of this book that tells about those signs and you will find a pretty good description of the kind of men that attract you.

When astrology does not work, it is usually because we are looking for the wrong information. The sun sign gives information on a certain part of the personality. It describes the conscious part of the psyche. It expresses who one believes himself to be. It will tell how one thinks and solves problems. It will tell what motivates one to act. It will tell where a person's energy in life comes from.

The sun sign alone cannot tell you whom you will be "compatible" with. It can predict strengths and weaknesses in a relationship. It is very good at predicting what common interests a couple will share, what their arguments will be about, and what patterns they will fall into in daily life.

Astrology can predict whom one might fall in love with. (The moon, Venus, and Saturn are the big indicators for the love bond.) However, for that you need a complete chart for both parties, and an astrologer with top-notch chart analyzing skills.

And is it not more fun to fall in love on your own without any astrological assistance?

Astrology should never become a substitute for your own experience. Rather than using astrology to anticipate and manipulate the future, it can most effectively be used as a tool toward understanding what lies underneath events and relationships in your life—past, present, and future.

This book will not tell you what signs are compatible. Instead it will describe the challenges and joys that await couples with specific combinations of sun signs. This book will discuss what the various bonds between signs feel like.

One thing astrology teaches is that everyone is lovable. No one is unsuitable for having a relationship. It is just a matter of finding the right partner. It is my hope that this book can help you in your search.

How to Use This Book

Loving Your Man

You already know how to use this part. This part will tell you what to expect from each sun sign when it comes to relationships. It runs from first encounter to breakup.

This is a good place to look if you are trying to snare someone of a particular sign. Or if you are trying to figure out why it did not work out with your ex.

There is info on how a sign handles safe sex, coming-out, and gay parenting. You will find that each sign has its own way of looking at these issues and at how to be a gay man in this new millennium.

The Five Faces

There are many different kinds of individuals within any sign. There are also many different kinds of gay men. So it can be hard to figure out how a particular guy fits into this whole astrological thing.

This may help. Look at the *Five Faces* section of any sign in this book. Each of these sections describes five gay archetypes and how that sign might express itself through those archetypes. Decide which face is closest to the man you are thinking of, then check how that description matches up with the man.

The Relationships

There are seventy-eight different combinations of signs in relationships. (Unless you count ménages à trois.) Each is described here. As mentioned in the introduction, you will find the joys and challenges of each pairing described.

It would be a mistake to discourage any of the seventy-eight pairings from giving it a try. Every one of them will work for *someone*.

gay
astrology

The Signs

LOVING YOUR MAN
AND THE FIVE FACES

Aries

LOVING YOUR ARIES

For a car, going from 0 to 60 in a second is a good thing, but when a guy goes straight from "Hello, what is your name?" to "Do you swallow?" you kind of wish *he* had an emergency brake.

Not every Aries is stupid enough to actually voice his every smarmy thought, but he is thinking them. He considers every man he meets a potential notch on the bedpost.

That is until he decides a guy is lifelong love, soul-mate material.

If it were not for his childlike openness, he would be insufferable rather than cute. Aries even looks like a toddler as he rushes around with herky-jerky staccato steps, tripping over furniture, never at rest. Mr. Ram is always in a hurry, because he wants to cram as much living as possible into each day.

Even if he takes his time in coming on to you, he will not waste his efforts on small talk. If this is going anywhere, he needs to know that you can stimulate his mind as well. He will solicit your opinions, challenge them, then lead you over an intellectual obstacle course.

Then he will decide whether or not to sweep you off your feet. You can be as aggressive as you want in your pursuit of Aries, but in his mind you are a passive prize waiting to be won by a guy with cajones.

ATTRACTING AN ARIES

The techniques for nabbing Mr. Ram are counterintuitive. The man wants everything NOW! NOW! NOW! but only values men who make him wait, wait, wait. If you are too eager for him, he will write you off as a nobody with no life of your own. Though it appears that Aries wants to dominate his mate, it is the struggle for dominance that excites him, not the actual achieving of it.

For Aries the world is a battlefield and the most emotionally powerful relationships are combative. He is like a puppy who bites and claws at his brothers for the fun of it. The unconquerable man keeps his interest longer than the one who rolls over and plays dead.

For Mr. Ram, your other interests and commitments can be fascinating obstacles to winning you—but only if he believes he has a chance to win. If he feels that you are a hopeless cause, he will give up and move on to the next guy.

In romance, Aries does not show the same impatience he does elsewhere. If he thinks you are a possible big love, he will go as slowly as necessary. He fears that sudden moves might provoke from you a no that you will not be able to take back.

Two fantasies color Mr. Ram's love life—that of the knight and that of the patron.

Aries likes to see himself as a knight in shining armor rescuing others from danger. He is a sucker for a hard-luck story because he imagines that he is the one who can supply a happy ending. Standing up for another against injustice or relieving undeserved poverty arouse Mr. Ram's protective instincts, which are only a step away from love. Even if these actions only translate to yelling at the guy who stole your parking space, or buying you a drink, they still move him. When starting a relationship, Aries likes to know that the other person will be better off for having him on his side.

The flip side is that Aries wants a patron of his own. Bills, housekeeping, cooking, health, and the everyday concerns annoy Mr. Ram. For every one of these areas that he handles competently there is another that he makes a mess of. This sign feels that it should be above the practical and the common, so, though he will not admit it, Aries dreams of finding a man who will buy his groceries, balance his checkbook, and sweep the dust bunnies out from under his bed. He will overlook many character flaws in a man who is willing to take care of him.

DATING

If you show a lot of enthusiasm for Aries' interests, he will pretend that he cares about yours. The only sure way to make him really care is by the element of surprise. A spontaneous trip to a hockey game or the Philharmonic can kindle an interest in sports or music that a planned trip will not. Anything spur-of-the-moment or adventurous can sway him.

In the normal course of dating, Aries considers himself a Henry Higgins, expanding your limited horizons. You might have written a book on the ballet, played in a rock band, and won the Tony, but Aries still thinks you knew nothing of culture until he showed you the way.

Meeting his friends, you will probably find them quite different from what Mr. Ram described. He is an abysmal judge of character. Aries' personality is obvious and out front. Since he thinks that everyone is like himself, Aries expects that what you see is what you get. The suspicion necessary for noticing hidden layers is alien to Mr. Ram.

Every Aries believes that he has a special destiny. Love is often part of it. As you spend more time together, if you notice Aries telling friends cute stories about you rather than about himself, that means you have become part of his special destiny. That means it is love.

Though Aries is malice-free, he can hurt the ones he loves. The problem is that he often does not notice the feelings of others unless they write them in neon for him. Even when he is aware of your feelings, he is more concerned with your concrete actions than with the emotional state you are in. So your pain and indignation do not count until you slash Mr. Ram's tires.

When you do act on your feelings, Aries will be relieved, since your earlier hints and innuendos mystified him. He needs open conflict. Though he screams and yells louder than you, do not worry that he will end the relationship. Real Aries anger is silent and icy. When he stares at you wordlessly and turns to the door—only then do you need to do repair work. And it is not that hard to do, since Aries likes to be the big man and forgive.

During your fights, he may lash out with vicious, wounding comments. However, when it is over, Aries will expect full forgiveness from you. Unable to bear a grudge himself, it does not occur to him that your resentment might linger.

Aries treats each day with you as a new beginning. He forgets the wrongs you have done him—and the good. By ignoring the past, he hopes to be able to fall in love with you all over again.

Clueless as this sounds, it actually works for him.

SEX

Instant arousal. Instant turnoff.

The unpredictability of the Aries libido is a source of delight and frustration to his lover. You never know when it will start, when it will finish, or what will happen in between.

Since he is easily bored, Aries needs to switch between being top and bottom, and to rotate his fetishes. If you are the kind of guy who likes to find a position and stick to it—or if you like to find a room of the house and stick to it—Aries is not your man.

There are few things you cannot persuade him to try. For him, experiencing something for the first time with another man is an unshakable bond. Even though his memory is usually poor, he can catalog the first time he ever tried any sexual act and recall in vivid detail the man he did it with.

His sexuality is restless and never satisfied, since the act itself is never as good as the ultimate extreme he pictures in his mind. Aries does not realize that fantasies cannot be real, so he blames his own lack of prowess for limiting the pleasure you share. The erotic braggadocio is a cover-up.

Safe Sex

Thought and communication have no place in sex. Or so he thinks.

For Aries, sex is about relating through the body. If he has to talk with you, that turns the transcendence down a bit. It is best to make the negotiations before the lovemaking momentum gets going. If Aries needs to stop for discussion, he might not get going again.

Aries wants to make love like you are the first two people to discover it. Rote fantasies do not work—originality is demanded. Mr. Ram adores the exchange of bodily fluids, but if a form of erotic play is new to him, he will never miss the old in-out.

Since he started having sex so young, you would expect him to be more confident. And the guilt-free abandon he demonstrates in flagrante makes him seem a total bandit of the sheets. However, Aries cannot accept the limits of the body. This is wonderful when working out since it allows him to exercise beyond his strength and push through exhaustion (though this is a good way to injure yourself). It is less wonderful in bed because by not accepting the limits, Aries cannot see the possibilities—he is often embarrassed by his body in the slower, more tender parts of lovemaking. The abandon he shows during the heated moments is how he transcends this—he turns off his brain to become an animal.

LIVING TOGETHER

If you do most of the chores that keep the home running, then why does it feel like *his* place?

Aries just naturally makes all the big household decisions himself. It is not that he considers himself smarter than you. It's just that the quality of your judgment never comes into his thoughts at all. When Aries acts it is full steam ahead, undistracted by the courtesy and fear that makes most partners hesitate.

To make your plans for the home come through, you can try to convince him that your ideas were actually his ideas—though I suspect that only works if you are living in a sitcom. The best method is to simply do what you want to do. His philosophy has always been that it is easier to ask forgiveness afterward than to ask permission before. This philosophy will work for you as well. It is being part of your scheme and having to follow your lead that threatens Aries' equilibrium. A fait accompli is just dandy with him.

At this stage, you are becoming part of Aries' mission in life. The competition between you is limited to who makes the decorating decisions and who does the dishes. Out in the world, you could not have a stronger supporter than Aries, and he is determined to see you make your mark—even if you do not want to. For Aries, if it is not me-against-you, then it has to be us-against-them.

When Aries does not get the recognition he deserves, you will hear him give vent to great bitterness. The eternal optimist is more crushed than the cynic when he finds out that life is unfair. At these times, you will be required to play the parental role, to build up Aries to face the world again. Aries is supremely image conscious, and the only thing worse for

Gay Parenting

Though Aries wants to be a hero to his child, he does not expect the child to be a Mini-Me. It is the individuality of the child that Aries values.

Aries is a terrific companion and guide for any child, but is short on coddling skills. He will stay home from work to make the chicken soup when the little one is sick, but the moment the temperature breaks, the kid had better be ready to make up for the missed softball practices. Mr. Ram puts too much pressure on himself as a gay dad to out-butch the straight dads. This forces him to be tougher than necessary on his child.

Because he sees his child as an investment in the future, Aries will do anything to provide the best opportunities. Few parents have the energy to work extra hours for tuition, then drive to soccer practice, then help with homework, then read a bedtime story after fetching the little one umpteen glasses of water. But Aries will not let himself do any less. Even if he gets little support from his family or community, Mr. Ram has the stubbornness and the stamina to do it right.

him than losing his confidence is if others can see that he has lost it.

The routine of living with you destroys some of Aries' illusions. He thought the two of you were going to sleep intertwined every night and be out dancing every weekend. Then he learns that it takes work to keep a relationship fresh. Though Aries may be lazy around the house, he is not emotionally lazy. He can make a concentrated effort to keep you emotionally satisfied—if he can figure out what it takes to do so. If he makes mistakes it is because he is dense when it comes to reading you, not because the effort is lacking.

So give the guy a break and be explicit.

BREAKING UP

Admit it. You got away with a lot.

Aries usually does not notice when his partner hides something from him. So you can go along being adored by Mr. Ram while secretly doing the super, holding Satanic rituals in the basement, and/or planning to move to Nepal.

But then you drop a chair on his foot or break a door—and he knows it is all over. Aries looks for symbols all the time. When he found a pair of potato chips stuck together he said it meant the two of you should also be one, but this time the symbol signifies the end of your relationship. You can argue that he is reading too much into a small detail. He is. But Aries often reaches the right conclusion for the wrong reasons.

Right or wrong, what Aries believes is always more important than actual facts. That is why documentation of debts and promises he has forgotten do not phase him—if he has truly forgotten, you cannot convince him they exist.

For Aries the best defense is a good offense. He fights dirty, making irrelevant but venomous comments designed to hit you where you are most vulnerable. Though he has always been there with a helping hand, and though he is no stranger to self-pity, your very real needs are now framed as selfish malingering.

When you fight back in a clear, cold, focused manner, Aries does not understand how you could be so destructive. Focused negativity is incomprehensible to him, because his darker actions are always impulsive and never planned. Using strategy to demolish his arguments seems to him to be unfeeling and black-hearted.

The difficulty you face while arguing is that Aries can sympathize but he cannot empathize. He can see the bad things that have happened to you, but he cannot imagine what it is like to be you. So he remains firmly lodged in his

Coming Out

The truth is like a hand grenade in Aries' pocket. If he keeps it there and trips, he can do himself a lot of damage. If he pulls it out, he wants to throw it at someone and see it explode.

Staying closeted takes a huge effort on Mr. Ram's part—and is usually unsuccessful. Though Aries likes to think he is so big-time butch that no one would guess he is gay, most people get a whiff of lavender from him since he is no good at pretending.

Coming out is an aggressive act for Aries. The aggression is how he resolves his ambivalence about being gay, since even the queeniest Aries has a machismo thing going on. If no one gets upset that Aries is gay, he will force the issue until they do.

Being semi-closeted does not work for this sign. It has to be all or nothing.

own point of view, unable to look at the situation from another perspective.

Any rupture with Aries can be repaired with well-spoken apologies—except one. If you make Aries doubt himself, he is gone. In most conflict Aries' response is first anger, then hurt. When he doubts himself, there is no anger, no hurt, only silence. He has no defense but to turn his back on you and walk away.

THE FIVE FACES OF GAY ARIES

DRAG QUEEN ARIES

The divine Miss Ram is a star and the world owes her a living. At least that is what she says. Others would be embarrassed to admit such high self-esteem but Drag Queen Aries is proud of it.

Yet if she really loves herself that much, why does she wear her femininity like a chip on the shoulder? Her manner is a mocking parody of womanly softness.

Too much drama makes a diva draining company after a while, no matter how generous she is with the compliments. Aries' need to be center stage makes her keep upping the couture ante until the look-at-me impulse triumphs over taste.

Though she may turn into a sloppy harridan by sunrise, her vivacity keeps her trotting around in her stilettos long after more sensible girls have gone home to soak their feet.

By the next night, she has purposely lost the number of that guy who seemed like such a good idea twenty-four hours earlier. Sometimes getting the number is enough and actual sex will add nothing to her conquest.

DOMINANT ARIES

Nothing for Dominant Aries is as exciting as having another man looking up at him with the word "Sir" on his lips.

Aries loves to go where his bodily impulses lead him. The freedom of being a dominant top lets him give over completely to his impulses. He can get carried away, but when things get dangerously intense he turns on a dime, shifting to some other type of play.

Sometimes the orders get spit out too fast for the submissive to follow. Sometimes the submissive fails to satisfy for other reasons. Rather than ruining the scenario, this enlivens it. In fact, a defiant bottom that needs to be humbled is Mr. Ram's favorite kind. After all, topping a pussy-boy is easy; turning a butch guy into a pussy is an accomplishment.

It is not the ingenuity Dominant Aries shows in devising humiliations that is frightening. Rather it is the obvious emotional satisfaction he gets from debasing others. Yes, it may just be a game, but the game is real.

ACTIVIST ARIES

You cannot keep a good man down, if he is Activist Aries. The discouragements and setbacks that make other men give up bring out the best in this boy. When he knows that right is on his side, he will never take no for an answer.

Every Aries needs a cause to get behind, because he believes that one man can make a difference—if that man is him. Impatient with group action and the political process, Aries does what he can in everyday life to bring about change. After all, you never know if writing to your congressman does any good, but when speaking face-to-face with your neighbor the effect you have is plain.

Though Aries never loses energy, he can lose interest. The quality of the opposition is what decides it. The opposition is like a sex partner in that there has to be chemistry. A bad fight is like bad sex—it is best to leave ASAP, without waiting for breakfast.

GUPPY ARIES

A man who hates paperwork and has trouble following through on what he starts should not succeed in corporate life. Yet Guppy Aries does quite nicely for himself.

Though Aries has no interest in being a good little worker bee, making the boss man glad, or winning the affection of subordinates, he does have an ornery competitive spirit. The need to prove himself motivates Aries to throw himself wholeheartedly into what is for him an alien environment.

Aries thrives on the concrete recognition that the business world gives. Inner satisfaction is fine, but the titles, promotions, and raises are even better. Though not adept at negotiating backroom office politics, Aries' instinct for jumping in when others screw up propels him upward in the company hierarchy.

He shines most at the beginning of a project. His imagination and energy jump-start new enterprises. The opportunity to be a pioneer, to do something never done before, is irresistible to Aries.

Seeing himself as ahead of the crowd, Aries is unconflicted about being out at work. Anything that sets him apart from his coworker is good in his view.

GYM BUNNY ARIES

Unless he feels good about his body, Aries will not feel good about himself. So though Gym Bunny Aries starts out trying to bulk up as a macho challenge to himself, it has mental health benefits as well.

But what really hooks him is the looks he gets from other men. Aries is vain about his appearance but is also ashamed of it. Then, when he goes through the effort to sculpt himself into something magnificent, he no longer feels shame—he has earned the right to be vain, stuck-up, self-involved, and egotistical. If other guys have a problem with his attitude, it is because they do not have the balls to go to the gym and do what he did.

The Gym Bunny Aries thinks that sensitivity, gentility, and vulnerability are for sissies. His muscles are his armor. He would do better, though, to let down his guard.

After all, a man's worth can be measured by things other than body-fat ratio and dick size.

Taurus

APRIL 21–MAY 21

LOVING YOUR TAURUS

No subtlety here.

Taurus's come-on is explicit and clear. If you are not equally direct, you will see clouds of confusion in his lovely liquid eyes. The hints and coyness that usually go with flirting will not work.

A solid man with solid values, Taurus lacks the surprising quirks and intriguing depths that can make a first meeting scintillating. However, his honesty and sexual stamina make him an excellent candidate for Mr. Right (or for Mr. Right Now).

He may be a little thick around the middle and slow moving, but it is clear that he knows how to use his body when he wants to. And it is kind of cute how seriously he takes everything you say. Give him a chance. Most men are not what they appear to be—Mr. Bull is.

Once he has decided that he wants you, Taurus is forceful. Still, you need to help him along. He belongs to the one-line-fits-all school of seduction. The tactics he uses on you are tried and true, having been tested successfully on many other men before you. If you respond to him in an unexpected way, he may not know what the next step is. So stick to his script. It should be easy, since he makes it plain just what he expects of you at each stage of the game.

ATTRACTING A TAURUS

It helps if you are pretty. And available.

There is no game-playing with Taurus. He wants you because he finds you physically attractive and thinks you are willing to have sex with him. Though he likes a little bit of holding back, he will not pursue any man who seems truly unbeddable.

That does not mean he is easy, though.

He is afraid of being taken advantage of, so before he invites you into his bedroom he wants to be sure you are safe. The easiest way to win his trust is to buy him things. Since he is not very intuitive, he looks for tangible proof of another man's feeling and character. Spending money to buy things for him (especially big, sweet, edible things) is a clear sign that you value him as a person.

Taurus understands money more than emotion, so he often looks at himself as a commodity for sale. Though Mr. Bull does not rule out poor boys as possible lovers, rich men who can spoil him have the advantage.

Materialistic though he is, do not worry that Taurus will dump you for the nearest sugar daddy. To him a commitment is a commitment. If he says he will stay with you, he will. However, this also means that you, right from the start, will be expected to live up to your words. If you lie or weasel out of a promise, Taurus will start thinking of you as untrustworthy. And once Mr. Bull pigeonholes you, it is nearly impossible to make him change his opinion.

Taurus is the sign least interested in the murky depths of human psychology. Yet it is also a sign that is suspicious of things it does not understand. Thus when he meets a man whose character is filled with contradictions and mixed motives, Taurus runs the other way. He is also dismissive of people who are unlike himself. Mr. Bull wants security and comfort; those who live for abstract principles seem flakey and those who willingly choose poverty seem irresponsible. Remember that Tauruses are herd animals that want to be with like-minded creatures and not with anyone who will challenge their worldview.

For all his levelheadedness, there is a side of Taurus that yearns for magic. Though he claims not to believe in unseen forces, he wants to be swept away by something more powerful than himself. Because his sex drive is strong, it is usually in the romantic arena where Taurus feels himself controlled by the unexplainable. Passion can and will make him abandon common sense.

DATING

Taurus divides men into two categories: possible lays and possible boyfriends. How do you know which you are? If he enjoys hearing about your exploits with other men, you are only a lay. If he touches you in a way that says "Back off, he's mine" the moment another man looks at you, you are boyfriend material.

The difference is possession. You have probably noticed the pride he takes in all those things he owns. He watches you like a hawk in his apartment to make sure you will not break anything. Mr. Bull thinks of those he cares about in the same way—they are precious objects to be jealously protected.

If he cherishes you, you will see it in his actions more than his words. His idea of romance is old-fashioned on the heterosexual model. Heart-shaped boxes of candy, roses, and breakfast in bed should tell you where the relationship is going. Physical affection also will tell you his feelings. If he loves the feel of your skin, that means he loves you.

When he does speak, believe what he says. (Do you really think he has enough imagination to lie?) No Taurus can say "I love you forever," then dump you the next day. His words are his bond. He waits to speak until he is ready to commit.

Also, Taurus is a savvy negotiator. He knows that if you put your feelings on the table first, he is in a better bargaining position to get a commitment out of you. He may be falling for you, but he will not let you take advantage of his feelings if they are not mutual.

Though he prefers to stay at home with you, it is easy to get him off his butt and out the door if you promise to buy him a big meal in a good restaurant. (Chocolate and cheese are his major weaknesses.) You will also find that he enjoys nature and the great outdoors. However, he is lazy, so do not expect him to jump at the prospect of a ten-mile hike in the woods. New activities in general will not excite him. Stick to the familiar—if he liked it once, he will love it a second time.

When your Taurus starts doing anything that you do not like, NIP IT IN THE BUD, *IMMEDIATELY!!!* He is a creature of habit, so if you do not like him pinching your ass, playing loud music, or whatever, make absolutely sure to let him know the first time. Each time he repeats it makes it much much much harder to get him to stop. Highlight this paragraph and read it at least once a day, because it contains the most important advice you will ever get for dealing with Mr. Bull.

On the plus side, if you become a habit with Taurus, he will stick by you through the worst difficulties and work hard to keep you in his life.

SEX

The hang-ups and insecurities that trouble the sex lives of other men do not trouble Mr. Bull. For him it is simple. You look good, it feels good, so why not?

Taurus expresses himself better with his body than with words. So even though mutual pleasure is enough to justify lovemaking for Taurus, the act will never be empty. All his feelings will be evident in his touch.

Fantasy does little for him. Mr. Bull is into the real thing. He actually enjoys the taste of sweat and the smell of cum. Thus all your make-believe filthy talk will do little, but showing some skin will drive him wild. He is a man with few kinks other than a huge fetish for real, live, naked flesh.

Taurus lovemaking is long and slow. But it is not gentle. All the passion that he conceals in daily life under a calm front comes out sexually.

Once he begins, it is hard for him to stop. He will suck and suck on that one spot that drives you mad for what seems like forever. Taurus lives in the moment, and if the moment is pleasurable he will extend it beyond every normal limit.

Though he never seems to lose interest in sex, you might. Because he does not enjoy exploring new sensations, love-

Safe Sex

The practical side of Taurus accepts the necessity for safe sex. And after the first few times, he stops thinking about it and does it automatically.

The temptation happens when Taurus feels the only way to keep some wild cutie is through high-risk behavior. When Taurus is horny, he believes the guy who says, "I was just tested and I am negative." Also, when in a relationship, Taurus's talent for denial lets him ignore signs of a partner's infidelity.

The wiser Taurus uses his inborn stubbornness to steamroll those who would have him go raw.

making can get stale. The unfortunate part is that Taurus is not very observant and may think you are perfectly satisfied. You need to talk about sex and your needs. Unlike other men, Mr. Bull will not be offended if you voice your concerns. With his matter-of-fact approach to sex, you can speak freely about your erotic desires. You can even make requests and he will not mind. He might not fulfill them, but he will not fault you for asking.

LIVING TOGETHER

Taurus would prefer that you move into his place, as long as you promise never to touch his things. He hates moving and he hates sharing, but he hates being apart from those he loves even more.

Living with Taurus is living with beauty and comfort. He has a passion for interior decorating. Though his taste is far from cutting edge, his rooms have a lived-in elegance with excellent feng shui. However, though he has many stubbornly held opinions, those on household decor and management are the most stubbornly held. In other words, you are stuck with his good taste whether you like it or not.

Even the poorest Taurus has certain little luxuries that he will not do without. Though this may seem spendthrift, he will not give them up. Mr. Bull rarely indulges in the self-criticism or second-guessing that might force him to change his behavior.

Mr. Bull is oblivious. You can hint that he should pick up his dirty clothes. You can try guilting him into buying the groceries. No result. Though he understands that he has obligations toward you and the home, Taurus will not go out of his way to figure out what they are. You must tell him exactly what you want from him in so many words.

Then of course you will face the wall of Taurus smugness. There will be remarks about how silly little you expected him to read your mind. Then, if you make less than him, he will remind you that he is the major breadwinner for the home, so you had better make up your financial deficit by doing extra housework. In the Taurus mind it is he who pays the bills, who calls the shots.

Still, daily life with Taurus is calm since he hates being angry. (When he gets mad he transforms into the Incredible Hulk and cannot control himself.) Mr. Bull sits back in his special chair with a beer, chips, and the remote and ignores any danger or discontent that could disturb his ease. To him, if there is no easy solution then there is no real problem. When you do him wrong, he finds it easier to forget than to forgive.

The rock-solid stability that Mr. Bull gives the relation-

Gay Parenting

Mr. Bull can be insensitive and selfish. And he hates anything that disrupts his routine. He's not the sort of man one expects to be kid-friendly.

But fatherhood transforms him. A Taurus will give to a child unsparingly. Quality time and family rituals become the center of his life.

The stability and routine of the Taurus home makes any child feel secure. The rules are clear and sensible. There are lots of hugs and affection. And a Taurus parent with his childlike sense of fun makes an ideal playmate. It is a kid paradise.

Mr. Bull will not let prejudice prevent his child from being part of the community. By ignoring the stares and disapproval, Taurus deprives bigots of their power over his family.

When his child grows into adolescence and rebels against the family, Taurus suffers more than most parents. Tempers will flair; Mr. Bull's love for his child is never in doubt, but it will be a stormy time.

ship makes it easy to put up with his faults. Especially since he makes few demands on you other than patience, respect, and loyalty.

BREAKING UP

Whichever one of you calls it quits, the underlying reason for the breakup is that you changed and he did not. When a Taurus gets pushed to adapt beyond his ability, it gets ugly.

After taking you for granted so long, Mr. Bull is genuinely bewildered by your changing needs. He is not faking that tone of injured self-righteousness when he demands that things go back the way they used to be. Since all the evidence of your dissatisfaction went right over his head, he is convinced that some outside force has stolen you from him. And "steal" is the word. Taurus thinks of his loved ones as belonging to him. No possession can leave on its own. Some thief has to come along and take it.

Taurus is slow to anger but when it happens the explosion is volcanic. He does not care where you are, who is listening, or what the consequences will be. Even in the most mild-mannered Taurus there is a threat of physical violence when he is mad. Expect slurs to be flung at you, since Tauruses are prone to bigotry. If you have not seen the dark side of Taurus before (which is very possible) you will be shocked by this nasty-minded thug calling you "faggot."

Even more shocking is how lovey-dovey he can act after calming down. Taurus is a firm believer in the power of make-up sex. He will pull out all the stops in hope of keeping the relationship together.

When the end happens, be fair in settling financial obligations. For Taurus everything is black or white. If you cheat him in some small way, he will be convinced that you have cheated him on a larger scale as well. He is not interested in

---

Coming Out

As long as he is getting money from his family, he will not come out voluntarily. Abstract principles of honesty and empowerment mean nothing to him when there is a chance he might get cut off.

In a workplace that has no nondiscrimination policy, he will keep mum. Unless there are lots of other gay men around. If being open means that he can be one of the boys, then he will do it.

Taurus has trouble keeping lies straight, so being closeted takes a good deal of effort on his part. But only when it becomes more of a bother to conceal his sexuality than to reveal it will he come out.

---

the reasons behind your actions, but only in the actions themselves. He will extrapolate from there in the most paranoid way he can.

Because Taurus does not like to probe too deeply, he is unlikely to ever fully appreciate his role in the breakup. However, that does not mean the two of you cannot be friends. Unless he returns your gifts—if he does that, it means he never wants to see you again.

THE FIVE FACES OF GAY TAURUS

DRAG QUEEN TAURUS

There is nothing ambivalent about this man's self-image. He is a girlie-boy and accepts his femininity totally, without guilt, and without wanting to be any way different.

He tends to be more a matron in his persona than an

ingenue. This is not because he lacks the looks, but rather because his style has all the straightforwardness and self-confidence of a grande dame.

Ms. Bull is not quick with the repartee. His drag persona is made up of a limited range of unimaginatively stereotypical gestures and inflections.

Yet these feminine failings do not matter after the music starts.

When this girl starts dancing or singing, something inside gets liberated. Take her for a turn on the dance floor and watch that thick male body become the essence of soft womanly power.

Drag Queen Taurus's lack of temperament, and her earth-mother warmth, makes her popular with the other girls. She gets the love that wittier, faster, nastier drag queens miss out on.

DOMINANT TAURUS

The man is a pig. He sits back and expects sex to be done to him—with no effort on his part. There is a fine line between dominance and laziness. Dominant Taurus rides that line.

With few preliminaries, he comes out and asks for what he wants. Then he demands it again. And again. And again. Like some leather Teletubbie.

And he cannot take no for an answer. He will ask for that one thing again and again, as if your answer would change five minutes later.

If you are a repetition queen, this is your man.

In spite of all this, there is something thrillingly butch about how easy he is in his body. Though he is superconscious of your looks, he seems completely unconscious of his own appearance. As if the denim accidentally happened to show off his package like that.

But be careful with this one. He sometimes gets so caught up in his own pleasure that he does not realize when he has gone past your limits.

ACTIVIST TAURUS

What could be hotter than to stand tall with a bunch of guys all wearing the same T-shirt and battling evil? For Activist Taurus—nothing! It is as much the camaraderie as the cause that keeps him fighting.

Though economic issues and job discrimination make his pulse race, Taurus is not a tilting-at-windmills kind of guy. His style is to find what changes are actually possible and concentrate on them. He prefers taking part in a direct-action demonstration or designing snappy, persuasive graphics to canvassing and lobbying.

Taurus makes a better foot soldier than leader because he tends to demonize his opponents. When he says that politicians are committing genocide in the U.S.A., it is not rhetoric. He really believes it and feels that compromise with such evil men would be immoral. This makes negotiation difficult. But as the muscle behind a leader, his oversimplified worldview gives him the energy to keep on pushing.

GUPPY TAURUS

He may seem like a nine-to-five drudge but he knows how to party.

Guppy Taurus feels that all the hard work justifies all the fun. This man spends most of his income on fancy food, fancy clothes, and fancy home furnishings. After a hard day at the office, who can sleep on cotton sheets? Not him.

Love is also a form of self-indulgence to him. Being with someone beautiful and comfortable is as pleasurable as sitting in a beautiful and comfortable chair or buying a beautiful and comfortable Armani.

He wants a man who can enjoy the same things he does. If the man knows what fork to use with each course, so much the better. Above all, he wants a man who is an escape from the competition and tribulations of the working world.

If you can bring balance to his life, Guppy Taurus will gladly share his material goods . . . after he makes you jump through hoops to prove you are not a gold digger.

GYM BUNNY TAURUS

He may have started working out to improve his looks. Or maybe it was because working out is what gay men are supposed to do. But over time his gym routine evolved into something Gym Bunny Taurus does for its own sake. Tauruses find comfort in the regularity and predictability of their gym schedule.

And they get to see cute guys. The advantage the gym has over the bar is that bodies are in use. Taurus likes to see how men move, so the disco and the gym are his favorite cruise spots. The gym is best, though, because the clothing is skimpier.

In the gym, you know what to do now and you know what you will do next. Taurus likes that. The boredom that makes many men abandon their fitness regimen never bothers Taurus. He is committed to his body. He likes feeling its strength and he loves testing it.

And besides, burning off all those calories four times a week means he can eat whatever he wants, whenever he wants to.

Gemini

LOVING YOUR GEMINI

It is your first conversation.

While talking to you, he is scoping out the room for other men.

In case you missed it, he then jokes about scoping out the room for other men.

Then he quotes at length a review of some new Broadway show. Catching sight of a leatherman prompts him to outline for you the steps in the tanning process.

By now you think he likes you as a friend and is not looking for anything more, when a string of double entendres tumble out of his mouth to make his intentions clear.

You are ready to go home with him, but he runs away to catch an old acquaintance he sees leaving.

Where do you stand with him?

Even he does not know.

Gemini is a perpetual motion machine powered by contradictions. He can be sharing without being generous, open without being totally honest. He is sometimes warm without caring and cold without hating. And in an instant his mood will change.

Geminis are always cute, though rarely gorgeous. The attraction is not in their looks but in the excitement of their mercurial temperament. Gemini bends the truth and has the attention span of a bumblebee—everyone he meets knows it! But they do not mind, because he charms them into thinking they are as smart and funny as he is.

ATTRACTING A GEMINI

Mr. Twin is a man who never outgrew his terrible twos. He still looks at the world with the same fascination and curiosity that a small child does—which will either delight you or make you want to yell *"Grow up!"*

The Gemini mind is restless, so he does not like to get bogged down in messy emotions. One might say he lacks depth, but that would not do justice to the epic scale of Gemini's superficiality. To him life is a grand hunt for interesting autobiographical anecdotes and fascinating tidbits to contemplate and share. To classify some of what he finds as "important" and some as "trivial" would restrict the freedom of the hunt. For this reason, everything from the theory of Freudian psychotherapy to the color of his new toothbrush carries the same weight in Gemini's mind. He needs to be anchored by a boyfriend who responds with strong emotion to the things that matter most.

Fortunately for Mr. Twin, he is attracted to men who are deeply emotional yet will not burden him with talk about feelings. Still, Gemini's man cannot be a completely silent type. You will notice that Mr. Twin frequently interrupts others when they are talking. He also like to be interrupted himself. Because Gemini is in a constant search for new ways to link ideas, he thrives on having his thought process diverted in unexpected ways. Let him go on his own way and he gets bored. For him the most exciting man is one who voices interesting challenges and positions contrary to his own.

If Gemini is attracted, it is in part because he sees you as a caretaker. If he stays, it is because you give him a long leash. Gemini's purpose in life is to connect to as many people and things as possible. His casual relationships and his on-the-go-lifestyle are meant to keep him from getting stuck in a situation which would limit his ability to connect. A man who can plug him into a new circle of friends, introduce him to new types of art, and surprise him with unexpected thoughts (as well as take care of him) will find a niche in Gemini's life. On the other hand, a man who threatens to restrict Gemini's access to the big world does not have a chance.

Here is a person who knows what everyone thinks and feels—except for himself. Gemini constantly contradicts himself, trying on various attitudes in search of the one that feels right. The signals are mixed because he does not know what he wants. Let your come-on be lighthearted and half-joking so he can indulge his ambivalence before he says yes.

DATING

His model for romance is more *Bringing Up Baby* than *Romeo and Juliet*. The mushy stuff is too embarrassing. When he goes for candlelight and roses, it is a tactic to get something from you. When Gemini is at his most sincere, he is at his most quirky.

Forget about planning dates more than a couple days in advance. Gemini is allergic to scheduling and would rather play it by ear. If you want to do something with him, plan it yourself and spring it on him last minute. If he already has committed to something else, make him cancel it. As you probably already know, bagging out is Gemini's favorite sport.

The above may make Gemini sound like a bad date, but that is not the case. Mr. Twin views the world as a giant amusement park. He takes nothing seriously and can find the fun in anything. So what you do does not matter. Gemini will work hard to amuse you—and himself. He can make coffee in a diner a memorable experience as he rags on the other customers and the decor.

Though Gemini likes to tell the same stories over and over, he does not enjoy having the same date over and over. If you ordered in Chinese food and watched videos last Saturday, try to come up with something different this week. Since Gemini infallibly knows where to find the best parties and latest hip spot, this is not much of a chore.

Gemini looks at other men as puzzles to work out. If you give him the same clues over and over again, he might think that your solution is too simple. Keep it fresh with changes of setting and by sharing the full range of your personality. Be careful, though. Mr. Twin keeps no secrets, so whatever part of yourself you show him will be public knowledge within days.

When Mr. Twin is there, he is completely there for you. But he is not always there. If he says he will call Tuesday, you can be sure he will call Monday or Wednesday. Or next week. You can complain about Gemini's disappearances, but it will do no good. Either he needed solitude or the company of other friends. He will never ignore the need for time away from you. In fact, he may be bewildered why you are always willing to be around him.

Often Gemini evades your questions about his feelings. He turns pain and frustration into sarcastic jokes. Sometimes he outright lies. But it is never his intention to lie. Gemini does not relate to others through any subtle currents of emotion. The glances, sighs, and touches that other men use to express what cannot be said are not in Gemini's repertoire. He relates through words. If he cannot name a feeling, he cannot express it (and probably does not even think it exists). So he rewrites his inner life to fit some punchy, clever phrase he made up. He does not know that it is not the truth.

SEX

You have to lube your mind before you can lube anything else. You need to be alert enough to enter into his humor, since innuendo and dirty jokes are the Gemini idea of foreplay. And afterplay. And during play. (Did you really think that sex would shut him up?)

Even in a committed relationship, the sex feels casual. For Mr. Twin, sex is fun. Period. It is not mystical or emotional, it is just another great activity the two of you do together. Gemini is proud that sex never overwhelms him. He loves the lunchtime quickie at work because it proves that he can start and stop at will.

Due to his detachment from the act, Gemini is less possessive than most men. If he were to catch you in bed with

Safe Sex

Wow! He can finger you with one hand while putting on a condom with the other. And a good thing too!

No Gemini is entirely forthcoming with his sexual history. His selective memory will not let him be. Even though he can quote verbatim conversations from twenty years ago, he honestly cannot remember everyone he slept with.

So you will want to be strictly safe, which luckily is easy with Gemini. It is the connection between you that gets him off and that connection need not be physical. He enjoys talk and fantasy almost as much as touching.

With time, he might want to go bareback "just for a change." You can put him off without any sweat, since he does not have enough follow-through to actually insist on it.

another guy, he would probably get more turned on than jealous. Okay, he might pretend to mind at first—before suggesting a three-way. After all, Gemini is always looking for a new thrill.

The same unshockability ensures a wild sex life. There is nothing this man will not try. With his excellent physical coordination Gemini picks up any new sexual technique easily. However, all the kinks and positions are like toys to him. (Toys are like toys, too.) He will be into this one now, get tired of it, and be on to the next. As in every other part of his life, he has an insatiable need for variety.

Remember that Gemini is a highly distractible sign. Just as spontaneously as his arousal arose, it could disappear. Seize the moment (and him). If you run to the bathroom during a session, you may return to find him answering his mail. Which would be a tragedy for you, but not for him, since he finds social intercourse as satisfying as any other kind.

LIVING TOGETHER

However much he denies it, you are now officially a couple. So let him pretend that nothing has changed just because you share a roof and a bed. The world knows the truth.

Gemini wants to appear single because he fears the stagnation of a settled life. The nights out with his friends, the trips he takes alone, and those strange days when he hardly says a word to you are all meant to prevent the relationship from falling into a routine. Paradoxically, the more he has a life outside of the relationship, the more stable the relationship will be.

The reason it took so long for him to decide to move in was that he needed to find some advantage to the arrangement that outweighed the stagnation factor. That was hard for him. He still has one foot out the door and will always have one foot out the door even if you stay together for fifty years. So do not press your luck with the commitment factor. He is there—be happy.

You will need to make sure that the bills get paid on time, since Mr. Twin will either procrastinate or forget. His inability to understand schedules shows in his pattern of overextending himself then not following through. By now you have observed his extraordinary ability to organize information in his head. If only he could organize a to-do list and do it—instead of letting you down.

The biggest disadvantage of having a Gemini beau is that he is immune to the emotional manipulation that is the bread and butter of most relationships. Without the power of guilt on your side, you need to use reasoned argument to persuade Gemini. However, this does not mean that Gemini will be equally rational in his approach to you. His tactics are those of a used car salesman. Slippery rhetoric and highly charged words are his tools.

Gay Parenting

Raising a child seems like another flaky Gemini project that he will soon tire of.

But that is not so. Gemini identifies strongly with children in general and is devoted to his own child's well-being. Though Gemini is too erratic for regular meals and a strict bedtime, he provides a stimulating home environment that encourages the child's intellectual growth.

As a gay man, this father knows what it is like to be pressured to conform. Gemini gives his child much freedom to follow his or her own talents and interests. He wants his child to have an education that provides a wide array of options for following his or her own bliss.

Often you will ask yourself what Gemini gets from you. He has so many friends. He has little regard for home life. He seems embarrassed by your affection. What role does your relationship have in his life? Love for Gemini is salvation from his fragmented self. For all his self-mockery, he does not really look at himself—unless it is through the eyes of someone he cares deeply for. Through you he learns who he is.

BREAKING UP

Obligation has little meaning for Gemini. His commitment to you is one day at a time. Those days can add up to years. Or not. If he stays with a man it is because he wants to. If he does not want to, there will be no foot dragging or pretense.

Of course, the type of relationship he is happy in might make you want to bail out.

Mr. Twin is used to ambivalent feelings. He likes them. So the love/hate partnership that feels like a roller-coaster to hell for most men is a wowie thrill ride for him. Though he usually prefers more emotionally sedate pairings, he can get into volatility if it means interesting heated arguments.

Confrontation he can handle, but simmering resentment will kill his affection. Baffled by your half-hidden feelings, Gemini's response to them is deviousness. Rather than taking action to solve a problem he does not understand, he sneaks around the issue and hopes you will not notice. Somehow he expects this to strengthen your bond.

Underestimating problems in the relationship is common for Gemini. Rather than getting to the root cause, he looks for some pop-psych classification that fits your situation. Once he has described the problem, Gemini is done. He does not think that any more probing is needed. He believes that by making excuses he can heal any wound he inflicts on others.

Only hard experience can teach him otherwise.

Coming Out

The idea of a double life is very appealing to Gemini. And he is very good at maintaining his cover. He easily remembers what lie he told to which person, so staying closeted is easy.

Gemini will turn over in his mind the pros and cons of coming out to someone. But in the end he makes the decision on the spur of the moment and just blurts it out. Usually it comes out when Gemini is trying to make some point and cannot get through to his listener in any other way.

Being a charmer, Gemini can find the words to use that will put others at ease. Coming out for him is a smooth seduction, not a strident confrontation.

After you have been apart for a while, Gemini will make friendly overtures to you. You will find he lays no blame on you and bears no lingering grudges. (Face it, it takes a lot more concentration than he is capable of to hold a grudge.) He always regarded you first as a friend and second as a lover. He feels that just because the lover part did not work out, does not mean you should give up on the friendship.

It may get sticky when he comes on to you after the breakup . . . and he will. But whether you choose to bed down with him or not, you can be sure that Gemini will always be there if you are up for a bit of fun.

THE FIVE FACES OF GAY GEMINI

DRAG QUEEN GEMINI

You can see the man in the woman and the woman in the man. Gemini likes living in the ambiguous gray area between two opposites, so being a she-male is just dandy for him.

Drag Queen Gemini has been playing dress-up since childhood and thinks of all clothing as costume. Even when he goes out in a business suit, he wears it like a form of straight drag. (And this girl can be way butch when she puts her mind to it.)

Her quick wit and love of gossip makes her the hub of any party. Friends also love the way that her drag persona keeps evolving. Anytime you see her, she reveals some unexpected facet.

Constant partying interferes with Drag Queen Gemini's everyday life. Fortunately she has many irons in the fire, so when she loses a job, an apartment, or a lover she can easily find a replacement. Still, like our gay patron saint, Judy Garland (also a Gemini), there is a little-girl-lost quality here that all the brave smiles cannot hide.

DOMINANT GEMINI

Dominance is a game for this man. He loves taking whatever you throw at him and incorporating it into the scenario, as if he were an improvisational actor. Dominant Gemini is ingenious at finding new twists to old kinks. Intensely verbal, his commands are not your usual leatherman grunts, but rather a hot haiku whose words are skillfully chosen to bind you into submission.

It is disconcerting to hear him parody his own sex talk as he smokes afterward. But it is the artifice of the role-play that turns him on. If he ever took the roles seriously, he would find himself unable to perform. When he laughs at you during sex, it is not to humiliate you. He genuinely finds the whole setup hilarious.

His special skill: Spanking.

Dominant Gemini's slap can be soft as a kiss or hard as iron. Overall his physical control is virtuosic, but his open palm is pure genius.

ACTIVIST GEMINI

Activist Gemini does not so much fight for his cause, as sell it. He enjoys a good debate, but he enjoys persuasion even more. The man has a gift for making both his allies and enemies reexamine their assumptions. His prowess at twisting the words of his opponents into pretzel logic comes from being able to hear what they actually are saying, unclouded by Gemini's own biases. This also translates into an infuriating habit of playing devil's advocate, just when you want him four-square behind you.

Gemini is equally involved with both his comrades and opponents. His interest in the individuals in both groups is what keeps him involved. Because of his dispassion, Gemini has no problem sleeping with the enemy—literally or figuratively. When he wants a man or wants an issue resolved, Gemini will do whatever it takes, even if it seems shady.

GUPPY GEMINI

He loves having one foot in the straight world of business and another in the gay world of fun. Gemini has gotten where he is in business through hard-core networking. Which is the exact same thing he does at the bar and gym—though with a different end in mind.

Gemini is famous for his multitasking at work and at play. In the office he can work out a budget on paper while negotiating a contract on the phone. In bed, he can work that spot at the base of your throat with his tongue while opening you up with one finger and fondling your cock with his other hand. Same skill, different setting.

In both arenas Guppy Gemini is better at short-term than long-haul because he has more energy than stamina. However, he is so seductive that he leaves both lovers and colleagues with a smile on their face—so who is going to complain?

GYM BUNNY GEMINI

Sex is a great way to meet people.

And Gemini is very social. The best part of being buff is that any man is available for you. Having his choice is worth all the sweat and misery it takes to have that body.

The repetition and persistence needed for concentrated exercise is sheer drudgery for Gym Bunny Gemini. It becomes bearable only when there are others around to talk to and gawk at. This is not a home-gym type of boy.

Because Gym Bunny Gemini tends to neglect his warm-up and not get enough sleep, he frequently injures himself when working out. The problem is that he is really uninterested in his body for its own sake, thinking of it as a tool to help him get to other things that interest him more.

Gym Bunny Gemini is cheerfully promiscuous. Guilt will never impede his pleasure, but sex itself it not his ultimate goal. Neither is a serious relationship. For him sex really is a good way to meet people, so the chat over brunch the next morning is as important to him as what went on the night before.

Cancer

LOVING YOUR CANCER

His voice is as soothing as warm milk. Soon you are revealing to Mr. Crab secrets that you never tell strangers.

Maybe it is that undercurrent of melancholy you can feel even when meeting him for the first time. No matter how happy Cancer is, you always know that he is grieving for the loss of some paradise.

But what that paradise was he will not say.

It is hard to be indifferent to Cancer, because there is some indefinable quality about him that evokes strong emotional responses. In conversation Cancer gives very little hard data about himself, but you still feel you know him. Cancer is much more comfortable telling you anecdotes about friends and family. These stories imply much more about Cancer's personality than he is willing to share with you directly.

But what they imply only raises more questions.

While Cancer's sensitivity and warmth toward his circle is evident, you have to wonder how he can throw so much of his energy into tracing the intricacies of other people's inner lives. Does he love them that deeply? Or is he merely using them? Can someone so strong be living vicariously through others? Where would you fit in if you became part of his life?

As you sense him responding to your unspoken questions, you know that this mysterious man has the power to reach all those hidden corners of your heart.

Will you let him?

ATTRACTING A CANCER

If you remind Cancer of his old boyfriend, you are off to a good start.

Cancer is always looking for a vehicle to his lost past. He bought this shirt because it is like his old one and that car because it is like the one his mom drove as he was growing up. A boy who reminds him of some past affair has a very real (if very strange) advantage.

The clincher though is need. The deep pain and psychic injury that scares most men off attracts Cancer. He wants to be needed, so your weaknesses count more with him than your strengths. At any given point in this relationship, one of you will mother and the other will be mothered. The roles may be consistent or they may switch periodically. But without at least one of you needing nurturing, Cancer cannot see you as a viable possibility for a relationship.

Unfortunately Cancer is prone to the fantasy of turning a poisoned apple into Prince Charming. With a little love, he believes anyone's life could be turned around. So though he usually plays it safe, you may find Mr. Crab passing you up in favor of Mr. Scumbag.

An even bigger obstacle you face is that Cancer does not give off obvious emotional signals. This is not a consciously manipulative choice. (Cancer manipulation usually involves the display, not the hiding, of emotion.) This is just Mr. Crab's nature—he is indirect, so emotions and desires are signaled in obscure ways that are inscrutable to the uninitiated.

Love takes time for Mr. Crab. He is warm, but he is wary. When not pursuing his fantasy wild boy, Cancer looks for men who have settled down, have a little money, and know their direction in life. Because he is not afraid to commit, Cancer wants a man dependable enough to be worth committing to.

DATING

Without a meal in there somewhere, it will not seem like a date to Cancer. Though he can be stingy, he is always willing to splurge on a good meal. The prejudices that color all his opinions are doubly strong when applied to food, so do not make a reservation for sushi unless you are sure he eats fish. Go with what you know he likes.

You know things are getting serious when he cooks for you in his home. The home is his sanctuary, and only those close to his heart are allowed extended visits. The Cancer home is haunted by memories and mementos. Because Mr. Crab sees himself as the sum of his past, when you handle his baby picture, you touch something at the core of who he is. To protect that core self, he cannot let just anyone into his home—figuratively and literally.

Once you get into the Cancer inner circle, he will become completely protective of you. His attitude is that the rest of the world can go screw itself, as long as his friends, boyfriend, and family are safe and sound.

However, being inside also means that you will witness his tantrums. For Mr. Crab, his feelings will always justify his actions, however wrong they appear by any objective standard. As long as his outbursts are sincere, he believes his emotional displays are perfectly all right.

Realize, though, that the show of emotion is strategic.

Unless he is after something, Cancer expects you to intuit his feelings. In fact, his first response when hurt or depressed is to hide in his room, not to seek comfort—that is until he realizes that his sadness might inspire feelings or action on your part. Still, you need not ever feel bad for Cancer's misery, because his psyche moves in cycles, so some other emotion is bound to be on the way.

The one constant is Cancer's prodigious hunger for affection. If you ever withhold your love, he will turn himself inside out to get it again. His emotional demands, though, are not unfair, since he throws a constant stream of tangible love in your direction as well. The way he anticipates your needs and reads your moods feels psychic—because it partly is. Cancer can channel your heart, to feel a bit of what it is like to be you. In a very real way, he lives within and through the people he cares for.

And if he does care, you will know that Cancer is ready to take this relationship to the next level when he brings you home to his family at holiday time.

SEX

Orgasm, schmorgasm.

Sure, Mr. Crab likes to come just as much as the next guy. But without the prospect of a little cuddle time after the spurt, all that bumping, grunting, and flying fluids seems pointless.

Though Cancer will indulge in recreational sex at times, he ultimately finds it unsatisfying. Without emotion attached, sex is like a plate of whipped cream with no dessert underneath. It sounds like fun, but it is merely sticky. For him sex has to be a vehicle rather than an end in itself.

The real end is to feel cared for and safe. Thus Cancer is very sensitive to the environment around him during lovemaking. Anxiety about time, an uncomfortable bed, an argument, or a mis-timed fart can ruin the experience. Long, luxurious foreplay ensures that Cancer can drop his defenses and slide into the erotic moment. Pamper him. Give him a deep sensual massage. Or let yourself become passive so he can pamper you. There are no quickies with this boy, so you had best give in to the pleasures of a slow, long night of love.

His nipples are unusually sensitive and he loves using his mouth. The big turn-on is when you caress him with the same gentleness and undivided attention that a mother shows her baby. In bed, Cancer *is* a little boy, needing reassurance and nurturing. His style will become playful when he feels secure enough with you to share a few of his numerous fantasies.

However, Cancer also has a little boy's pride in his physical prowess. Thinking that Mr. Crab's Barbara

Safe Sex

Often feeling betrayed by his body, Cancer does not trust his health to take care of itself. Precautions are part of his nature.

Given that Cancer likes taking responsibility for others as well, it is likely that he will be a nag on the issue of safe sex. He wants to know your past sexual conduct even though this gives little indication of your present HIV status. And he probably will not believe you are telling the truth anyway.

After time, he might be tempted to unsafe activity if he thinks it is the only way to hang on to his boyfriend. Whichever decision he makes, Mr. Crab will be torn apart by having to choose.

Cartland attitude means that sex has to be pink and fluffy is a mistake. Let him take charge and those high-pitched moans will deepen into animal grunts. A Cancer top gives special satisfaction because he not only gets inside your body but inside your mind as well. This lets him fulfill your unexpressed desires and fantasies.

LIVING TOGETHER

Being the commitment slut he is, Cancer will gladly give up freedom and independence for the sake of a reliable husband and a good kitchen.

The home makes very few demands on you. Somehow Mr. Crab makes sure the bills get paid, the garden tended, and the floor swept without you needing to give it much thought. Sure you may contribute labor and money, but Cancer does all the planning. Though he constantly complains about the effort involved, Mr. Crab elbows you out of the way whenever you try to take a more active role in household management. By keeping you lazy and fat, he thinks he can prevent you from ever leaving him.

Mr. Crab sees isolation as akin to death. His connection to you is strong, but it is not the only one he has. Every relationship is precious to him and the need for physical clutter is manifestation of this. All that junk has meaning as a small thread in his web of relationships. As he grows more sure of your ongoing commitment, the hoarding may lessen or confine itself to stockpiling of foodstuffs. Or not.

The kitchen is where the action is in a Cancer home. Preparing food and eating together are central to your life together. Without that kind of home life, Mr. Crab will feel rootless and only half-alive. For Cancer, physical and mental health go hand in hand. When he is upset, he is likely to feel ill. When he is ill, he is likely to feel emotionally unbalanced. The boundary between his inner and outer worlds is blurry. Even the boundaries between himself and others can be blurry.

In his mind, you are now Mr. Crab's responsibility. He feels that he is the cause for each of your emotional states. He also feels that your physical well-being depends on him. It can be hard for him to stand up for himself, but he is absolutely ruthless when fighting on your behalf. The trouble is that he believes that he knows what is best for you better than you do yourself. So his aggressive attack on your behalf could actually be directed at you, since your judgment is obviously not up to his. If you try with reason and dispassion

Gay Parenting

Motherhood becomes him.

With a child, Cancer finds energy and purpose for his life. His boyfriend is decisively bumped to second place by the new addition to the family. The child becomes an obsessive priority for Cancer, and everyone else hardly rates anymore. Ambivalence toward the child by friends or family is seen as betrayal.

Cancer regards any questioning of the fitness of gay parents as an invasion of privacy. And since Cancer works so hard to be a good parent, questioning his fitness is not fair.

Cancer's take-charge attitude can make his partner feel left out. A child may also polarize roles in the home, with Cancer playing the "woman." Still, he is so good at creating a warm, nurturing home environment, it is hard to argue for more balance in the roles you play.

Anyone who does well by Cancer's child is good in his eyes. They are now a package deal, and the most important half of the package is the smaller one.

to convince him of your view, he will still take it personally and be hurt. It is a no-win situation. Your only consolation is that even if you repeatedly go against his wishes, he will still remain loyal to you.

BREAKING UP

The make-or-break moment comes when Mr. Crab's attentions grow so smothering that you yell at him, "Get a life!"

Cancer discovers who he is by living through others. Free-spirited individualism is unnatural and unnecessary to him. How the two of you face up to his needs and the burden it places on you will determine whether or not the relationship survives. If you work out a balance, you will be together for a long time. If not, the breakup will be filled with bitterness.

Being so dependent on others is not easy. Cancer often rebels against the intensity of his attachment by becoming critical. The theme of his snipes is that the loved one owes Mr. Crab since he sacrificed his individuality. That the sacrifice was willing does not matter because Cancer sees his love as somehow obligating the one who receives it.

With his eye ever turned toward public relations (since he expects the whole world to be as judgmental as he is), Cancer does not want to appear the villain when the time comes to part. If you are lucky, Cancer will turn to passive-aggressive withdrawal of affection, which is designed to force you into calling it quits, thus allowing Cancer to appear the victim.

The less pleasant alternative is for Cancer to turn his anger and frustrations inward. If this happens, you will see an erosion of self-confidence as he assumes the blame for everything wrong between you. If you have any decency, guilt will reduce you to a state not much better than his.

Coming Out

Telling his mother he is gay is a turning point in this boy's life. Whether she is accepting or rejecting will color his view of his sexuality and how readily he will come out to others in the future.

Cancer feels no responsibility to share his identity with the masses, so he wants to choose where, when, and to whom to come out.

His biggest fear is that coming out will separate him from his community and family. The fear is groundless. His instincts for how to do so without compromising his dignity or making enemies is dead on.

The clincher is usually a serious relationship. As secretive as Cancer is, it is difficult for him to conceal his boyfriend from the other important figures in his life.

When one of you moves out, expect to spend a long, long time dividing up your possessions. Looking back with nostalgia is his weakness and you should let him indulge it here since it will soothe his anger toward you.

The loneliness of breaking up is more than sad for Cancer. Since his life's meaning is wrapped up in others, there will be a period where he will lack direction. Binge shopping and binge eating ensue. With time, though, he will heal and heal completely. But he will not forget the despair he went through. So if you wish to remain friends, it will take a lot of work and a lot of patience on your part. You must also accept that Mr. Crab will never trust you again.

THE FIVE FACES OF GAY CANCER

DRAG QUEEN CANCER

Yes, a man can get PMS.

It is the switches between sweetness and irritability that give Drag Queen Cancer an authenticity that others lack. Since men of this sign view women with such high regard, it is not surprising that they would try to emulate them in *every* way.

It is not just the dress that makes this boy seem like such a girl. He treasures his inner woman and lets her out at every possible opportunity. His home is frilly and his manner feminine. Even when dressed butch, the underwear is still embarrassingly femme.

Cancer did not make up his feminine persona. He learned it in early childhood. (That explains the retro feel he exudes.) His wardrobe and pet phrases come from his mother. Even his bust, which he so endless fusses over, is strikingly similar in shape and size to that his mother shows in old photos. When turned out in his finery, he presents to the world an idealized picture of her.

Could any mother have asked for a better tribute?

DOMINANT CANCER

Hiding vulnerability under a mask of toughness is the oldest trick in the book. But it works for Cancer.

Dominant Cancer feels himself under a constant assault from the world. If he let himself, he could dissolve in the soupy mess of other men's emotions. Early in life he learned that it is best to erect a wall that can prevent them from overpowering him.

The stern parent role allows Mr. Crab to distance himself from other men while taking control over them. It also lets him replay childhood family traumas—except this time

Cancer has the power. Scenarios in which submissives are completely dependent on him and strive for his approval are the most satisfying.

At times, Dominant Cancer might consider switching roles to be a slave himself. However, unless he has had the chance to experiment in that role when young, he will continue on the same mean-ass path until he is too old and arthritic to lift a dildo.

ACTIVIST CANCER

Activist Cancer comes to his position through emotional empathy rather than rational thought. His principles are an afterthought invented to justify his action. It is the sight of people in trouble that first motivates him.

With a sure instinct, Mr. Crab presents his views to wring the maximum emotion from the hearts of those listening. This makes him an excellent recruiter and fund-raiser.

At times his condescension may alienate friend and foe alike, but he can never alienate the people he is trying to help. The affection he shows them is unfaked.

A firm believer that those who do not learn from history's mistakes are bound to repeat them, Cancer feels that the key to our future lies in our past. He is not interested so much in leaving behind some monument or achieving some personal power. Activist Cancer wants to change individual lives for the better.

If Activist Cancer does not give enough focus to his own personal life, he can turn fanatical. More than most people, he needs to have a home base which belongs only to him and from which the concerns of the world are excluded.

GUPPY CANCER

A crab needs a shell for protection. For Guppy Cancer, that shell is money.

Unless the business is family-owned, he cares less for what he does than for how much he makes. If the pay is good, he will do his damnedest to make sure he hangs on to that niche. If the pay is bad, Mr. Crab will change careers if necessary to improve his bank statements.

Guppy Cancer has the intuition for safe but lucrative investments that will build up the security he craves. He does not want to make a killing, but rather something that will work out over the long haul.

In the office, Cancer wants to be able to hide from his coworkers. He fills his office with barriers to separate himself from any who dare enter. He also fills it with items that symbolize security: Photos of family, instant soup in the drawer, and that favorite coffee mug turn his desk into a second home.

Privacy in the workplace is important to him—as long as it is his privacy. Guppy Cancer puts his nose in the affairs of those under him, but is shocked when employees respond in kind.

GYM BUNNY CANCER

What spectacular pecs! Their perfect roundness gives a soft quality to Gym Bunny Cancer's hard body. Abs remain a problem area since his concern with proper nutrition sometimes becomes an excuse to overeat.

When in emotional distress, Cancer finds it hard to keep up maintenance on his body. It becomes a vicious circle since his loss of definition feeds his depression. However, the familiar faces at the gym and his routine are often enough to pull Crab Boy out of his downward spiral.

Though he loves the admiration his body gets, Cancer feels it is not enough because he is suspicious of physical attraction. He wants to be loved for who he is inside, but he is shy about sharing his inner self with the world. Sure, he can play the casual sex game, if he withholds some part of himself.

Eventually he will find a man who is like that boy he loved and lost back when. Then he will not be able to stop himself from opening up.

Leo

LOVING YOUR LEO

Leo is very aware which of the five faces he is showing. Whether it is hip-hop, couture, lumberjack, or guppy, he's got a definite look and he knows it.

He feels your eyes on him. Getting attention is his life's blood, so he can sense you watching him like a cat senses a nearby mouse.

Then he looks at you.

His large, open features seem to reveal all as he confidently makes eye contact. Yet he will not cross the room to introduce himself. Does he have a boyfriend? Does he not like your looks? What is going on?

Every astrology book will tell you about Leo's confidence, but few describe his peculiar shyness. Both come from the same source: Since he believes the universe revolves around him, Mr. Lion is convinced that we all gossip about him for hours when he is gone. When you are the star of any scene you enter, it is important that you play against a strong costar—not an extra. Rather than risk making an error, since the eyes of the world are on him, Leo will wait to see what you do.

So make the first move. Let him know you are available. Leo is not going to risk rejection, no matter how attractive he finds you.

ATTRACTING A LEO

Flattery will get you everywhere. If you don't believe it, try a little experiment. Pay him a small, easy compliment, such as "Your hair looks great today." Then watch his eyes get bright and his smile broaden. Try working your way up to more outrageous compliments. Maybe tell him that physically he is an updated version of Michelangelo's David—only better looking. Yes, the Lion Queen will believe any compliment you hand him.

There is no need to feel guilt about manipulating Leo's vanity. Anyone who puts that much energy into his appearance is just asking for it. In his mind, your compliments just show what good taste you have.

He's a snob. He wants to know that what he has is the best. That includes you. Either your looks, intelligence, style, humor, warmth, or *something* has to make you stand out in Leo's eyes. Choosing you is a sort of declaration of values for Leo, a way of saying what qualities matter most to him.

In his fantasies Leo loves snatching some handsome boy away from a rival. In real life that scenario will send him running. Sure, he would like to prove himself a better man than a rival, but he does not want to encourage any direct comparison of himself with another. For a one-of-a-kind guy like Leo, that would be beneath his dignity.

Since the two of you are not in "competition" and there will be no "comparison," Leo feels comfortable trying to prove himself better than you. That does not mean you should hide your light under a bushel. Being superior means nothing to him if you are faking inferiority. He needs to win fair. Leo gets turned on by a smart, tough, and sexy guy bowing down to him. Twits and wimps leave him cold.

Generous himself, Leo respects the same trait in others. So do not try to play him cheap. It may cost a few bucks to get yourself a Leo. Make it clear that you expect to pay for the first date. Bring him some gift. He is expecting to be treated like a lady.

However, there is a part of Leo that loves playing the sugar daddy to boys in genuine need. If you *really* are poor, he will appreciate the daisies you stole from the garden next door as much as a Rolex from another man. With Mr. Lion it is especially true that it is not *necessarily* the money you spend, but the thought that counts. One well-chosen trinket can land him.

DATING

The spark that Leo feels now will determine everything that follows. For Leo, new love is the best love. Unfortunately, you can only have one first kiss, but Leo will commemorate every other first as a milestone in your relationship. That is his way of keeping it new.

Even though for Mr. Lion nothing will beat the thrill of the first day he discovers your passion for cold sesame noodles and your allergy to chrysanthemums, it would be a mistake to think that he wants you to introduce excitement into the relationship. Leo does not need or want you to broaden his horizons. If he is good at dancing, take him clubbing. If he enjoys films, take him to the cineplex. If you love weekend rock climbing expeditions and he has never tried it, do not drag him along. Eventually he will want to come along, but it has to be *his* idea.

Leo flees from the control of others. Though he wants to fall in love, he is afraid of being trapped in a constricting relationship. This is why you cannot move the relationship forward until he is ready for it to move on. This requires a high degree of attentiveness to small signals that he probably does not even know he is giving.

So notice him. That is all any Leo wants anyway. He wants to be seen for who he is. He wants his desires acknowledged, even if they are not fulfilled. Notice his habits and his body language. Learn to anticipate his needs. In this relationship, you will get no satisfaction for any of your needs in any area until he gets his first. Then you will get yours back, tenfold.

Where Leo excels is the romantic gesture. Because he believes he is the reincarnation of Prince Charming, he has been practicing the moves his whole life. The restaurant will be just right, his conversation insinuating without being gross. When his hand slides to your knee, the move is sweet and warmly sexual, not an under-the-table grope.

After you have gained his trust and won his affection, Leo will be up-front about what he sees in your relationship and what he hopes for its future. He has no hidden agendas. In fact, if you suggest that he does, Mr. Lion will be deeply offended. Again, notice him. Accept his affection. Take it all at face value—this man is not out to make a fool of you. At least, not on purpose.

Leo lives on a big scale. His life is a Cinemascope adventure and you are his leading man. Your private times will have the atmosphere of an old Hollywood love scene (or an MTV video). Keep the settings dramatic and upscale, make the reservations in his name, and he will be around for a long time.

SEX

Bringing strong men to their knees is a Leo specialty. The secret is in his smile. No, it is not his smile's radiant warmth but rather its sincerity. Who would deny a man anything when he seems to enjoy it so much?

Being desired is the biggest turn-on for the Leo man. In the bedroom, he doesn't want love—he wants worship. Reverent licks up his thighs, astonished gasps as you hold his pecs, heavy breathing at his every touch, and serflike begging for his cock or ass will do the trick.

It may sound like lovemaking with Leo is one-sided, yet nothing could be further from the truth. Leo wants to be your sensual muse and inspire you to surpass your wildest imaginings about what sex can be. This man believes that he can bring others to the very pinnacle of pleasure, and in trying to prove it, he becomes an extremely attentive lover. And after Leo has decided that you are the one, your pleasure will be his pleasure (and vice versa).

Most gay Leo men have fantasies about seducing straight men and virgins. Partly the idea appeals to Leo's vanity, but mostly the turn-on is because Leos do not want to share. Mr. Lion wants to be the only man ever to experience his lover's body. Leo does not want to have sex with you—he wants to *be* sex to you.

Of course, with such high expectations for himself comes

Safe Sex

It disturbs Leo deeply to think that there could be any danger attached to something that gives pleasure. But he would never want to bring harm to anyone and he has a playful sexual imagination that can make safe sex big-time fun. If you just tell him that you need him to be strong to keep you from slipping into unsafe practices, he will feel honor-bound to protect you from your darker urges.

a smidgen of insecurity. He gets upset if you don't acknowledge him as the most fulfilling lover you've ever had, so exaggerating your reactions during sex is probably a good idea. If you lose interest or need a break, you can fake it—he wants so badly to believe in his own prowess that he will be convinced by even the phoniest moan.

LIVING TOGETHER

So now Leo has decided that you are perfection. (Well . . . not quite perfection, since you cannot bear his children. See the *Gay Parenting* box.) Permanence matters to Mr. Lion, so he is ready to set up house.

Living together is easy if you just remember that your home is his castle. It is up to you to make sure that there is toilet paper and that the bills get paid on time. Do not bother him with the petty details, since he will just ignore them and make you frustrated.

Of course, Leo will always be there to second-guess your decisions about running the home. As you probably know by now, Leo loves to give advice. Though he would not dream of organizing the storage closet himself, he is an expert on that (and most things) and will not hesitate to give you lots and lots of really, really helpful advice—even when you are too stubborn to ask for it. How considerate of him! Though he hates the drudgery and routine of making a home, he needs to feel that he is in charge of how things are run. On those rare occasions when he does lift a finger to help, it will usually be preceded by the words "I can't believe I have to . . ."

But living with Leo is not thankless by any means.

Leo will not express his appreciation for your household management in words, but he does notice. If you wonder why he planned the surprise trip to the Cape or bought you the ring, it is just his way of saying thank you.

His flirting would not be an issue were it not for the insane jealousy tantrums he throws every time you look at another man. The Leo double standard is a given. By being extra attentive, you can make it more bearable, but you can never make it disappear entirely. As much as Leo needs stability in a relationship, he also craves freedom. Your monogamy is the stability. His flirting is the freedom.

If you have problems in the home, speak up. Demands and ultimatums will not work, but a simple request or a quiet discussion of your needs might. Though Mr. Lion is undeniably self-involved, he does have a generous spirit. He wants to know that he has the power to make you happy.

Gay Parenting

Sooner or later, your Leo is going to bring up the subject of children. However comfortable he is with his gay identity, deep down every Leo wants his own biological Leo Jr. This is important to him, so try not to laugh when he broaches the topic.

Whether the children are his own or adopted, Leo leaps into the father role with gusto. He will save every last finger painting. He will be there for every swim meet. In the wildness and willfulness of children he sees a reflection of his own drive. Because he identifies with them, it is hard for Leo to be a strict parent. This means that it is up to you to be the disciplinarian. Leo will make sure that the kids learn to throw overhand. You have to make sure they eat their vegetables.

Because he considers himself the exception to any rule, Leo is well suited to face the special pressures of gay parenting. When confronted with disapproval, Leo's confidence and obvious love for your child will go a long way toward changing people's attitudes.

BREAKING UP

It could be that his double standards and jealousy finally get to you. (He can flirt, but you can't.) Or maybe he thinks that you are not making him your number one priority. Though lions mate for life, sometimes a relationship with a Leo has to end. The breakup can be painful or painless, depending on how you choose to play it.

If your relationship is supposed to be monogamous, but is not, all is not necessarily over. Your Leo can be emotionally completely faithful to you while fooling around on the side. It is important for a Leo to feel that he is still virile and desirable. Some flings are merely a way for a Leo to bolster his self-image. Other men may have his body, but you have his love. Whether that is enough is up to you to decide.

Though Leo likes to claim credit for all the good things in the relationship, he will not take the blame for the bad. Challenge him and you will see his smug, pompous, and

Coming Out

When a Leo has trouble coming out, it is usually because he is afraid of losing the respect of others. When a Leo feels secure, coming out is easier. It will also be easier if Mr. Lion understands how important it is to you that your relationship be out in the open. You might also flatter him by saying that when someone like him comes out, it changes how straight persons view gays. True or not, this argument will make sense to him.

However, the strongest appeal coming out has for Leo is a chance to separate himself from the pack and to establish an identity apart from his family. Leo needs to be his own man standing on his own two feet. Coming out is his opportunity to establish himself as just that.

infuriatingly self-righteous side come out. His memory for every mistake you made at every stage of the relationship will astonish you. It will be up to you to take a step back and remind yourself that bombastic self-assertion is Leo's way of conquering insecurity. Any anger you show will lead to nasty scenes in restaurants and movie lines. (Oh, yes, Mr. Lion wants an audience for the dramatic fight scenes.)

It does not have to be that way. Sure, he can get angry; sure, he can remember everything you have ever done wrong—but Mr. Lion loves to forgive. Take the blame yourself for the breakup and your Leo will become magnanimous and generous. Soon he may even start matchmaking for you.

Leo hates to think that he is ever wrong, so he will not want to admit that you were a mistake. This means that it is possible to be friends, even if the breakup was bloody. It also means that you may occasionally have sex. Do not think that this means he still loves you. Mr. Lion just wants to prove that he has still got it.

THE FIVE FACES OF GAY LEO

DRAG QUEEN LEO

How can you pick out the Leo in a line of drag queens? He is the one with the biggest hair. While the Lion Queen spends as much energy on clothing, shoes, and makeup as the next girl, it is his wig that is his true love.

There is no mistaking Drag Queen Leo for a real woman. His inner girl is a fabulous fantasy figure unlike any real person, male or female. It is not the clothes or repartee you remember. It is the larger-than-life perfection of this gal's personality.

His drag character is like Leo's child. He loves her, cherishes her, and protects her. When she is threatened, he will hide her, only allowing her to come out in those situations where she can shine for all the world.

Even an only moderately femme Leo, who never does drag, will feel that his feminine side is like a precious gift. When he reveals this part of himself, he will demand that it be given respect.

DOMINANT LEO

Face it—there are few men who do not look silly in leather. It just looks fake and costumey on them. And there are even fewer men who can say things like "Pleasure me, slave boy. *Now!*" without inspiring more laughter than fear.

But somehow for Leo it works.

All the accoutrements of dominance seem a natural extension of his personal power. He can lead the straight and narrow life all week long, and yet transform himself into the daddy of all evil cowboys on Friday night in a way other men cannot.

It is easy to submit to Dominant Leo because of his aura of control and because it is clear he will do nothing to surprise or hurt. However nasty he is, what you see is what you will get.

The need to dominate is common to all Leos. Most just do it with more subtlety.

ACTIVIST LEO

The world is so lucky to have a man like Activist Leo who can send it spinning out of its orbit.

Or so Activist Leo would have us believe.

Activist Leo fancies himself a leader. But he does not expect to change the world through reasoned argument, behind-the-scenes wrangling, or diligent ongoing effort. He is a leader who does not even believe he needs followers. He thinks he can change the world himself by sheer force of personality. And after five minutes with him you might agree.

His motives are sincere—he really wants to do good for others. Ego comes in because he thinks he can do more good than anyone else.

Do not fall for his anti-fashion fashion statements. He goes for grungy only because he knows he can get away with it. The Lion knows that ripped jeans, klunky boots, and a dirty T-shirt only make his magnetic attractiveness shine brighter by contrast.

GUPPY LEO

His motto is "Nothing but the best—for me." That sense of entitlement would be infuriating, if he were not so charming.

Even in a gray-flannel corporate culture, his innate sense of style stands out. And if it does not, he will point it out to you. It is wrong, though, to assume that he loves his BMW, Armani suits, and Palm Pilot for their own sake. To him they symbolize his accomplishments. Guppy Leo loves showing off the results of his hard work for the same reason that a cat loves showing off the mice it kills.

Ultimately, the whole fast-track life is just a game for him. Watch his eyes as he clinches the deal and you will see the same glee a little boy has winning a slot car race. Part of his daring and success comes from his ability to not take business too seriously while applying himself to it wholeheartedly.

Mr. Lion knows how to let his personality define the job and not let the job define his identity.

GYM BUNNY LEO

Is there anything more charming (or more dumb) than Gym Bunny Leo?

Since he puts so much effort into making himself desirable, Gym Bunny Leo considers it an insult if he does not get noticed. He is trying to transform himself into the kind of man he himself is attracted to. The problem is that Leo thinks we all look for the same things in men that he does. So this boy does not realize that all the posing and flexing he does in social situations is more silly than impressive. But silly is kind of cute, too. (Isn't that so unfair?)

This boy is so transparent in his bids for attention and his narcissism. Yet it is his obvious need that attracts, even more than his impressive physique (though that does not hurt either).

Though he is trying to build a big man's body, it is his little boy's heart that slays them. It is typical of Leo to recognize his own charm but not quite understand its source.

Virgo

LOVING YOUR VIRGO

You have been under observation—even if only for a few minutes. No Virgo acts on attraction alone. He needs to see exactly what you have to offer.

If he has a one-night stand in mind, he will check out your movements to see how you handle your body and surmise what to expect in bed. If he has dating in mind, he looks at the whole package—your body, your clothing, how you interact with others—for clues to your personality. Mr. Virgin is now certain he knows what you are about inside and out.

Unfortunately, he is wrong.

Still, what he thinks he knows gives Virgo the confidence to take a few tentative steps in your direction.

Mr. Virgin knows how to make the most of his young features and physical grace. With low-key charm, he concentrates on putting you at ease rather than forcing himself on you. He plays the perfect audience, appreciative of who you are, so there is no need to pretend you are anything you are not.

Of course, his Stepford-wife niceness can alter at any

moment. The second you shade the truth or unthinkingly let some inaccuracy cross your lips, he will leap down your throat to rip the offending words out of your vocal cords before the sentence is complete.

Then it is back to niceness as if nothing had happened.

ATTRACTING A VIRGO

Other men look for a relationship that offers security, but Virgo looks for safety.

Virgo tries to be the master of his own fate, so he has no need for men who will take care of him emotionally or financially. He is much more comfortable playing the sugar daddy himself to a man with potential, than depending on a boyfriend for his future security.

But he does need to know that his man will not hurt him. And Virgo defines the word "hurt" broadly.

In his world, the shifting ground can swallow him if the bolts from the blue do not strike him down first, so Mr. Virgin views any surprise as an assault. With perfect poetic irony, he is drawn to self-expressive men who act rashly and do not take their responsibilities too seriously. Thus he does not trust his attraction to you (or anyone) unless he can justify it by measuring you against his boyfriend checklist. Yet even if you meet his standards, you are not in the clear yet.

Mr. Virgin likes to know that if he does x, then y will always be the result. He wants to know that he can learn how to operate you—that you will always respond in a consistent way. Unexpected behavior on your part is a "hurt."

He asks for little else besides consistency. Virgo does not need the most beautiful or most sensitive man in the world, as long as he can comprehend your behavior. In fact, your flaws are an important factor in winning his love. He enjoys them because they make him feel needed. Virgo pretends to have all the answers, so you do not have to. Asking him to solve your problems for you will only strengthen the bond between you.

Honesty works with Virgo. Being brutally self-critical, Virgo knows his own good and bad points better than you ever will, so the flattery that turns other men's heads only makes him suspect that you are deceitful. When you do try to lie, get your story straight and practice it, since Mr. Virgin will zero in on the tiny details that contradict each other. Or better yet, be truthful, because in time he will always find the things you hide.

Though intensely sexual, Virgo will look for an excuse not to get started with you. He fears that his own sexual passion will lead to bad judgment. As a guard against the force of his emotions, Virgo likes to think of relationships as deals. If he is certain that he is receiving good value in return, your chances with him are that much better.

DATING

Be on time.

Not every Virgo is the persnickety neatnik described in pop astrology, but most are as obsessively punctual as those books say. And he looks upon your lateness as a signal that you do not consider him important.

He will maintain a certain formal reserve when the lights are on, even if you go at it like panthers in the dark. Virgo resists being taken for granted and losing his independence. By keeping the ground rules strict, he hopes to maintain his identity separate from you.

Dating can make Mr. Virgin feel a twinge of guilt. Though not noticeably selfish, he feels it is a disservice to himself to get involved with someone else before he has smoothed out his own psychological wrinkles. The idea that another could help in this process never occurs to him. Even if it did, he would flee before asking for help. Doing it himself means that much to him.

Though he will make the reservations and pick you up, Mr. Virgin hates to decide where to eat. That would deprive him of the great pleasure of raking you over the coals for making a bad choice. Do not take Virgo criticism too much to heart. In a sick way, it is a positive sign, showing that his trust in you is growing.

However, with Virgo, criticism is a one-way street. Just because he tears you to shreds in public does not mean you have the same privilege. Be discreet! Keep in mind that though he never admits to a mistake, he knows when you are right and it tortures him.

When selecting an event for a night out, remember that Virgo likes to imagine he is improving his mind as well as being entertained, yet he abhors pretension. (You see how he has set it up so that nothing can satisfy him?) The nitpicking afterward is Virgo's favorite part of the experience—even if he loves a film or concert, he must find fault to really enjoy it.

The only thing that escapes complaint is nature. Virgo loves nature, whether it is in the form of flora or fauna. Even he would not dare criticize the design of a shoreline or a woodpecker's beak. Get this man out in the woods and you will see a new side of him.

Though he values his own self-sufficiency and hates ineffectual men, Virgo wants you to need his help. When he fusses over your health and organizes your tax records, he is showing his love in the best way he knows how. A natural-born assistant, Virgo knows that most men do not deserve his service and is happy to find one that does. Still, he has a strong need for physical affection and appreciation that you would be foolish to ignore just because he is too modest to mention it.

SEX

Contrary to stereotype, Virgo is no prude. It is his practicality about sex that puts men off. When a man wipes off the headboard seconds after orgasm, you forget how hot it all was up until then.

Sex drives Virgo so strongly that if he did not sometimes put the brakes on, he would never leave the bedroom. So he holds out as long as possible. His fear is that if it gets too good, too fast, then his libido will make him your willing slave. Which is probably correct, because sex is easy for Virgo but the emotions that follow can be overwhelming.

When you do bed Virgo, you will find that as in other aspects of life, he leaves nothing to chance. His sexual technique is prodigious even when he is not in the mood. He has an extraordinary ability to anticipate your sexual needs, so you will have a fabulous time . . .

But something is missing. Until Virgo can admit to loving you, the sex is merely gymnastics. Good gymnastics, it is true, but not the meeting of souls that the best sex is. Also, Virgo's pleasure is often neglected. He can read your needs but cannot communicate his own.

Safe Sex

He knows more about safe sex than you ever will. He knows more about staying healthy in general. It is one of his favorite obsessions.

The cleanliness of safe sex also appeals. Virgo adores sex but not the mess it makes. After disposing of a condom, Virgo is ready to go back at it—and no shower is necessary!

Be aware that you cannot trust Virgo to tell the truth about his sexual history. He is more likely to tell you what he wishes his past had been than what it really was.

Unlike with other signs, you can count on sex with Virgo improving over time. As he grows more comfortable with you, he will give more of himself and be more willing to take. His technique, which was always superlative, becomes filled with emotional content. It is worth waiting for.

Though Virgo shrugs off more casual physical contact, he needs it. The little caresses and hand holding mean a lot. He knows that he is good in bed, but sometimes feels ugly when the lights are on. The reassurance of a peck on the cheek heals any number of his psychological wounds. So even if he gets embarrassed by your affection, do not ever stop showing it.

LIVING TOGETHER

It is baffling. No matter how many times Virgo shows you the right way to do household tasks, you insist on doing them wrong. What is the matter with you?

Lucky for you that Virgo does not mind shouldering the larger share of the household burden. It is like having a live-in maid and super in one person. In fact, when feeling low, Virgo finds sorting and rearranging to be therapeutic. However, it would be ill-advised for you to try the same. Even a messy Virgo knows where every one of his possessions can be found. Should you misplace even an unimportant item, Virgo paranoia will read all sorts of evil intentions into your action.

Anger often arises from the very justified fear that lovers are out to exploit Virgo. However, though Virgo thinks fast, he acts slowly, which means that his responses are often out of synch with what is happening at the moment. A whole backlog of anger can pop out over what seems like a minor incident.

Life with Mr. Virgin is not necessarily stormy. He works to earn your love. Knowing the value of a good public image, he supports you in public. At home, he manages your schedule and helps you follow through with your plans. Whenever you have a work issue, Virgo is there to aid you in resolving it. Virgo can identify the pattern in a welter of details and organize the chaos. He will learn himself whatever skill you need, then teach it to you.

He does not want credit given for what he does; he is happy to be the power behind your throne. The joy for him is in meeting the challenge. It is important to him, though, that you understand what he does for you. Since his self-esteem is always taking body blows, any concrete way you can show appreciation is worth it.

Or at the very least, take seriously his hygiene and diet obsessions. And listen when he goes into minutiae about his work.

Gay Parenting

Having a child is definitely not a political statement for Virgo. It is a job. Though unflappable on the surface, inside he is in a constant state of blissful panic worrying how he can do the best for his precious young one.

Virgo has an innate respect for the individuality of children. He understands that the child did not choose to have gay parents, so that he cannot foist gay politics on him or her. So while he tries to pass on the life skills necessary for living in a bigoted world, Mr. Virgin will never embarrass his child.

Though respectful, Virgo is a hands-on parent. He will do anything to get his child into the right school. His impulse to perform tasks for loved ones can make for one lazy youngster.

Still, as a result of Virgo's efforts, none of the world's discord will disturb his child's happiness.

Most of all, encourage his ambition. Virgo limits himself to reachable goals unless his man dares him to let his vision soar. This is the one thing he will accept your help with.

BREAKING UP

Virgo is happy to place himself at the service of a bolder and more imaginative man. However, Virgo will then resent the man for using the power that he himself gave over.

While the pairing works, it works. Then the Virgo talent for steadily improving on what he has is in play. But when circumstances start to turn things sour, Virgo is ill-equipped to reverse the tide. He can get damn ugly when his resentment overpowers his love.

Virgo is a master of the preemptive strike. Because he sees himself as something of a wimp, he cannot imagine how anything sweet little defenseless Virgo does could possibly hurt such a rock-solid tower as you. In his mind, Virgo thinks he is merely restoring balance and is oblivious to the injuries he inflicts.

Because he is unable to see the forest for the trees, any argument becomes a listing of grievances rather than a substantive effort to get at the root issue dividing you. Even when Virgo wants to improve the relationship, his efforts are cosmetic. If you want to salvage things, you have to get it rolling then hope Virgo climbs on board. It is best to make your expectations clear. If he knows what the ground rules are, he can decide whether or not he wants to stay. If the ground rules are unclear, he will probably leave because the relationship lacks focus.

If it comes down to a choice between fighting for you and leaving, he will always leave. The dramatic scenes are too nerve-wracking for him. His natural gift for acting allows him to deceive you so that you think that matters have been resolved. To Virgo, the deception is simple self-defense, protecting him until he has the wherewithal to walk out.

His final departure is carefully timed. Mr. Virgin has saved his money and gotten a place to stay before you are even aware what he is considering. He will guilt himself over how he could have tried harder, communicated more, etc., but this is because he enjoys worrying. In his heart, Virgo believes he is doing the right thing.

Though he is still self-righteous in regard to you, on some level the lessons of your breakup do sink in and his behavior will change. After he has had a chance to reprogram himself with another boyfriend, he will look back with greater objectivity and understand his share of the blame for your relationship's failure.

Coming Out

Whether in the closet or out, Virgo can easily rationalize his choice. In reality, he is guided by expediency more than ethical or political concerns.

Since he is terrified at the prospect of being fired, being out in the workplace is a loaded issue for him. Coming out to his family is surprisingly less stressful.

Virgo does not want to be "the gay guy" at work. He prefers to fit in with the crowd. Since he can flawlessly mimic the straight lifestyle and is such a valued worker, no employer would see through his cover.

Though he does not want to be the first out man, Virgo will support efforts by other gays to end discrimination in the workplace. But only if there is a practical strategy in place for bringing about change.

THE FIVE FACES OF GAY VIRGO

DRAG QUEEN VIRGO

Ms. Virgin can steal the moves of her idols and subtly improve on them. It is called *taste*—which is something this gal has plenty of.

She presents the complete package. Her talents as a seamstress, makeup artist, and hairstylist set Ms. Virgin apart from other drag queens. Virgo is not a frilly femme type because she knows that simplicity sets off her aloof yet earthy beauty best. Again, that is called *taste*.

Though Virgo very consciously crafts his drag, there is an element of abandon. In the workaday world, he is such a serious presence that you could never in a million years picture him in heels. All those libidinous, silly, and histrionic impulses which embarrass him in daily life spurt out through the persona of Miss Thing. No longer Mr. Passive-Aggressive, the girl is Ms. Aggressive-Aggressive. When this diva slings the dirt, run for cover, because nothing can hold her back when she is running on a bitch jag.

DOMINANT VIRGO

Untouchably masterful, Dominant Virgo knows that what is withheld is as erotic as what is given.

His composure while whipping, pissing, or slapping is almost inhuman. Virgo needs to keep his personality in check to do the evil that he does. Having a slave goes against his every instinct, which is just what he finds so addictive about it. The danger of doing something so wrong feels so right.

Men who do not play his way are banished. Virgo knows exactly what he wants and will not settle for less. Since the dominant role is designed to counterbalance the flexibility he displays elsewhere, Virgo cannot compromise here.

Punishment is a major part of his scenarios. Inflicting

physical pain makes Dominant Virgo all warm and fuzzy inside. Though he is always looking for a new twist, he has a strong memory for what has pleased you in the past, and the ability to repeat it exactly.

ACTIVIST VIRGO

Making a real difference in the lives of others is what Activist Virgo is about.

It is strategy that excites the Virgo activist. No pie-in-the-sky dreamer, he fights for what is possible rather than some abstract ideal. However, Activist Virgo likes to ally himself with more visionary types.

Virgo has a special ability for keeping things humming within the group. His organizational skills and sensitivity to interpersonal politics see to that, along with a desperate desire to make things happen.

Political passion is an escape from personal passion for this man. When marching with a phalanx of comrades, he does not need to choose any one as a significant other. Being a slut for the cause keeps Virgo's physical needs satisfied without any messy emotion.

The holier-than-thou attitude thaws when Virgo is forced into more direct human contact. People in trouble release repressed emotion. The sick or homeless that he comes in contact with see an unguardedly generous side of Virgo—but it is not as if he were going to date *them*!

GUPPY VIRGO

You are what you do—if you are Guppy Virgo.

All his energy is focused on his career. It might seem that the long hours and stressful conditions might preclude having any personal life, but for Virgo the professional is personal. His relationship to his boss is as important as his relationship to his father or to his lover.

Mr. Virgin would like to move to the top, but prefers being in the back office to being in the public line of fire. He is like a cockroach—though loyal, Virgo covers his butt so that the mistakes of the regime are never attributed to him and he can outlive all those who foolishly stick their necks out.

In truth, give Mr. Virgin power and fewer mistakes will be made. With an inborn ability to analyze data, Virgo's judgment in business affairs is sound. He is unclouded by the vanity that distorts the perception of more edgy entrepreneurs.

Until he nabs a boyfriend, Guppy Virgo is a magnet for office gossip. He does not mind. After building such a solid life for himself, Mr. Virgin is in no hurry to risk it with some stud.

GYM BUNNY VIRGO

The mirror is his enemy.

No matter how good he looks, it is never good enough. Though Gym Bunny Virgo begins working out for health reasons, the beauty challenge soon becomes a factor. Though not vain, he wants to maximize what he has got.

It is reassuring to Virgo to know that if he exercises, results happen. He soon learns what routine is most effective and how diet can improve performance. Anyone not satisfied with their trainer will find Gym Bunny Virgo always glad to give advice. Though his brutal critique might make one wish he were less forthcoming.

When at the gym, Virgo is not thinking about sex. His workout plans are too rigorous to allow for distraction. The only reason Virgo looks at the other men is for comparison. Measuring his body against theirs and their technique, Virgo ups the intensity of his efforts. The hunt for bedable hunks has its own time and place. Staying focused is how Virgo achieves excellence.

Libra

LOVING YOUR LIBRA

He is pretty. Very pretty. True, his face lacks the distinctive features that would make him stunningly memorable, but that makes him more approachable than any strikingly idiosyncratic beauty would be.

Still no one would ever deny that he is one damn pretty boy.

When you speak with him it becomes clear that he is extremely intelligent, even if his ideas are a bit bland.

He is a comfortable man. Cute enough. Smart enough. But not threatening in any way. You might think that this one is too good to be true.

And you would be right.

When you first meet Libra, his deflector shields will be up and he will be practicing evasive maneuvers. He will withhold his true self until he knows what kind of man you want. Then he will emphasize those parts of his personality that you will most love.

But that may be quite a few dates away. At first meeting he is checking you out. He wants to know if you are involved (and perhaps hiding that he already has a boyfriend). He is subtly throwing out conversational topics that will give him a clue to your feelings about commitment. He is examining your clothing to get a sense of your personal style.

Fail to meet his standards and you will go home alone—without his number.

ATTRACTING A LIBRA

Fairness is everything for a Libra.

Minutes after meeting him you know that he is bringing looks, smarts, and highly developed interpersonal skills to the table. And he knows you know.

So his question is: What have you got for me?

He is not a gold digger looking for a sugar daddy. It is not money he is after. He just needs to be certain that he will not be the only one supplying juice in this relationship. So your artistic sense, your humor, your ambition, your ingenuity, or something has to match and balance what he has to offer.

It is only fair.

If you think this is going fast—it is. But for Mr. Balance, every meeting, every date is an audition for long-term commitment. He was sizing you up as a possible Mr. Right before you said one word to him.

So who is Mr. Right? A man who fulfills certain necessary functions: Libras hate expressing anger and negativity. So they look for men who will fight their battles for them. Mr. Right must play bad cop to Mr. Balance's good cop. Watching you kick butt (so long as it is not his) is thrilling to Libra. He loves looking at the world through others' eyes, and the more different those eyes are from his own the better. He is looking for a man whose drive and courage allow him to vicariously experience things he would be afraid to go through himself.

Libra almost always puts others first. He needs a man who will put him first. His need for reassurance and praise usually goes unfulfilled because he spends so much time reassuring and praising others. If you want him, let him know that you value him.

The difficulty you face is that it will take time for you to get to really know Libra. He makes a big show of openness and demands that you reveal yourself to him. But the revelation of the Libra man's true self is a slow tease.

And because he is such a good tactician and such an excellent liar, you might not even realize that he is concealing anything. Yet Libra is hiding qualities in his character that he fears will scare you off.

One last note: Look good. Libra will rule you out on the basis of aesthetics faster than for any other reason. (Libra quote: "He has everything it takes to be a great boyfriend—but those shoes . . . I just can't. Someone might see me with him. Someone might see me . . . with him and his shoes.")

DATING

You know Libra is serious about you if he has another boyfriend. When you are "the other man," it means that Libra thinks you are a potential Mr. Right and an improvement on the guy he has been seeing.

Since Libra hates being single, he will take on almost any willing man if there is no one else in his life. These men are not potential Mr. Rights. They are Mr. For-the-Time-Beings. They will be dumped when a better guy comes along.

So the only guarantee that he *really* likes you is if he is prepared to boot someone else.

However, Libra has so much trouble making decisions that it could take months before he resolves the situation. In the meantime he will use his looks and charm to string you along, knowing full well he is a wonderful trophy to have on your arm and loving it.

Libra likes to see everything in its larger context—

including you. He will want to meet your friends, visit your place of business, and learn the history of your past relationships. He needs to know what your life is about and whether it is one that he wants to be part of. Though he loves the dating phase of a relationship, because it is the phase where expectations and emotions are the most simple, he sees it as a probationary period leading toward something else.

When going out with Mr. Balance, remember that ambience and style are more important than substance. The decor of a restaurant matters more than the food. The cinematography of a film is more important than the script. Libra always thinks that what looks good *is* good. However, Libra will love to argue about the merits of any piece of art and will usually take the view most contrary to yours for the fun of argument. Libra loves debate—as long as the subject is not personal.

Though he loves being the consort more than being the king, Mr. Balance will absolutely not stand being taken for granted. Gifts and picking up the bill are important. Spending "quality time" matters. Libra has a built-in calculator tallying up how much time you spend with him (and how much time away from him with other friends) and what you spend *on* him. While he seems so laid back, letting you choose what to do and where to go, this guy does not miss a trick.

But oddly enough, in his quest for peace, harmony, and a man of his own, Libra will often seem to ignore the inequities in the relationship. However, they do disturb him, so he will refuse to move the relationship on to the next level.

Then things will stay status quo—until a new boyfriend shows up.

SEX

Mr. Balance is the boy who practiced kissing with a pillow when he was a teen. It might have made more sense to practice on another boy or the family pet, but that is not the Libra way. Libra needs to create the full fantasy image for himself (and be sure he has the technical skills to pull it off) before he could attempt to make it real with an actual living creature.

In other words, the ambience and ritualized foreplay are all part of it for him. The incense, the music, the mood lighting—they help him surrender. And for Libra, sex is always surrender, even when he is playing the dominant top. Even then, he is losing himself inside of your desires and inside of you.

Once he has taken that step, you will never find another man more willing to follow you wherever your erotic imagination leads.

As you deep kiss, you will taste his freshly brushed teeth. Mr. Balance is very aware of how he looks, sounds, smells, and tastes during sex. That is why he combs and colognes before hopping into bed with you for the night. If you want to hang on to him, you will need to be equally aware of your aesthetic appearance while lovemaking.

There is a secret about Libra sexuality of which even he

Safe Sex

They do not wear rubbers in Harlequin romances. So the mechanics of performing safe sex seem out of place to Libra.

However, the solution to his awkwardness is to use the occasion as an opening to act out one of his vivid fantasies. His imagination can transform a condom into something magical, and basic frottage into a wild new kink. The hardest part is to make him feel secure enough to begin sharing fantasies.

But once he starts sharing, he will never stop.

is unaware: The boy has the instincts of a whoring slut. Lest that sound a wee bit harsh, let me explain. If you hand him an expensive gift or give emotional support, he will put out soon after. He convinces himself that your sweet gesture inspired affection on his part. In truth it is simply payback. Which leads to the sticky conundrum of Libra love. It is impossible to tell whether a Libra has sex with you because he loves you, or whether he thinks he loves you because he has sex with you.

LIVING TOGETHER

It is odd how once you move in together, the word "I" vanishes from Libra's vocabulary. It is even odder how a man who had so much trouble saying what "I" wanted can now demand what "we" want with no difficulty at all.

Becoming a couple has liberated Libra, allowing him to become the man he was meant to be. Or so he thinks. As time goes on, you will find that Mr. Balance is full of grand ideas about what it means to be lovers, but has no clue about the day-to-day nitty-gritty of relationships.

His saving grace is that he tries. Libra has seen friends and family members in relationships bound together by money, habit, desperation—everything other than love. Libra wants your relationship to shine out as an example to them and to all the world. And he is willing to work to make it happen.

To Libra, a good relationship is one without conflict. He will overlook your quirks, flatter you, go behind your back, and outright lie to you just to keep peace in the relationship. He will even rewrite history. Past squabbles are never mentioned (or even remembered) when Libra recounts your life together. This makes it easy for Libras to remain in abusive relationships. Past hurts are covered up and the covering up is pure joy for Libra. Mr. Balance never feels so fulfilled as when he is smoothing things over. To him, his denial is proof of his love.

Libra hates to look within himself because he fears the strong emotions that lie beneath his placid exterior. But he will look within you. He observes your patterns of behavior and infers what motivates them. He can read your moods. In part this is self-protective. Libra is not wise in the ways of human nature and is afraid you might do something that could surprise and hurt him. So he studies you till he knows you better than he knows himself.

Once you live together and he really knows you, his unspoken demands on you become greater. You probably will not notice. You will assume that it was *your* idea to spend more time together, build the shed, and organize the

Gay Parenting

For Libra, parenting is about connection to the community as much as it is about nurturing the child. He loves the birthday parties, parent groups, and school fund-raisers that connect your lives to the lives of your neighbors.

Mr. Balance works hard to teach his child restraint when dealing with anti-gay bigotry. He is proud to see his child taking the high road when others show disrespect to the family.

His favorite times are those when the child confides in him and asks advice. His child's trust and their ability to communicate on a deep level is Libra's greatest source of joy.

Libra parents have an amazing ability to think things through from the child's point of view. That is why they think they can escape from painful adolescent rebellion. They cannot. Adolescent angst will blindside your Libra, so be ready to pick up the pieces.

weekly brunch. Libra is an expert at eliciting voluntary service, because he makes others happy to be on his team.

BREAKING UP

When Libra breaks up with you, it is quick and clean. When you break up with Libra, the process is as convoluted and painfully bloody as beating a baby seal to death with a teaspoon.

"Why me! Why me!" bleats the Libra.

After all, you are annihilating his entire sense of self and destroying his trust in the order of the cosmos. He'll get over it, but that is what you are doing.

So why did it happen? Did Libra's carefully stage-managed "compromises" with you begin to seem like manipulation? Did his inability to decide on a course of action and stick to it make running a household impossible? Were you annoyed at your lack of privacy? Did he get too possessive? Did you

Coming Out

Libra will refuse to come out to people whom he thinks would be uncomfortable with it. He can respond effectively to homophobia, but only when forced to.

Support is important, to give Libra strength in coming out. Libra loves being part of a team, so if he feels that the entire gay community is working with him on coming out it will be easier. When he feels alone, Libra can always find an excuse to stay silent.

The opportunity to share his love for you with the world is the main reason Libra wants to come out. Of course, the moment he walks into a room with you, he is out, since you are so obviously a couple.

feel like he was stealing your friends from you? Did his habit of telling you what you feel get to you?

These are all common problems in relationships with Libra. Most of them can be easily discussed with Libra and he will try to change. If you want out, these are just excuses. The real issue with Libra that ends relationships is the need to be the perfect couple. You might begin to suspect that all the efforts Libra makes to strengthen the relationship are not for the sake of his love for you, but his love of the relationship itself. You feel this as a coldness at those times when you need him to treat you as a unique individual.

Throughout your life together, he has defined himself as half of an "us." Now that you are gone, he does not know who he is anymore. The man who was always the calm rational one in the relationship turns into a nut job. His out-of-character ranting and self-pity spring from this feeling that he has lost definition and identity.

The only cure is for him to find a new lover or best friend to spend time with. This new relationship will give Libra the sense of purpose that your departure has deprived him of. And the speed of his recovery, when he finally finds someone else, can make your head spin.

THE FIVE FACES OF GAY LIBRA

DRAG QUEEN LIBRA

Straight men hate the Libra drag queen because she is so . . . attractive. She has everything het men want in a woman and more.

To begin with there is that astoundingly beautiful face. Her features have a perfection not seen much outside of Renaissance painting or Hollywood films of the thirties. Okay, she does overdo the cosmetics a bit, but the results are ravishing.

There is a perfection to her words and actions as well. Drag Queen Libra understands the woman's role better than any woman does. She combines the archetypes of Barbara Billingsley and Brigitte Bardot to become the madonna/whore that straight men dream of but never expect to meet in real life.

No real woman could be so soft or so endlessly fascinated with masculinity. Ms. Balance flatters and fawns a man so much that he leaves any conversation with her feeling like Jeff Stryker. If any gal can make Mr. Straight America question his sexuality, this is the one.

DOMINANT LIBRA

Clothes make the man. Leather makes the daddy.

Some actors need the right costume and props to play a role effectively. That is also how it is for Dominant Libra. When he puts on his leather cap and holds that whip, he can just feel his natural sweetness melt away as he turns into one mean hombre.

With Daddy Libra you do not need a safe word. He has a natural instinct for knowing when limits have been reached. Though he may push the envelope, he will not cross the line. Libra understands that though the fantasy is that the top has complete control, the reality is that the master/slave relationship is a mutually agreed on contract in which both sides have obligations. Even in the height of his excitement he remembers that he and his victim are working together.

Libra is skilled at many types of role-play, so do not be shy in telling him your desires.

ACTIVIST LIBRA

Activist Libra has been successful in nudging bigots away from their prejudices and bringing warring factions of his own comrades to consensus. With his gentle diplomacy he is far more effective than his storm-the-barricades brothers.

What is his secret?

Libra can enter into the mind of anyone and learn how they think. His arguments are all based on the personal logic and mental habits of the particular person he is speaking to. Thus Libra's words are as utterly sensible to the listener as something he himself would have said.

Libra gets frustrated, though, because his insight into others brings him the knowledge of how rarely people live up to their ideals. The danger is that this might lead to cynicism, which is ugly in a Libra. The cynical Libra is both manipulative and self-righteous. The only antidote is for Libra to develop compassion toward (and a sense of humor about) those who talk a good game but behave badly.

GUPPY LIBRA

Where most men see a corporate chaos, Libra sees order. To him the shifting alliances, the contract loopholes, the mergers, the buyouts are grand ballet and he is a lifelong dancer. Watch him negotiate office politics and ingratiate himself to the right people while devising a strategy to squash the competition. That boy can move!

Libra understands that no businessman is an island. For this reason he moves ahead by careful planning rather than naked competition, which could damage the intricate network of business relationships he has set up. By instinct he is a team player, preferring partnership and joint decision making to hotdogging it as an entrepreneur.

The guppy Libra does not want to sacrifice his personal life. He understands that a career without a decent home life or a home life without a meaningful career cannot satisfy him. Balance is all for this man, and this stability gives him staying power in business and in romance.

GYM BUNNY LIBRA

Have you ever seen such a perfectly round and perfectly symmetrical butt?

And this is one gym bunny who will actually talk to you even if you have a little flab around the middle. He probably will not go home with you, but he will not make you feel ridiculous for taking a shot at him.

Most profoundly superficial men are not this sweet.

At the gym, he works for appearance rather than strength. He has an odd obsession with body symmetry, seeing disproportions between his right and left sides that are invisible to the rest of the world.

Too bad that this boy can never feel completely satisfied with his looks. Or with the looks of the men he goes out with. He keeps thinking that if he could just build up that one problem area he could get a cuter boyfriend.

He wants love, but confuses it with lust. It will take a big heartbreak to make him grow up.

Scorpio

LOVING YOUR SCORPIO

It is a powerful thing to meet someone who recognizes you for who you really are. So even if Scorpio creeps you out with his blatant stare, you cannot resist him because he gets what you are about. Before he knows your name, he gets what you are about.

As any Scorpio will tell you, his first impression is always right. Mr. Scorpion does not understand what the big fuss over love at first sight is all about, because that is the only kind of love he knows. The moment he saw you, he wanted you.

But do not think that will make things easy for you.

While your psyche lays itself bare to Scorpio, his remains hidden to you. His immobile, set features betray no emotion that he does not consciously decide to let you see.

So you cannot even tell if he likes you.

In fact, the more Scorpio wants you, the less he will show his feelings. Mr. Scorpion fears that if you knew the degree to which he desires you, then you would tease him and manipulate his emotions to get your way.

Besides, he knows that his air of mystery is kind of sexy.

ATTRACTING A SCORPIO

Scorpio is looking for a sparring partner. Maybe that is why he likes his men a little bigger and beefier than he is. Beating a ninety-eight-pound weakling is easy, but taking on a big bull really means something. So just because Scorpio likes to be in control does not mean you should let him walk all over you. Fight back and fight hard. Then let him win.

Passivity and laziness turn Scorpio off. He is a keen observer of human failings and is compassionate about most of them. But men who do not take an active role in shaping their own destiny can never hang on to him. He can forgive a fighter for losing, but he cannot forgive a man for refusing to make an effort.

Physical attraction is never enough for Mr. Scorpion. Chances are that he attempted some wild, purely physical relationship in the past and got burned. It is hard for Scorpio to give his body to a man without also giving his heart.

You are probably more practical and more materialistic than Scorpio. That is what he likes about you. And dislikes about you. Mr. Scorpion is used to wanting things. He is used to working stealthily to get those things. (Notice how he is using those same sideways maneuvers to get you.) There is something about a man who goes directly for what he wants that is thrilling and monstrous to him at the same time.

For all his toughness, Scorpio is afraid of you. If he shows his inner self and offers you his tenderness, it is possible you will reject him, or even worse, laugh at him. The laughter is especially painful since it implies that his feelings are beneath your concern, and for the Scorpio man, his feelings are his whole self.

To avoid your scorn, Scorpio proceeds slowly. Even if he is red-hot for you, he campaigns with a cool head and with infinite patience. He tests your emotion in subtle ways. Then he works out a strategy for winning you based on the results.

Each step of the way he gives himself an out so he can end the pursuit if he needs to without embarrassing himself.

While he is delighted to know you want him, Mr. Scorpion will be scared off if you go after him too aggressively. Either he will suspect some ulterior motive or fear that you will overpower him. Of course the alternative of playing it cool could make him play his part even cooler, sending the relationship into the sub-Arctic zone.

Best try to follow his lead and pray you are reading the situation right.

DATING

You may think it is romantic how he calls you every night you are apart, but the truth is that he is checking to see if you are at home. Surely you must have noticed how anxious he was to meet your old boyfriends, visit your family, and house-sit for you? If you are smart, you realized that he was running a background check.

The guy has trust issues.

And with good reason. When Mr. Scorpion focuses all his intensity on you, it is so exhausting that the temptation is strong for you to spend a night with a lower-maintenance kind of guy. Especially when Scorpio pulls one of his disappearing acts and cannot be reached for days at a time.

Resist the temptation. However well you cover your tracks, Mr. Scorpion *will* know what you did. He might discover it through his usual snooping, but more likely his psychic radar will do the trick.

Though you are expected to put up with his hot and cold moods, yours frighten him. They remind him that he cannot control your feelings and that you might one day stop caring for him. So when he isolates himself for a few days, he is recharging his batteries, but when you do the same, you are abandoning him.

There is an irony here, since any man will feel himself changing when involved with a Scorpio. Scorpio is the sign of transformation, so you will find your sexuality, what you want from a relationship, and your personal habits transforming as you date him. But these same changes, that he is the catalyst for, convince him that you are drifting away from him. So he becomes more critical of you and clingy, which actually might drive you away.

During the dating stage, Mr. Scorpion needs heavy reassurance. Though he will sometimes withhold sex and affection, you will certainly lose him if you do the same.

Often his withholding is a conscious strategy. In other cases, it is simply downtime. Scorpio is deeply introspective and frequently needs time alone with his thoughts to process what is going on in his life.

Mr. Scorpion can criticize you with brutal frankness and terrifying accuracy. If you try to be equally brutal in return, it will not have the same effect. Any criticism you level at him he has already leveled at himself, so he will not be shocked. The best you can hope for is to get him mad.

Scorpio love is profound, yet not sentimental. Without all the gooeyness our culture associates with love, you might easily misjudge the depth of Mr. Scorpion's feeling. When you are in the midst of a crisis, Scorpio will easily express his feelings toward you, but at all other times he will expect you to intuit his emotion without any help from him.

SEX

If you expect Scorpio to be the ever ready, hot-and-heavy sex king of the zodiac that other astrology books describe, you will be disappointed.

Scorpio is not easy. In *any* sense of the word.

When sex happens, it will be wake-the-neighbors wonderful, but do not expect it to be a regular feature of your dating routine.

For Scorpio, sex is never casual. He regards it as an almost mystical experience, which cannot be taken lightly. He believes that during sex every mask is dropped and partners reveal their true selves. He expects the passion you share in bed to make up for all the crap (and for all the dry periods) you put each other through.

Does it?

Mr. Scorpion finds sex emotionally complex, but physically simple. Scorpio has given all the varieties of sex much thought, so linking bodies is not that difficult for him. As a boy, he fantasized new ways to join bodies like other kids fantasized new ways to fasten Lego blocks together. It is easy for him to dip into his repertoire and find something that will please his partner. Mr. Scorpion pities men who have to resort to sex manuals for help.

Scorpio is willing to experiment, but for him the excitement is not in finding new positions and kinks for their own

Safe Sex

As if sex were ever really safe.

Scorpio understands that though one can minimize risk, one can never eliminate it altogether. But since the body's vulnerability during the act is far less than the soul's, Scorpio can face it head on. No precautions you take will destroy the mood as far as he is concerned.

Often, Scorpios go overboard, insisting on wearing one condom on top of another or some other ridiculous precaution. This is because this sign fetishises danger and thus enjoys imagining that the risks involved are greater than they are.

sake. He wants something that will force both of you to get in touch with newer, rawer emotions during sex. The Scorpio attraction to discipline and bondage is due to the effect they have on the psyches of the participants. If you find such acts comfortable, Scorpio will not be interested, since the whole point is to push the envelope.

Scorpio is the most naturally monogamous sign of the zodiac. That is not to say that Scorpios never cheat. They do. But giving all their love to one man is a cherished ideal for this sign. Keeping sex exciting for the two of you matters more than anything to him.

LIVING TOGETHER

He may bellyache that your relationship is getting too routine, but settling down is good for Mr. Scorpion. All he ever wanted was to know you better. Now that he has bought groceries and done laundry with you, he does.

Though it may not feel that way to him.

Scorpio is still convinced you are hiding something. Part of the reason he likes living together is that it makes it easier to monitor you. You may think that he let up on the spy action, but in reality he has just gotten more subtle about it.

Scorpio can handle crisis and danger, the ups and downs of a fledgling affair. It is security that baffles him. He searches for some problem between you that he can obsess about. Often he zeros in on infidelity, because now that you have made the commitment of living together, Scorpio is even more frightened that someone will steal you away. (Notice how Mr. Scorpion is more comfortable imagining a rival than considering that you could go sour on the relationship with no outside influence.)

There is no need for Scorpio to manufacture arguments, since there are enough real ones between you. Shortly after moving in, there is bound to be a huge fight over control of the home. There have been power struggles in the past, but this one is key. If it is not resolved, Scorpio's resentment will poison the atmosphere of your home.

It is wise to let Scorpio have one small corner for himself alone. He needs a place to be grumpy, gloomy, and glum. Even when you are a couple, Mr. Scorpion needs the privacy to indulge his dark side.

If you have lasted with Mr. Scorpion this long, you already know what a bad loser he is. It is important in all arguments to let him save face, even if you win. He must come away with some concession on your part or he will make you pay somehow.

Lest it seem that life with Scorpio is hell, it must be said that this man's loyalty is superhuman. He knows that all this petty business is petty. Unless you screw up royally, he will never withdraw his emotional investment in you. Count on him being with you in good times and bad till the bitter end.

Gay Parenting

Straight Scorpio men love going through pregnancy and childbirth with their partners. Your Scorpio will investigate surrogates and pre-birth adoption since he also wants to be there with the birth mother.

Once he has the child, he is fiercely protective of it both physically and psychologically. Mr. Scorpion is vigilant to prevent teachers and relatives from influencing the child's mind in any way he disapproves of.

Scorpio does not feel obligated to win anyone's approval for how he raises his child. As long as the child grows up happy and secure, he is satisfied.

BREAKING UP

When you do a wrong to Scorpio, very soon after he will do an equal wrong to you. That is Scorpio justice—a quick, clean payback.

It sounds vindictive. It *is* vindictive. But payback must happen for Scorpio to forgive and move on. If you do not pay for your crime, Scorpio will carry around lingering resentment. So there are the cutting remarks. There is that icy coldness. There are those times when he is there but not there. There are the restrictions put on you. There are the mind games. All of these are (in Scorpio's mind at least) not aggressive acts but the restoring of a balance that you (not he) have upset.

Time and sex will heal the wounds.

The one sin Scorpio can never forgive is betrayal. In most instances betrayal means infidelity. But it can mean any act by

Coming Out

Since sexuality is central to Scorpio's identity, being out should be a given. Except that we are dealing with a sign that also loves secrets.

Coming out feels artificial to a Scorpio because he appreciates the complexity of sexuality. He finds that the terms "gay" and "straight" are not specific enough to mean anything. Is he gay like Liberace or gay like Herman Melville? Mr. Scorpion expresses his sexuality not just in bed but in how he walks down the street, how he signs a check, and how he eats a danish. When sexuality is so omnipresent, the word "gay" is not enough.

Mr. Scorpion uses coming out as a tactical move more than a political statement. He will wait for the moment that the revelation will have maximum impact. If coming out will not have any immediate effect, Scorpio might just keep quiet.

which you make money, drugs, or another person a higher priority than the love you share with Scorpio.

Once he knows that the relationship comes second with you, it is over. Nothing will soften his hard heart after betrayal.

Breaking up unleashes Scorpio's inner beast, which he held in check while you were together. Get ready for focused fury and an insidious stealth assault on your confidence. Scorpio turns revenge into an art form. It will make the old paybacks look like a weekend in the Hamptons. Fear of abandonment haunts Scorpio, so when you leave (or betray him), you become, in a very literal sense, his worst nightmare. The only way to avoid his wrath is to not let him think of you that way. Remember that Scorpio is by instinct a healer and does not want you to be his enemy.

First, you have to accept the blame that is honestly due you.

Second, have a plan for the future. No Scorpio will tolerate a man (other than himself) who wallows in misery. He wants to see you suffer, but he also loves to see people rise above adversity.

Third, let him know the experience of losing him has changed you. You will not get him back, but he will respect you for learning your lesson. This can be the beginning of a lifelong truce with your Scorpio ex-lover.

THE FIVE FACES OF GAY SCORPIO

DRAG QUEEN SCORPIO

What a scary bitch she is!

Her flat voice is pitch-perfect to utter sarcastic barbs. Her eyes are designed to mentally undress men and expose their shortcomings. Her thighs are a Venus flytrap ready to snap shut on the unwary.

She turns femininity into a sharp weapon capable of castrating any poor soul who gets in her way. The softness and the coyness of the traditional lady is not for her—she is drag queen, hear her roar.

Few can match her quick wit, but when she is not in full-throttle Joan Collins mode a certain spontaneity is lacking. This girl has a lot of heart, but she has had to bury it to protect herself against those who want to hurt her. What she did not realize is that by pretending to be tough and pitiless, she would become tough and pitiless.

As usual, a Scorpio's worst enemy is himself.

Love can save her, but only if she is willing to admit that she is in love.

DOMINANT SCORPIO

Many men need a whole ritual, props, special clothing, etc., to psych themselves into dominance. Not Scorpio. Though he enjoys all the accessories of power, he has enough juice to pull it off without them. Just look at him in daytime life—he uses the same tactics with the dry cleaner, the busboy, and his secretary that he uses with his submissive partners.

Pure unadulterated power is like crack to this guy. It does not matter whether he has the power in bed, business, or with his family—he loves it all. The problem is that law and etiquette forbid him to wield it as freely as he likes.

Except in the sexual arena where there is no shame and few rules.

He enjoys his power to turn you on as much as he enjoys the power to bend you to his will. So going through the motions will not satisfy him. His partner's moans have to be real for him to get hot.

ACTIVIST SCORPIO

He does not believe anything the media, the politicians,

the military, the lawyers, or cute guys tell him. The scary part for Scorpio is recognizing that he himself could become just as dishonest. His crusade to save mankind and his drab sense of style are both attempts to preserve his own integrity.

His obsession with uncovering the truth makes him see conspiracies in the government and in his own family. He would seem like a total wacko if he were not smart enough to keep his most outrageous theories to himself. As it is, you will find him merely over-intense and over-earnest.

It is hard for him to face his own destructive tendencies, so this boy projects them out. By fighting monsters in society, he can avoid looking at those demons within. However, since we do need men like Scorpio to heal society's ills, this is a pretty positive way to be in denial.

GUPPY SCORPIO

It is hard for Scorpio to play the good employee. But he will if he believes that he can rise to the top, where no one will ever order him around again. If he feels stuck at the bottom, he will leave a company and change his career without a second thought.

This gift for decisive action and bold risk taking gives Mr. Scorpion a fair shot at success. His independent thinking may make him the odd man out in a corporation, but Scorpio likes being a maverick.

Separating his work from his private life keeps Scorpio from feeling overwhelmed. After all, it is not money that he is really after, but the ability to control his own life. If work had an adverse impact on his private affairs, Scorpio would feel defeated.

Business is fun for Scorpio as long as other people's money is involved. Though his instincts are entrepreneurial, he gets lonely when he is the sole investor.

GYM BUNNY SCORPIO

He loves to see desire in men's eyes. It does not matter whether the desire is for himself or for another, he just likes being around horniness. It makes him feel alive. Some go to a spa, but this Scorpio goes out to a bar to reenergize his spirit.

His own desires are wildly unpredictable. Often he will go after some unbuff troll that anyone else would write off as too, too icky. Yet other times he will ridicule a much cuter guy for presuming to hit on him.

Scorpio is fascinated by the body. He is as interested in the process of building muscle as he is in looking good. He is very conscious of diet as well. If he is feeling stressed, though, there is a danger of overexercising in an attempt to regain control of his life. There is also a tendency toward eating disorders.

Mr. Scorpion is trying to heal himself. His workouts are aimed at overcoming a very specific physical problem. Often, though, this injury is one that only exists in Scorpio's imagination.

Sagittarius

LOVING YOUR SAGITTARIUS

Sagittarius is always hitting on men who are out of his league. Often he is rebuffed, yet he is never discouraged. As insecure as he is about his big butt, and though failure is always possible—or even likely—Sagittarius does not want to let an opportunity go by if there is even the slightest possibility of something magical happening.

His laugh may be a bit big for the room. The swooping gestures are also outsize. This cowboy seems unable to contain himself indoors. Maybe out on the range (or at least in a backyard) his high energy would seem robust and graceful. In here, however, he just gets dirty looks as he bumps into people and knocks over drinks.

Still, it is hard to get seriously annoyed at Sagittarian blunders because the man is just so gosh-darn sweet. When someone is so open, trusting, and willing to expose himself, getting impatient would be like shooting a puppy through the heart. And he is so persistent that the attention is flattering. Or harassing, depending on your point of view.

Sagittarius is looking for the next big thing. If he decides that you are it, he will spare nothing to make you happy.

ATTRACTING A SAGITTARIUS

You have to let Sagittarius be Sagittarius. Do not let him see you roll your eyes when he goes on and on about that trendoid over-aestheticized hot spot. Or when he delivers the inside dish on you-know-who. Or when he crusades for his latest pet cause. To mix metaphors, if you rain on his parade, you will be out in the cold.

Sagittarius is a man in search of something to believe in. His love of new fads and fashionable social causes stems from the hope that each new thing might prove to be the "one." He is that way with relationships too. Sagittarius does play around, but keeps hoping for true love.

However, every relationship disappoints Sagittarius in some way. He can envision the perfect relationship, but neither he nor any partner is perfect. Thus he is happier pursuing you than catching you. Before he has caught you, he can persuade himself that you are a god. Once he has you, he cannot deny your flaws.

So how do you make him believe in you? And continue to believe—even when he knows the truth about you?

You need to be hot action in every sense.

Mr. Horseyman is drawn to energy. He prefers younger men or, at the very least, men with a youthful, forward-looking spirit. Your aspirations count more with him than your actual accomplishments. Noble failures are more noble than failures in his eyes. It is willingness to give new ideas and experiences a fair chance that matters.

Any connection you have to fame or power helps. Sagittarius wants to be at the center of the big picture. Plug him into an important network, introduce him to persons with impact, and Mr. Horseyman is yours.

The human body in motion is his obsession, so let him see you dancing or playing some sport. You do not need big muscles, but you had better be able to use the ones you have got.

Most of all, Sagittarius needs to know that you will not suffocate him with expectations. He feels that being in a gay relationship should be an escape from the role-playing of traditional heterosexual pairings. He needs to see that a relationship with you will not hamper his freedom, but rather can become a passionate adventure shared by two.

Sounds great? Unfortunately Mr. Horseyman feels that this vision of a great gay life exempts him from the little things like being sensitive to his partner. You have already heard him put his foot in his mouth. Wait till he zeros in on your weaknesses.

DATING

As a charter member of the radical hip set, Mr. Horseyman has a lot more riding on where you go on dates than you do. You are going out to be with him. He is going out to be seen. That cute little café will not work if it was hot two weeks ago but not anymore. Only the latest will do. His "Been-there-done-that" attitude might tempt you to set up a series of stay-at-home-with-takeout nights. If you do this, Sagittarius will stop thinking of you as a real date. For Sagittarius, going out with you literally means "going out with you."

However, he is always willing to take a chance on some place or activity he has never heard of before. The idea of discovering the next big thing gets the Sagittarian pulse racing. Also remember that Sagittarius has a wide range of interests, so a day at the zoo can appeal just as much as a night at the Philharmonic. Keep the activities varied and you will keep his interest.

When Sagittarius is in high-gear fun mode, he is an entertainment juggernaut of astonishing single-mindedness. He will brave any danger and risk social ostracism for the sake of fast, furious fun. If you hesitate before the bungee plunge or slow down for a brief meditation during a ten-mile hike, Sagittarius will be on your ass to quit moping and get with the program.

Though Sagittarius can be thoughtless when in a fit of enthusiasm, he is not an ungiving boyfriend. True, he does think any bad fortune you have is your own fault. True, he does mistake tactlessness for honesty. True, he acts like a snotty teenager whenever you are the least bit critical of him. Yet Mr. Horseyman does want to bring you joy. He will gladly pay the bill, buy you presents, and call just to say he thinks you are wonderful. As long as his generosity can be a pleasant surprise, he will be generous. The moment he thinks you expect it—or even worse, need it—the generosity will dry up.

Mr. Horseyman is a shiny happy person who hates being around depressing people. Though he loves to love and loves to help others, he dreads being depended on. If you do not have the resources to take care of your own emotional distress, Sagittarius finds it hard to trust you.

Though sadness sends up red flags for him, little else does. Sagittarius is gullible. You can lie like Satan with no danger of being found out. Sagittarius is impressed by big talk—both yours and his own—so you probably will find yourself spouting whoppers that you would never attempt with another man. Even if he does catch you, he forgives easily as long as you do not act all gloomy and conscience-stricken about it.

SEX

Call him a stallion—he will like that.

The Sagittarian models his sexuality on that of barnyard animals. He may be too much of a Boy Scout to actually achieve his uninhibited, anytime, anywhere, wild, brutish ideal . . . but a boy can dream, can't he?

Sex with Mr. Horseyman vacillates between the sacred and the profane. One second he is cooing in your ear about the physical expression of spiritual love, the next he wants you to boink him on the dining room table.

There is no guilt and no fuss with him. Anything that gives pleasure is good in his eyes, and ceaseless experimentation is a given, so forget value judgments and timidity. Any new kinks or interesting places to do it will meet with his approval. Just realize that Sagittarius may not ever be able to duplicate any particular version of sex, even if it made you gaga. His talent is novelty, not repetition.

Just because he cannot always repeat a particular technique does not mean he peters out. Sagittarian sex can go on

Safe Sex

Take nothing for granted with a Sagittarius. His commitment to you could change tomorrow. As could his commitment to safe sex.

Every day he is with you, it is because he decides in that moment to stay. Every time you have sex, he must decide anew to be safe. The safe sex routine that other couples fall into is not for you, since there is no pattern to what part of the house or what specific type of foreplay takes place. This means running to the nightstand and back when you are playing in the kitchen. Add in Sagittarian clumsiness and it is a sure thing that the wrapper will not open. (And he may not have had penetration in mind anyhow.)

So now that you are both soft, you have to start all over.

The temptation to go bareback (given the logistical problems) is great. The best you two can do is be prepared for the unexpected—though the heavier responsibility will fall to you since Sagittarius likes to play with fire and considers himself immune to the illnesses the rest of us face.

for a long, long, long time—if he does not have another appointment somewhere.

Overbooking can wreak havoc on Sagittarius's sex life. If his schedule does not allow for lovemaking, you can still get him. He loves seeing a body in motion, so just find someplace private and dance for him. If you grind a hot lap dance for him, he will grind one right back. Spontaneity only gets him more aroused, so it will be easy to get him to scrap the schedule for boffing.

Though Sagittarius likes to vary acts, positions, etc., you will notice that he shows especially remarkable skills in the mechanical engineering aspect of anal sex. Whichever role he takes, he has an innate ability to organize your bodies so that weight and thrust achieve maximum impact with minimum discomfort. Had Catherine the Great's stallion been a Sagittarius, she might still be with us today.

LIVING TOGETHER

Before you moved in together, he made promises about what your life together would be like, cocooned in domestic bliss. You should have known by now that promises Mr. Horseyman makes in the heat of the moment will rarely be fulfilled.

For him, home is where you store your clothes.

Sagittarius sees a settled home life as a jumping-off point for new adventures, not an end in itself. When the home dominates his world, he considers it a prison. His values are just different from those of other men. He is more afraid of failing to reach his potential than failing financially. His drive is to make an impact, not to acquire material things (though he might get some of those too). Keep him focused on his dreams and do not let your relationship turn into a long conversation about bills and mortgages—unless you are ready to skip ahead to the *Breaking Up* section.

Emotions run high with Mr. Horseyman in the house. Out in the world Sagittarius is always a broad-minded gentleman. Behind closed doors he is often a self-righteous twit. Convinced he knows what is best for you, he ascribes your mistaken judgment to some character flaw. It would be easy to shrug it off were it not for the fact that he has accurately described an actual character flaw of which you are acutely aware.

The most infuriating part is that after the fight is over, it is completely over. The display of emotion exorcises it, and whatever fueled his anger is gone without a trace. Sagittarius bears no lingering resentment and no guilt. Though he loves high drama, scenes of tender pathos bore him so he will not apologize for injuring you.

Sagittarius will not be mushy with you. He and you will never be joined at the hip. Instead, he shows his love by allowing you the same freedom he wants for himself. Even at his most overbearing, Sagittarius wants you to stand up to him and be your own man. His hope is that, even if you are

Gay Parenting

In most of life, Sagittarius acts first and thinks later. If he really considered how hard it is to be a gay parent, he would never do it. So it is good that he plunges right in, since parenting is an immensely rewarding experience for this man.

He is very concerned with the child's moral development, yet he does not lay down strict rules. Instead, he teaches by example. This is not always helpful with very young children, but it pays off in the teen years. If Sagittarius is adopting, it is worth considering the adoption of older children, since he has such success in helping them move toward adult independence.

not tied by any sense of duty, you will choose to be with him because you just plain want to.

The alternative of you staying because of a sense of obligation would humiliate him. (Notice how he goes out to the movies when you are stuck home with the flu—it is the same principle.) He considers your presence in his bed as proof of your love. And he expects you to recognize his presence as a pledge of love to you. That way he never has to come out and say "I love you," which would really embarrass him.

BREAKING UP

If you want to push Mr. Horseyman's buttons, give him an order. Or, better yet, an ultimatum. Sagittarius can overlook any sin except the attempt to control him. Even if you win, you lose, since he will bolt at the first opportunity to escape a restrictive relationship.

The harder you try to hang on to Mr. Horseyman the more he will pull away. Your jealousy will become an excuse to cheat. Unfounded accusations of any kind offend him so much that he will do what he can to become what you fear he is.

It was clear from day one that he could not keep a secret. When the relationship hits the fan, he has even less reason to keep your dirty laundry in the drawer. Friends will hear the litany of your faults revealed as he tries to win them to his side. If they remain loyal to you, he will just dig down deeper for even worse dish on you.

To avoid the wrath of Horseyman, you need to placate him. Absolve him from guilt. Tell him that it was not his pomposity that tore the two of you apart. Nor was it his immaturity. Nor his irresponsibility. Nor the broken promises. Nor his self-involvement. Nor was it his concern for all people who were not his lover, at the expense of the one man who was. Tell him that the blame lies with you and that you need his help to regain your self-respect. (Remember: His gullibility is your best ally!)

As much as he liked having an unconventional relationship, he will also like having an unconventional breakup. Since Sagittarius tends to look at the bright side, he might think of the breakup as a new beginning. The dissolution of old bonds and the possibility of new loves intoxicates him. That might not be great for your ego, but you should recognize by now that the newest toy is always Sagittarius's favorite. Your actuality cannot compete with his fantasy.

After a time, Sagittarius will want to be a friend. Any residual bitterness on your part will baffle him, since he will only be able to remember the good times you had together.

Coming Out

Though Sagittarius has an outsize personality that shines out through his actions, he reveals surprisingly little personal information in conversation. He thinks that the facts are unimportant and say little about who he is.

Thus it is easier for him to act like an obvious homosexual than to say in so many words that he is one.

Labels in general make him squirm—at least when applied to him. Sagittarius always likes to keep his options open, so how can he call himself "gay" when he might suddenly find a woman attractive? And how can he call himself "bisexual" if it is possible that he will never get involved with a woman?

When Sagittarius comes out, it is usually for moral or political reasons more than personal ones. He hates sticking a label on himself, but cannot bring himself to let down the cause.

THE FIVE FACES OF GAY SAGITTARIUS

DRAG QUEEN SAGITTARIUS

The persona may remind you of a little boy raiding his mom's closet, but this boy is a rebel in pantyhose.

It is the transgression of being a man in women's clothes and not the woman's role itself that thrills him. Inappropriate behavior is his chief delight in or out of a dress.

Though always outrageous, Drag Queen Sagittarius lacks the focused malice of a real diva. He may be hyper-dramatic in dealing with others, but he could never intentionally hurt anyone.

Instead he does all his damage by accident. Sagittarius is the archer who can shoot an arrow into the air, then watch in horror (and satisfaction) as it just happens to land in the heart of his enemy.

One mean booty-shaker, Drag Queen Sagittarius dances with spontaneous ease and grace. Then wipes out to land on her butt. One would say that drag releases the wild side of her personality. Except that she is exactly the same when butching it up.

DOMINANT SAGITTARIUS

If it were nice, it would not be fun.

Within every Dominant Sagittarius is an anger at every person who has ever dared to tell him what he could and could not do. In the act of dominating he is asserting his right to do as he pleases. The irony is that he treats the submissive in the same manner that he abhors being treated.

Dominant Sagittarius will take it to the very edge since danger is his aphrodisiac. In danger he expects to find an ecstasy that will lift him above ordinary experience. However, he is easily distracted away from the kind of ongoing sexual collaboration that can reach such a level. His love of public sex and his habit of divulging his sexual secrets too explicitly further remove Dominant Sagittarius from the ecstasy he craves.

Still, he will not give up. And since he is persistent he will at times reach a divine erotic madness—though not as often as he wants.

ACTIVIST SAGITTARIUS

He really thinks that the world can change and that human nature evolves for the better over time. The nuts and bolts of creating such change elude Activist Sagittarius—but the vision is there.

It is easy for him to make common cause with others whom he does not like. Though he cares for his fellow man, Sagittarius does not fight for people but for abstract principles. However, unless he associates with more practical-minded comrades who anchor him, Activist Sagittarius can slide into fanaticism.

Once Sagittarius crosses over to fanaticism, he will not want to go back to moderation, since the daring take-no-prisoners style that goes with monomania is frighteningly effective for him.

His high political passion leads Sagittarius to spread himself thin. This and a tendency to sacrifice today for the promise of tomorrow means this boy has trouble summoning up enough concentration to build a sustained relationship. But no potential suitor should let this deter him. Sagittarians can always change if they think doing so will lead to something fabulous.

GUPPY SAGITTARIUS

Sure he makes a lot of money, but he spends a lot too.

Between those long vacations in faraway places, those stupid trinkets, and the charitable donations, it is surprising he has anything left. He does not love work for its own sake or money as a status marker. What he loves is the control over his own life that his position allows and the fun he can buy with his money.

With his eye on the big picture, Guppy Sagittarius does not sweat the details—he delegates them. No one minds taking on the responsibility since Mr. Horseyman always gives recognition where recognition is due.

Guppy Sagittarius is a prime candidate for early retirement. Unless he can see some way that his work will benefit society, he will leave the workforce at the earliest opportunity.

He will be missed since his impish approach to business puts his associates at ease. And his departure will have an impact on the corporation since his daring strategies have mostly proved to be moneymakers.

GYM BUNNY SAGITTARIUS

Too much is not enough for him. This is one hungry boy. Hungry for life, hungry for excitement, hungry for men. In his quest for the ultimate he may miss a few smaller pleasures along the way, but Gym Bunny Sagittarius never slows down.

If it is new, fast, and men are pressed close to each other, he is there. The boy can smell a party five miles away. He knows everyone on the scene by name, even if they cannot remember his, because the circuit is his life. Some men might want to be more serious with him but Gym Bunny Sagittarius fears anything that is not strictly casual.

He prefers dancing and running to a gym workout, so his legs are strong and he can use those hips. But often as he exercises, he stops to ask what it all means. To convince himself that he is not brain dead, he pulls out his college philosophy texts and reads some Dennis Cooper.

Then he pours himself into his jeans and is off again into the night.

Capricorn

LOVING YOUR CAPRICORN

He has been watching you but will not approach. It is not that he fears rejection. It is that he fears everyone finding out that he was rejected.

If you make the first overture, he will still be afraid. This time the fear is that his friends will find your pairing ridiculous. What if they laugh at him!

It is a medically proven fact: Capricorns can die of embarrassment.

This is why getting started with them is so torturous.

The first conversation is polite, but noncommittal. You both feel the spark, but Mr. Goat leaves himself an out—will your next meeting be a date or hang-out session for two buddies? He keeps the question open.

Capricorn is more comfortable if you are introduced by a mutual friend whom he can pump for info after you are gone. Otherwise, he will scrutinize your clothing, social manner, and conversation to figure out your income, education, and ambitions. If you seem like a man going nowhere, the pressure will be off him. He can then pursue a casual relationship.

If, on the other hand, you seem to be a man of substance, it all gets more complicated—and slower. When Mr. Goat is trying to begin what he hopes will be a lasting relationship, he takes his own sweet time.

ATTRACTING A CAPRICORN

Most men fall in love with looks and personality. For Capricorn, your career, status, and ambition are also part of the package. He is not necessarily looking for wealth or power, but for someone who is "going somewhere." Inertia is a turnoff. Drive is hot.

Capricorn is most comfortable in relationships where the balance of power is uneven. Father/son, mentor/intern, and teacher/student are the models to go for. He can take either role (though he prefers the senior position). Allowing him to channel your drive is the surest way to enmesh him in your life. He does not look down on men who ask his advice. In fact, it is what he lives for.

Mr. Goat is also interested in your relationship to your family. While he himself has often strained relations with family members, he respects the family structure. He may trash his parents in conversation, but he will be there for them in a crisis. So though he does not want to hear that you live with Mom, he does want to know that Mom matters to you.

The attachment to family is an expression of Capricorn's need to belong. As self-sufficient as he seems, Capricorn struggles with self-doubt. Giving him the reassurance and acceptance that he needs seems like an easy path to boyfrienddom. It is not. Much as he wants what you offer, Capricorn is terrified of becoming dependent on anyone in any way. Early in life, Mr. Goat faced hardships (either emotional or financial) which convinced him that the world is a hostile place in which everyone is a possible assassin. What seems like love could be exploitation.

Because words lie, for Capricorn affection cannot be stated, it must be proven. Simple actions like wiping up his spilled drink or lending him a few bucks till he gets to an ATM have a large significance for him. Only in time, after quite a few dates, will Mr. Goat open up his heart to the possibility that you might just, if he is lucky, be a halfway decent guy. But you need to lay the groundwork now.

Because he hesitates and doubles back so much in his pursuit, you might think that Capricorn ends up with men as patient and cautious as himself. Not true. The buttoned-down Mr. Goat works overtime to fulfill the expectations of others, so it is poetic justice that he usually ends up with men who upset expectations and bring chaos into his life. As much as he voices disapproval, in truth he needs the vigor that a man touched by divine madness can bring out in him.

DATING

Sex and love, like everything else in the Capricorn universe, need to be earned by both parties. It may sound coldhearted, but Capricorn understands that every relationship is a transaction. The deal may be that A gives B his undying love in exchange for B giving A his, but the heartfelt nature of the emotions involved does not change the fact that a deal has been struck.

Dating is the arena in which the negotiation takes place.

Though this definition of dating sounds highly unromantic, Capricorn does believe in old-fashioned wooing. It is always hard for him to show his feelings, but he recognizes that now is the time to give you flowers, love notes, and other tokens of affection if he expects the relationship to grow.

Mr. Goat at this stage takes nothing concerning you for granted. Since he wants to see how you live, it is worth it to have him over for a home-cooked dinner—your efforts will be much appreciated. Visiting his home, your patience in listening to the stories behind his precious souvenirs will also be noted. The respect he shows you could be misconstrued as emotional distance, but it actually indicates strong affection. Far be it from Mr. Goat to be presumptuous (and possibly blow everything) with a man he wants to keep in his life.

The Capricorn's need to justify his fun can suck the spontaneity out of dating. Researching the "best" restaurant or the "right" movie eliminates the possibility of just stumbling across something delightful. Even if he does agree to a less structured date, he will have a backup plan just in case.

Work, time, and money are always topmost in Mr. Goat's mind. He expects you to be ever-ready to discuss work-related issues—in bed, on the getaway weekend—anytime. This will never change, so get used to it. He expects you to be punctual, or at least to let him browbeat you when you are late. Since condescension is his idea of a ripsnorting good time, you may as well let him.

If you consistently divide the check unfairly, or do not leave enough for the tip, you will not be browbeaten. No accusation will be made at all. Since you are obviously a gold-digging whore, you will be dropped. So watch yourself.

Though dating this sign is not 24–7 excitement, it is not stagnant either. The relationship is always moving forward, however slowly. If Mr. Goat cannot anticipate deepening levels of commitment in the future, he will walk out. But if you push things along too fast for him, he will suspect your motives. View the dating process as a taming process. You can with patience teach wild animals to trust you. But if you try to have them eat from your hand on the first day, they will flee forever.

SEX

Looking at the to-do list of a Capricorn friend for the weekend his boyfriend was in town, I once saw "sex" listed.

(Along with "sleep.") Like so many of Capricorn's actions, this one could be misinterpreted as a coldness. Who would need to be reminded to have sex? But the real reason for listing it was that sex was so important to him that he needed to make sure it was not edged out of a cramped schedule.

Just because Capricorn is practical about sexual matters does not mean that he lacks sexual feeling. Far from it. Mr. Goat regards sexual indulgence as the just reward for the self-control and self-denial he normally demonstrates. If he refuses to fuck during the week, claiming that he has to be up early for work, then just wait for the weekend. Deferred pleasures are approached with ecstatic abandon when their time is ripe.

If you get him at a vulnerable time, Capricorn will confess to a past with a few lost weekends of debauchery. He will not boast about them, but he does not regret them either.

Control is a feature of Capricorn lovemaking that can

Safe Sex

Anticipation is half the fun.

Capricorn loves mapping out the possibilities, so even picking out his best underwear and stocking up on condoms can get him aroused. The more planned the encounter is, the more erotic it will be for him, thus discussing what you feel safe with can be a form of foreplay. Also, when Mr. Goat has planned safe play, it is difficult to get him to switch to anything unsafe.

He likes his sex to be dirty and just a little sordid. Any fantasy scenario with a nasty subtext will satisfy him. Punishment and domination always work, whether he is top or bottom, even if there is no actual flesh-to-flesh contact.

express itself as Tantric sex, B&D, S&M, role-playing, or rape fantasies. Even among more vanilla Capricorns control will be evident in how he constructs each session like a well-made play. A succession of acts build on each other, leading inevitably to a satisfying climax. This does not happen by itself. Mr. Goat takes pleasure seriously and has studied the principles of erotic fulfillment assiduously. Aren't you lucky he has?

With Capricorn, everything improves as time goes on. If the relationship continues, he can stop trying to prove that he is a good lover and just relax in the knowledge that he *is* a good lover. Also, as he ages, unlike most men, Capricorn actually becomes more attractive. This gives him the confidence to be more playful and spontaneous in and out of bed.

LIVING TOGETHER

Love means never having to pay late fees. Because Mr. Goat is so good at making sure that the bills get paid on time and that expenses are fairly divided, his partner will want to abdicate household responsibilities to him. Do not do it!

If Capricorn does all the work, which he will do without complaint, he begins to think of the home as belonging to him. You already know he has problems with the concept of "ours" and is just as willing to be your commandant as your lover. He is still so scared that his credit rating, savings, and home could slip away that you need to demonstrate your competence over and over again. Then he still will not trust you, but might accept you as his junior partner.

Capricorn never feels completely grown-up until he has established a household of his own. His tremendous loyalty to you is in large part because you are working with him to create a secure home. (However ineffective he thinks your efforts are, here it is the thought that counts.) Since the two of you are now a family, he might finally let up a bit at work and focus more on spending time with you.

Vulnerabilities previously hidden from you will reveal themselves, since Mr. Goat only lets his guard down in the home. The depression and angry moods he hates showing will be played out in front of you. His pain is painful to watch, but at least the negativity is directed inward.

When Capricorn negativity is directed outward at you, it is like a psychic fart, mysterious in origin, permeating every room, that sends you fleeing into the open air to avoid suffocation. The silent treatment can be confronted but the resentment that hangs in the air can only be endured.

If you stand by your goat in the midst of his black moods, he will probably want to make your coupledom offi-

Gay Parenting

When Mr. Goat is ready to do the white picket fence thing with his 2.5 kids, he is unstoppable. The old slowpoke turns himself into an upright 1950s-style dad at the speed of light. He no longer has time for his gay brethren since he is so busy with the straight parents of his child's friends.

No Republican senator from North Carolina could raise his child with more traditional family values than a gay Capricorn. Mr. Goat sees his job as molding the child into a person who can effortlessly claim his spot in mainstream America.

Being a father comes easy to Capricorn. The school-marm attitude, the bullheadedness, and the authoritarian manner that can be off-putting in a gay bar are absolutely right for dealing with children. In addition, children bring out a warmth and silliness in Mr. Goat that no one else can.

Capricorn self-reliance can lead to self-centeredness. However, this is never a problem for a Capricorn dad, because his life is always centered on his children.

cial. Speaking vows in public is the crown of everything that has gone before. Capricorn has consciously and painstakingly built a life with you. Acknowledgment of that effort is important to him.

Is it any wonder?

All his life Capricorn has gotten attention for his achievements more than for his personality. If you have stayed the course this long, you must love him, not for the things he does, but for who he *is*. That distinction is one Capricorn takes tremendous pride in.

BREAKING UP

Capricorn is more interested in making the relationship work in practical terms than in fulfilling some abstract ideal about what a relationship should be.

Still, there are lines you cannot cross—even in the midst of a breakup:

1. Do not lie to Capricorn. There have been many times he has given you the brutal truth, though it would have been easier to tell you what you wanted to hear. He expects the same treatment in return. His short-term foulness is better than long-term distrust.

2. Do not blame Capricorn for your problems. Take responsibility for your own life. Mr. Goat has enough guilt to carry without having to trek your baggage around as well.

3. Be scrupulous with money. Capricorn never forgets a loan or a debt.

4. Do not tell Capricorn's secrets to the whole world. Those previously unspoken ambitions that he shared with you in the afterglow should stay private. When you disclose Capricorn's confidences to another, it is like throwing the poor boy's heart under a steamroller.

5. Do not mock Capricorn.

He was never an easy man to love. His incessant demands for reassurance, which you knew would not be reciprocated, were piggish. His emotional unavailability to you when you were in crisis was just plain wrong. However, unless you are some mean-ass Scorpio, you will never beat Capricorn at the revenge game, so do not try.

Because Mr. Goat knows what it is like to be misunderstood and treated unfairly, he wants to do better by others. If he has half a chance, he will give you the benefit of the doubt and end the relationship in a dignified manner. You must maintain a respectful manner even when seething inside.

Also, Mr. Goat hopes there is some way you can reconcile. Even if he initiated the breakup. He believes that everything in the world is in scarce supply, including love. After you walk out the door, he is not certain he will find any more. Be kind to him now, and he will remember it for a long time to come.

Coming Out

Though Capricorns mature early, they often have difficulty finding themselves. In their twenties, Capricorns usually feel like something is preventing them from becoming who they were meant to be. Coming out at this stage is usually selective, unless the Capricorn believes he has a mission that is tied to a gay identify.

After age thirty, Capricorn relaxes into himself more and being gay is easier. Capricorn will do nothing to jeopardize his job or social standing, so he may choose a semi-closeted existence if he does not live in a pro-gay community.

Later in life, after establishing himself, Capricorn becomes more free. A hard-won self-acceptance allows him to share more of himself with the world at large.

You will come out of a relationship with Capricorn with a stronger sense of what you want out of life and a more realistic view of where you actually are. Give him credit for how he has helped you.

THE FIVE FACES OF GAY CAPRICORN

DRAG QUEEN CAPRICORN

That awkward, shy boy has become an elegant, self-assured woman.

Drag Queen Capricorn escapes from a painful past through impeccable styling. A remote and distant beauty with a high-gloss glamour, her makeup is a mask which prevents the unfeeling comments of the common rabble to penetrate her sometimes thin skin.

This girl is never taken in by the show she puts on. She has a delightful self-awareness that her cool persona is completely artificial, which allows for self-parody.

Though she seems tough, Drag Queen Capricorn has a heart of gold. She loves taking younger and weaker creatures under her protection. She is the first girl to sign up for any charity event. And she is extremely generous with her criticism of anyone whose fashion sense is less defined than her own.

(Of course her own style, which she thinks of as classic, seems frumpy to the more outré. But we will not get into that catfight.)

DOMINANT CAPRICORN

The thrill of transgression attracts Dominant Capricorn. Pretending to be Mr. Nice Guy to the straight world, while doing foul perverted things in bed makes him feel superior to the ordinary folk. Giving out orders and meting out punishment to his submissives may just be role-play, but the role is one he thinks he deserves.

Bitterness fuels Capricorn's sardonic take on dominance. Few top men can do cruelty with the same sense of entitlement. Even when Capricorn avoids physically dangerous play, there is something frightening in the emotions he evokes.

Dominant Capricorn has no guilt about using money or drugs to buy sex. However, he does have shame about it and would be mortified if anyone other than the trick knew that he had paid.

Dominant Capricorn's mastery can only be toppled by snickering at his act. Other men can incorporate your mockery into their fantasy, using it to drive them to even higher dominance. Laughter pushes Capricorn out of the arena.

ACTIVIST CAPRICORN

Capricorn has a tremendous feeling for his fellow man. However, he is often uncomfortable in social situations. What to do?

Social activism allows Capricorn to touch lives without getting personal. Workplace issues especially interest him. Activist Capricorn is a keen political strategist with a savvy eye that can pick out the most winnable battles. But for him this is not enough.

The problem with political work is that every accomplishment can be wiped away in the next election. Activist Capricorn strives to create a more lasting change in society as a whole, even if there are few immediate benefits.

A naturally conservative personal style means that even his most outrageous positions will come across as nonthreatening and reasonable. Yet in his drive to push forward his agenda, Capricorn can become intolerant of those who will not cooperate with him. He can respect those who hold positions contrary to his own, but he cannot respect those who do not know how to play the game.

GUPPY CAPRICORN

Monday through Friday, he belongs to the corporation. From Friday night on he is his own hard-partying hombre.

During the week, he listens to the homophobic jokes of his superiors, puts in sixteen-hour days, and does whatever it takes to get ahead without objection. It is as if he can put his own personality on hold. On the weekend he lives in a blur of sensual pleasure that ends promptly at 9 A.M. Monday.

Guppy Capricorn lives with contradictions but sees nothing peculiar about his lifestyle. In fact, he becomes so used to self-denial that having his fun, without the dull grind preceding it, would be no fun at all.

In both parts of his life Guppy Capricorn likes to rely on himself, building his own career and finding his own fun without depending on any single mentor or buddy. He is results-oriented in both areas, willing to set aside the rules if two business partners or two lovers mutually consent to an unorthodox arrangement.

And if both parties agree to confidentiality.

GYM BUNNY CAPRICORN

If he is going to put all that effort into his body, the least he can do is enjoy it.

Maybe not, since he looks at it as a kind of Zen thing— if he can overcome his body's resistance, then he can overcome the world's resistance. When he works out, the result of his labor is visible. Walking around in tight clothing he is not showing off his muscles. Rather he is showing off the hard work it took to build up those muscles. Gym Bunny Capricorn is still too timid to be as much a player as he would like, but at least with that body he is noticed.

By creating a new body for himself, Gym Bunny Capricorn hopes to establish a new identity for himself, separate from his family. Eventually he will assert who he is through other means as well, but his body will always be the starting point.

So while he is grateful to the look that gets him laid, he is more grateful to the muscular definition that helps him define who he is.

Aquarius

LOVING YOUR AQUARIUS

You could not call him shy, so why is he not picking up on your obvious interest in him?

Aquarius more than holds his own in a discussion of the upcoming election or String Theory. However, when you corner him for a more intimate conversation, he becomes evasive. His impersonal charm evaporates when the contact becomes personal. The Aquarius *über*-dork will stare a hole through you at the bar, but will not ask for a date when you introduce yourself.

Aquarius lives in a clear-cut world of mixed signals. He gets them from others and he puts them out himself. The subtle, unexplainable rules that we use every day to dress appropriately, eat right, know who to come on to, etc., are for him a confusing mishmash of mystical nonsense. That is why this sign has the worst gaydar. You could be dressed like Liza Minnelli, ordering drinks from a bare-chested bartender in a night spot called The Cock, and he will still have to ask some mutual acquaintance if you might be gay.

His oblique semi-come-ons are an attempt to play the game right without embarrassing himself. When he finally realizes that you have been trying to encourage his advances, Aquarius will pounce on you like a horny teenager.

ATTRACTING AN AQUARIUS

You are going to have to work to get this guy.

Though he wants to be the cool, rational one, Mr. Waterboy is a self-contradicting, unpredictable, erratic, eccentric freak of nature. His principles are the highest, but his actions fall short. He believes in love, honesty, harmony, unselfish giving to others—as long as they do not disrupt his day.

This makes it hard to define just who the real Mr. Waterboy is. His words and his actions seem to come from two separate personalities. Aquarius is a suave raconteur who can effortlessly enthrall a party of friends for hours, but then becomes insta-geek when alone with another man. His inconsistency is the only constant about him, yet he thinks he is the one stable man in a world of Lucy Ricardos.

Aquarius views emotion as a quicksand that will sink anyone bestial enough to indulge in it. Passionate men are walking vats of quicksand seeking to lure Mr. Waterboy to his demise. Still the cool Aquarius wants the heat that such men bring into his life. Finding a man whose main passion is either for some cause or for himself rather than his partner solves the dilemma. Much as Aquarius scolds about selfishness, in truth he takes pornographic delight in witnessing an unabashed self-involvement he would never allow himself.

Somewhere in his head Aquarius has a Platonic ideal of what a good relationship is that bears no resemblance to actual human life. However, this ideal is more real to him than the raw desire that overcomes him when he finds love. So it will take more than simple attraction to hook him. His ideal relationship is largely mental bonding, so you need to let him see the measure of your mind. He loves debating on politics, technology, and art—any topic that is neither personal nor trivial. Aquarius is drawn most strongly to men who give him a fresh perspective. The quirks that make you feel like an oddball with other men are the very qualities that Aquarius will find absolutely fascinating.

Conventional wisdom says that if two men are friends, they cannot later become lovers. This does not apply to Aquarius. He does not see much difference between being a friend or a lover, so one will not preclude the other.

Because he feels that no individual relationship can possibly stack up against the fate of society and the world, Aquarius equates romantic love with outrageous egomania. Sentimentality and clinginess on your part will only confirm this view, sending him flying. Mr. Waterboy's nature is to stand outside of the norm, and he needs a man with an independent streak of his own. Aquarius is not a boyfriend for the easily embarrassed or the touchy.

DATING

You can call it "dating." But as usual, Aquarius redefines the term, just like he redefines "relationship" and "romance." On those occasions that he does go for the traditional hearts and flowers, there is a self-consciousness in his manner. When he is at his most sincere, Aquarius is also at his most weird.

Because he always invites others to join you when going out, then springs for the e-mail and the phone when you get home, you might think he finds you dull company. Do not worry. It is simply good old-fashioned fear of emotional intimacy. Mr. Waterboy fears that without chaperones to siphon off some intensity, you two could get too heavy.

Closeness will bring commitment, which Aquarius rightly fears. He takes all of his commitments (which are few) so seriously that their burden threatens to crush his little skull. In romance this burden is not so much panic at the prospect of choosing one man, but rather the terror of eliminating all other possibilities. You already know how important it is to him to keep options open if you have ever tried to make him decide when to meet for dinner. Do you think dating you at all is any easier a decision for him?

But once he decides, he is decided. Just try shaking his commitment once he finally, at long last makes it. Of course if you lack the patience, casual dating and casual sex are fine with him too. Just be up front with him about what you expect from the relationship. Aquarius will not hold your stated desires against you. However, he will damn you for any lies or evasions. He expects from you the honesty and openness that he aspires to. In return, Aquarius will try to be as honest with you as he can. Unfortunately, since his own emotions are usually hidden from him, that honesty can only go so far.

No matter what you want from the relationship, Mr. Waterboy will treat you the same as his other friends. To him it seems unfair that any man should get special consideration just because he is sleeping with him, or even because he is in love. As time goes on and you become a habit, Aquarius may elevate your position slightly—though he will always think of you as a friend first and a lover second.

Though Mr. Waterboy enjoys anything new and is a sucker for a good gimmick, he is not a trend whore. Sure, he likes to go where everyone else is going, but that does not mean his judgment will also follow the herd. He understands that neither mass popularity, snob appeal, nor the price tag can indicate the true value of something. Discovering something wonderful in a thing that others reject is a source of pride for Mr. Waterboy. A night out, wandering with no plans, trusting serendipity to let you stumble on something fascinating is the best date you can take him on.

However, you need to take his tastes as a given. Nothing

you can do will get him to change his opinion of MTV, Indian food, Caspar Van Dien, or any other cultural phenomenon. He will not try to change your personal biases and will resent it if you try to change his. Compromise is not a problem for him, but change will never happen.

SEX

Mr. Waterboy is uncomfortable with the animal side of human life. He feels contempt for physical needs like eating, drinking, and sleeping. He thinks physical illness is the body's insult to the mind.

So even though he enjoys sex, Aquarius feels somewhat ashamed of it since it involves cum, hair, the anus—all those things he would rather forget about. If he could somehow translate the antiseptic quality of cybersex to real life he would enjoy sex even more.

Because he experiences love in the mind, Aquarius does not take his lover's need for physical affection seriously. The man might very well be willing to lay down his life for you, yet never give a spontaneous hug. Besides, Aquarius does not give his other friends hugs—why should he give them to his lover, who after all is just another very good friend?

This is why Aquarians tend to be cold to their partners after sex. It does not feel fair to him to make any particular relationship "special" in that way. In fact, the more emotionally involved he is during the lovemaking the more he feels obligated to disavow it afterward. With time and commitment, however, the chill will lessen.

Mr. Waterboy brings the same unpredictability to sex that he does to everything else. The erratic nature of his sexual drive can make you alternately exhausted with his demands and lonely for attention. The limits of your endurance for sex or celibacy mean little to him since, as usual, he is running on his own unique clock.

Though he might be shy about making suggestions himself, any unusual kinks or fantasies you want to try will delight him. His sexuality is by nature adventurous, but you may need to build up his confidence in this area. When you do, Aquarius will reward you with the kind of ever-evolving, ever-energized sex life that most couples only dream of.

LIVING TOGETHER

If you are lucky, he is no Suzy Homemaker, preferring to leave the details of running the household to you. Aquarius worries that housework and maintenance could take over his life. In truth, most Aquarians are not very savvy on cooking, cleaning, and repairs—but a few men of this sign hide their lack of domestic talents behind a surefire "system." Those

Safe Sex

As if sex were not complicated enough.

Aquarius is scared enough about what can happen emotionally during lovemaking, so worrying about his physical health as well is a huge burden. Add to this his abhorrence of being told what to do, and safe sex becomes a troublesome issue for Aquarius.

It gets him mad.

However, the cleanliness of safe sex does appeal to Mr. Waterboy. Anything that removes him from the dirt of another man's body cannot be completely bad.

Mr. Waterboy's feelings about safe sex are as complex as everything else in his life. The pendulum swings both ways, so you never know whether he will curse at the condom or just use it without making a big deal. You can only be sure that he will not treat the precautions the same way he did last time.

Aquarians with a housekeeping system are rigid about it. These guys will help out around the house but insist that you do everything their way.

Better to have an Aquarius who lets you be the house-wife with no assistance from him.

Mr. Waterboy has trouble appreciating when a relationship has progressed into another phase. Moving in together means that the two of you now have a different kind of accountability to each other—which Aquarius will ignore. You will never know when he will be home for dinner or when he is leaving to visit his family without you. He wants the two of you to maintain your independence but confuses freedom with emotional distance. Aquarius does need time alone and time with friends apart from you, but you need to gently remind him that you are more than just a roommate.

With friends Aquarius is often willing to sacrifice his own needs, but with his live-in boyfriend Aquarius is much

Gay Parenting

Even many straight Aquarians would rather adopt than go through pregnancy and babyhood. The dependency of an infant has no charm for this sign. For Aquarius the fun of parenting begins when a child begins to assert his will. Aquarius sees his parental role as that of a teacher, sharing with his child a delight in discovering all the world has to offer.

Aquarius knows how to explain your relationship to the child and the child's friends in terms they can understand. While never lying about the stigma a gay family faces, he also helps the child develop pride in the differences that set your household apart from those around you.

more unbending. When he does give in to you, it is not out of love but because he fears that your anger will upset his own equilibrium.

Finances are often a subject for disagreement, because though Aquarius claims to be nonmaterialistic, he cares a good deal about money. He carries a budget in his head which he will not disclose to you until you violate it. In other areas as well, Aquarius has made firm plans without your knowledge. Only when you unknowingly screw his agenda will he reveal them. Then, after you know his plans, he will turn them around completely.

Aquarius's plans can blind him to reality. If Mr. Waterboy has an expectation of what will occur, he often does not recognize when something else entirely takes place. Then, when you give him a reality check, it appears to him that once again he is misunderstood, though in the right. This obliviousness is paradoxically a source of strength. It is what allows him to stand by you even when common sense would indicate that he should bail out. Aquarius is squarely focused on the best possibility for what the relationship can become rather than the failings of what it actually is.

Breaking Up

Mr. Waterboy sincerely believes that any conflict can be resolved by discussing it. Yet when he has reached his breaking point, Aquarius leaves without a word. He is more used to reversals of fortune than continuity, so the man who never quite knew how to keep a relationship going knows exactly how to make a clean break.

Aquarius stays faithful more because it is easy than because it is right. Falling in love is not something he does often, but when he does it rocks his foundations. If he falls for another while with you, even if there is no cheating, he will resent you until he gets over it. Still, Aquarius is rarely in a hurry to end a relationship and is even less rushed to start a new one, so it is possible to weather this rough patch.

There are two ways to decisively end the relationship. One is to simply absent yourself. If you are not nearby, or at least in frequent phone contact, Aquarius will not pine away for you. In fact, he prefers that the relationship peters out rather than face the Sturm und Drang of a confrontational ending.

The other way to break up is to increase your demands on him. He likes to imagine that after a time relationships take care of themselves. If the upkeep taxes him too much, then you will be seen as a liability. Though his love never quite disappears, Aquarius will amputate any relationship that threatens to pull him under.

Coming Out

Innate sexual orientation is a difficult concept for Aquarius. Though it goes against modern science, he likes to think that, at least in part, his homosexuality was a choice.

Though honesty is highly valued by this sign, getting along with others is valued even more. So Mr. Waterboy believes in being completely out but feels no guilt about being closeted. This is one of those things that make absolute sense to Aquarians but seem daft to anyone else. Ultimately coming out is a political act to Aquarius. He does not do it to improve his own life but out of a sense of responsibility to his gay brothers.

However, he does it completely on his own timetable, and any pressure on him will backfire, sending him deeper into the closet.

If Mr. Waterboy seems too calculating in matters of the heart, he is. More often than not he hurts himself most of all when leaving a lover. Since he tends to value the public face of the pairing more than the intimate support, Aquarius often severs an emotional lifeline because his lover does not fit in with his circle of friends.

With his eye ever on the big picture, Aquarius loses sight of the individuals who are closest to him. The intellectual bigotry (or moral rectitude) in the Aquarian psyche will not tolerate a lover who violates his ethical sense. Compassion comes easier to Aquarius with strangers than with lovers.

The one small mercy is that Aquarius does not bad-mouth his ex-lovers.

THE FIVE FACES OF GAY AQUARIUS

DRAG QUEEN AQUARIUS

This drag is not swish. It is gender-fuck. "After all," Drag Queen Aquarius asks, "has not the human race moved beyond the arbitrary labels of 'male' and 'female'?" This gal claims to express the androgynous ideal that all persons should be reaching for in the new millennium.

Ms. Waterperson gets along with just about every faction in the drag community, even though none of them understands a word she says or respects her fashion judgment. Still Drag Queen Aquarius is so sincere and unique that they cannot help but love her.

Drag Queen Aquarius follows underground designers and cutting-edge performance art for inspiration toward expanding the horizons of drag. Though she may be Queen Avante, the girl rarely works solo, because she knows that without the support of her sisters she is sunk. She sets her weirdness off by being seen with the kind of hokey drag she herself moved beyond ages ago.

DOMINANT AQUARIUS

Outlaw sex. The fun is doing everything that those in power say you cannot do. Dominant Aquarius sees his sexuality as a way to give the finger to a hypocritical society.

After all, if everyone is a consenting adult, then what is the harm?

The structure of the S&M transaction frees Aquarius in a way that ordinary social interaction cannot. As he understands it, the submissive's only role is to let Aquarius be Aquarius, allowing him to set the rules and define the limits.

In his quest for ultimate kink, Dominant Aquarius tends to forget the limits of the human body. Without thinking, he will make the clamps too tight or shove the dildo too hard. But some bottoms enjoy that sort of thing.

Being worshipped by a group of slaves is his favorite fantasy, though it is one that he is ashamed to admit to. However, when you see him at an orgy, you can be sure he is thinking, "If only all the other tops would leave, *then* I would have fun!"

ACTIVIST AQUARIUS

Nothing is sacred to Activist Aquarius. He will ruthlessly trample on feelings and destroy institutions if he believes such actions will help bring about a better world.

He is not intolerant of those who disagree with him. He just thinks they are dumb. He remains outwardly respectful because, though a revolutionary, Aquarius is more subversive than confrontational. He is so fascinated by his opponents that he studies them to learn what bad psychology could have made them so benighted.

Thinking that he knows what others need more than

they do themselves gives Activist Aquarius the confidence and energy to instigate real change. Sacrificing himself for the cause is easy since he has little sense of his own personal identity outside of his political beliefs and vision of the future.

GUPPY AQUARIUS

Mr. Idea Man is well liked throughout the office. Though he is a rising star, he has a nonchalant way of keeping tasks in perspective that puts all his coworkers at ease. Even the homophobes do not mind him, considering his homosexuality more of an eccentricity than a threat.

So much seems effortless. Mr. Waterboy is rarely seen studying reports yet he seems to know all the facts as if by osmosis. The latest technology also comes easily to him. Implementation and follow-through, however, are difficult for him. Though Guppy Aquarius comes up with the ideas that will move his company forward, his productivity comes in spurts. For sustained effort he depends on his support staff.

While the work is going on, he is a dedicated team player, although he refuses to follow the same rules as the other team members. After a job is over, when it is time for the kudos to be handed out, Mr. Waterboy will step forward to accept full credit for the success of the project.

GYM BUNNY AQUARIUS

By disciplining himself to work through the pain and beyond the boredom, Gym Bunny Aquarius hopes to elevate his consciousness. After a workout, his mind and body feel pure.

The look-but-don't-touch sexuality of the locker room also makes him feel all clean inside. Anytime that he can gawk or even have sex without having to remember anyone's name, Gym Bunny Aquarius is happy. It is not sex that makes him feel impure, but the whole messy game of pursuing it. He prefers a good back room or bathhouse where he can get off with no one pretending to be his friend.

He does not fall easily into a routine workout schedule since sleep difficulties and social commitments make it impossible to come at the same time every day. This is fine by him since he likes to see different bodies every time he goes. Each mass of sweaty bodies out there on the floor suggests a whole new cast for that orgy he fantasizes about.

Pisces

LOVING YOUR PISCES

When he is talking to you for the first time, he is drunk.

It might be on beer or it could be on something nonalcoholic. He could be intoxicated on the music, the room's general vibe, the wad of cash in his pocket, or your gorgeous eyes.

Whenever Pisces is in an outgoing mood, he is intoxicated on something. But even when he is outgoing, a part of him is held back—you can see him thinking things he does not say. It is as if he were partly somewhere else, hearing a secret symphony that you cannot tune into.

That is because he is.

What you are saying and doing with each other is the least important part of what is happening. There is a subtext, an unspoken exchange under the surface that most men are only semi-aware of. This subtext is Pisces' main focus; it is the secret soundtrack of his life.

Each Pisces has his own brand of weirdness, which makes him tolerant of the strangeness of others. There is no need to pretend that you are anyone different than who you are.

This does not mean meeting Mr. Fish is a comfortable experience. His sudden silences and nonsequiturs are frustrating to the more literal-minded. His inability to talk about his own desires and goals will make it almost impossible to figure out just what he expects from you—until you shut up and clue in to the telepathic messages Pisces is sending out.

ATTRACTING A PISCES

Mr. Fish does not confine himself to any one "type" because his attraction is not primarily physical. He is looking for a man who triggers strong emotion in him and this response is to the inner man, not the outer package. The kind of emotions stimulated do not matter because Pisces does not judge feelings as "good" or "bad." He just wants to feel with intensity, so powerful anger is better for him than weak joy.

Because most emotions are fleeting anyway, chances are that strong negative emotions will turn to strong positive ones and back. Pisces is fearless in surfing the ever-changing emotional waves. His only real fear is indifference, which seems a kind of death.

The Pisces need to reach out to others is often misunderstood. While it is true that Pisces will fantasize about any man he meets, he is seriously interested in only a few. However, his habit of giving emotionally to anyone in need—even strangers in a bar—leads men to think he is coming on to them when he is not.

And if he is single at the time, Mr. Fish will not do much to disabuse them of this notion.

Since he cannot conceive of life alone, if Mr. Fish has no strong family or social network, a man he only half wants is better than nothing. In other words, if he is new to town, he is easy.

To foster real love, though, you have to go down the

rabbit hole into Piscesland. In his world, how things feel is more important than objective reality. Ideas are linked by association more than logic. The world we see and touch is an illusion; the one we sense in our dreams is solid.

For most of us, the way we think, plan, and act is formed by the language we use to communicate. Pisces thinks in pictures rather than words, so his thoughts, plans, and actions are formed by pictures—the fantasy and memory images he carries in his heart. Early in life, Pisces learned that his world is for him alone—when he tries to share it with others, they either mock him or are baffled.

To win his love, words will not do, since he knows that words lie. You need to demonstrate in your behavior the same acceptance and tolerance he shows you. You need to enter his world with an attitude of respect rather than one of criticism.

Pisces feels much more than he expresses, so it will be hard to know just where you stand with him at any given moment. Be aware that he always knows how you feel. Your desire for him and the vulnerability it brings will draw him to you.

After all, Pisces always wants to be in love with something or someone—so it might as well be you.

DATING

The traditional symbol for Pisces is two fish, but a sponge might be equally appropriate. Mr. Fish absorbs the characteristics of the people around him into himself. You will notice as you date that your interests become his interests and your habits become his habits. Even any talents you have for things like math, music, or cooking become his talents as well.

Pisces does not think of this as losing his personality but rather as expanding it. For him, identity is infinitely variable and ever changing. He would not want to remain the same man all his life any more than he would want to wear the same underwear. Instead, Pisces would like to have a drawer full of identities that he can pull out and assume whenever he wants.

For this reason, though he seems to live for those he loves, Pisces will never belong to any man. You can be together for fifty years and there will be at least one self he never lets you see. Notoriously hypersensitive, Pisces protects himself by keeping a part of himself secret from everyone and safe from injury.

Given the above, what do you do with him on a Saturday night? ESCAPE!!!

The practical problems of making a living and getting along are huge burdens to Pisces. He wants more from life than is possible—he wants meaning, faith, and a feeling of wholeness few ever achieve. If through cinematic fantasy, Glenlivet, coke, the beach, or the pounding beat of the dance floor he can rise above mundane concerns for a short period, it may not be the transcendence he hopes for, but it will be some relief.

Make your time together something apart from the ordinary. If you are also an escape for him, the relationship will be more solid. Special restaurants, new clubs, and visits to hidden spots of natural beauty will rub their magic off on you. If budget is not an issue, Mr. Fish loves luxury and he loves being taken care of. An evening in which he does not have to consider the price of anything and can just wallow in the pleasure of fine food, fine wine, and sumptuous surroundings is like heaven for him.

Pisces is sensitive to his surroundings, so do not take him anywhere with harsh lighting, clunky decor, or ugly noise. Pisces' mind works associatively, so if he associates you with unpleasant places, he will come to think of you as unpleasant.

Because he is so easygoing you might think that Pisces has no mind of his own. Wrong. Pisces always has an opinion about everything. His seeming detachment is just a natural reserve about expressing his own thoughts. But he *does* think them. When your actions offend him, he may offer no overt resistance. Instead, he just disappears inside himself or drifts away. Attempts to dominate him are as useless as attempts to carry water in your hands. Very soon you will discover that he is gone and you have nothing.

Trying to extract commitments is equally difficult. Mr. Fish hates to give a definite yes or no, because he thinks of a promise as some fiendish trap. Your commitment will have to come first. After time, when trust develops, he will also take that step—but not before.

SEX

The point of sex, in Piscesland, is to dissolve the boundaries between one man and another so that they can become one. Mr. Fish finds his ecstasy as he merges into union with another.

Of course, when a man has such a mystical vision of sex it can be hard for him to discuss the nitty-gritty details about which positions are comfortable for him and which kinks are not. The easier alternative is to be open to anything.

Mr. Fish wants to know what excites you, so that he can become the lover you have always fantasized about. However, it would be a mistake to take undue advantage of this. Whenever anything becomes too much of a bother, Pisces loses interest. So, willing as he is to fulfill your wildest desires, if the demands become so heavy that sex turns into work, he will freeze up on you.

On the other hand, tenderness and affection can transform Pisces. In a loving atmosphere, his touchiness and secretiveness will become less pronounced and the dark moods will be fewer. Pisces responds best to relaxed and uninhibited eroticism. Time constraints and men with a limited repertoire will not satisfy him. Spend time together cuddling, sharing a bath, and just plain lounging, and watch where it leads—it will build up to Pisces lovemaking at its best.

Because he is sensitive to his surroundings, he will be happiest if you make your bedroom a sanctuary, with its own special lighting and music. Splurging on soft, sensual sheets will also help. Pisces has a rich fantasy life, and if you can get him to share it with you, it can help guide you toward making a home and making love in the ways that fulfill him the most.

Safe Sex

The mind is Pisces' most sensitive erogenous zone. His ability to enter fully into fantasy makes unsafe practices unnecessary.

Except for the fact that many of his fantasies are about risky behavior.

Sacrificing life and health for a few moments of ecstasy with a man sounds like a pretty good trade-off to Pisces. He may never act on it, but the idea of sharing everything—even viruses—with another man has an appeal for him. Mr. Fish wants love without limits of any kind on its expression. Though he knows that such love is not possible in this world, he still yearns for it.

Oddly enough, if Pisces falls for a man who is HIV-positive, he probably will not even fantasize about unsafe sex. It is the gamble of unsafe sex that holds the attraction, not certain danger. In such a case, the self-protective instinct will be stronger than sexual desire.

LIVING TOGETHER

It will never be even-steven.

Dividing up chores or taking turns is a bit too structured for Pisces to handle. For him, even putting out the garbage on Tuesdays and paying the rent on the first of the month are too confining.

Pisces prefers to do what is easiest rather than what is right and fair. In the past this worked in your favor, when he avoided confronting you over your faults and wrongdoing. But now that you live together, you may find yourself stuck with all the responsibilities that Pisces finds distasteful. Though Mr. Fish shows gratitude, you wish he had negotiated this beforehand rather than leaving you holding the bag.

This issue has a deeper significance for Pisces. Mr. Fish sincerely wants to be the practical guy, standing on his own two feet—but he also sincerely fears that taking complete responsibility for himself could isolate him from you. Hence he is both resentful of and happy for your assistance. Resolving this ambivalence is key, because the value of the relationship for Pisces is that it gives him strength, so if he acts weak within it, it is doomed.

One avenue for resolution is through learning to accept Pisces' help.

Mr. Fish's first instinct is always to aid those in need—especially you. When times are good, Pisces often does not know how to show his love. When you are in any kind of turmoil, Pisces will be right there, happy to counsel and give practical assistance. He is remarkably nonjudgmental, so you need never be embarrassed about your feelings. Many men reject Pisces' helping hand since he can be flaky. However, you will find that he is more than competent when doing for others—he only screws up when trying to do for himself.

You will be given much freedom, even though you live together. Pisces knows that you think his friends are strange and does not mind that you would rather not spend time with them. So even though he might be clingy at times, Mr. Fish respects that you will have separate social circles. He also is aware that each of you needs time to be alone.

The need for friendships and the need for solitude are easy for Pisces to acknowledge. However, he might feel it is selfish to impose anything else on you. Thus it is easier for him to ignore his needs for affection, household money, R&R, etc., than to express them. When his hopes for time with you or other plans are disappointed, he will say "It does not matter," or "Who cares?" but it does matter and he does care. Pisces can find fulfillment in self-sacrifice if it is for

Gay Parenting

Though it is impossible to insulate children against the pressures of the world, Mr. Fish tries. If he has his way, no child of his will ever know that anyone is against gay families. By creating a home filled with whimsy, warmth, and tons of make-believe, Pisces thinks he can protect his child against all the awkwardness and struggles of growing up.

When his child does get hurt, Pisces is always there saying the right things (though secretly he blames himself for any problems the little one encounters). He does not pressure his child as aggressively as other parents, but his hands-on, always sympathetic, unconditionally loving style of smothering can fuel equally violent adolescent rebellion.

Pisces must learn to be more laid-back when faced with a teen monstrosity. And since his love is never in doubt, in time his child will come around.

something that matters—when it is for the trivial reason of keeping peace in the home, it only breeds resentment.

Provide encouragement for Mr. Fish to be more direct with you about his needs and his complaints. If you do not foster self-respect in him, you are not the lover he needs. But if you do, he will stick to you like a barnacle.

BREAKING UP

Mr. Fish sees little difference between what is true and what might as well be true. The ease with which Mr. Fish tells lies to workmen, creditors, and neighbors might make you wonder how truthful he is with you. Especially since so many of his lies are meaningless fibs serving no useful purpose.

Nothing is simple with Pisces and this issue is no exception. Many times the lies tell a kind of truth, describing what a situation feels like subjectively to Pisces. Listen between the lines to hear what Pisces cannot bring himself to say.

Pisces deceives himself most of all. His ability to delude himself gives him the courage to continue when times are rough and to walk away from what anyone else would consider a good thing. Pisces is usually the only one hurt by his deceptions, since they eventually result in losing the trust of his lover.

Whichever one of you decides to end the relationship, just remember: It ain't over till it's over. Pisces still has a few surprises in store.

If you end the relationship, there may be a big scene with tears and begging until Pisces rolls over and plays dead. From that point on Mr. Fish accept all your charges and recriminations with no defense. Pisces is at his best when he is open to a range of possibilities. Once the possibilities are used up and it is clear that the relationship is headed for breakup, he has no energy to give you.

If Pisces says he wants out, he is really asking for you to

fix what is wrong between you. And you had better do so. When Mr. Fish has had enough and really decides to call it quits, he will leave like a thief in the night. There will be no second chance for you.

Even when the end is decisive, guilt lingers like a nasty stain. Pisces says nothing critical of you—but even if he did the dumping, it feels like it is all your fault. Pisces is a romantic with expectations so high that no lover could fulfill them, so why do you feel bad about being a disappointment?

Mr. Fish has an infinite capacity for feeling pain and making his ex-lover feel it too. However, he also recovers more completely than other men do. You may never be his best buddy, since Pisces has a long memory. But you have not damaged him for good—though he would like you to think that—so do not look back, and get on with your life.

Coming Out

The boy can pop in and out of the closet like a jack-in-the-box. Pisces feels no obligation to help the world put him in any particular category—in fact, he likes to confuse people by defying definition.

Because Pisces often feels that the world is against him and because his privacy is so valuable to him, he hates to put himself in the firing line by taking a stand such as coming out. However, when Pisces sees other gays or a special loved one facing discrimination, he feels that he has no choice but to come out.

Whether he stays out or not depends on whatever circumstances arise later, though he will always be ready to be out when it can help others.

THE FIVE FACES OF GAY PISCES

DRAG QUEEN PISCES

Every man thinks that he is the only one who really understands Miss Fish—and every man is right. Miss Fish is like a blank slate on which each of us projects our own inner drag queen. Drag Queen Pisces is not putting on a femme act. Rather she is channeling the eternal feminine. That is why Miss Fish does not inspire laughs or lust as much as awe.

All the work she does to look good gives Drag Queen Pisces a geisha-like quality, because she does not seem vain. It is as if she were working to create beauty, glamour, and wit for their own sake, and that she herself is the medium is merely accidental.

That is until she gets sucked into drag queen culture.

When Miss Pisces finds herself in the company of bitches, she can paint on Jungle Red with the best of them. To avoid this shallow pettiness, Drag Queen Pisces must not let herself become dependent on other drag queens for her social and sexual outlets.

DOMINANT PISCES

Pisces can feel the pain, longing, and weakness that is within each person that he encounters. That is pretty exhausting, so some Pisceans like to turn off the empathy, be selfish, and get in touch with their dark side.

Because Pisces blurs the line between fantasy and reality, his dark side can get really dark. Moderation has no meaning to him, so he drinks too much, parties too much, and plays too rough. He has no limits, so why should you?

In an ever-changing world, the roles of master and slave are an anchor for Dominant Pisces. In that relationship, each person knows how to behave and what to expect. Role-play is like an armor that protects Pisces against the dangerous unpredictability of sexual emotions.

Submissives have to get used to how easily Pisces slips in and out of his dominant persona. One minute he makes you lick the sole of his boot, the next he is offering to cook you breakfast.

ACTIVIST PISCES

Yes, Activist Pisces knows that he cannot save the world. But he hopes that by trying he can make things just a little better for someone.

It is the plight of the individual that motivates Pisces to work for social change. Though he might discuss principles and ideals, those are justifications after the fact. For Pisces, it all begins with an emotional response to people in trouble.

Mr. Fish does not care how he accomplishes his goals, as long as he accomplishes them. If it means cutting a few corners or ignoring the rules, so be it. While this makes him highly effective in bringing relief to the suffering, it can also create enemies among those in power.

Though it looks as though he has no personal life, Activist Pisces does not complain. He does not compartmentalize, so the work he does *is* a personal life.

And besides, Pisces knows how to shoehorn some fun into a busy schedule. A boy can be politically engaged and still enjoy fine dining, couture fashion, and sliding around on silk sheets.

GUPPY PISCES

His rise in the business world is not the result of ambition. It is the result of obsession. Guppy Pisces does not work for the money or advancement, but rather for the sheer joy of losing himself in intense activity.

He may have plans and projections to back him up, but

Pisces understands that business is an art, not a science, and that in the end you have to depend on gut instincts—which he has in abundance. Pisces' talent for spontaneously making the right decision is the secret of his success. Marketing is the area where Mr. Fish's business skills are sharpest. He just seems to know what people want and what ideas are in the air. If you ask him how he knows, Pisces cannot tell you. It happens by osmosis.

Though he throws himself wholeheartedly into his career, Guppy Pisces can only take it half-seriously. He knows that because economic factors are unsteady, everything could be lost, and if it was, Pisces would simply start all over again (after a few months of intense depression). His instinct for self-preservation prevents him from tying his self-esteem to business success.

GYM BUNNY PISCES

Because he loves excess, Pisces is susceptible to addiction. But not all addictions are bad.

Gym Bunny Pisces with his workout addiction has found a healthy outlet for himself. It is like meditation for him to go through the repetitions—which can go on for a long time since his endurance is strong.

Pisces' no-pain-no-gain attitude can lead him to ignore injuries and damage himself more. His feet are not strong, so Pisces should invest in the best footwear he can. He is also prone to dehydration. However, the biggest danger he faces is turning his muscle into a buffer against the world. When exercise becomes a form of withdrawal, it has no benefit for Pisces.

Fortunately the sweat and exhaustion of the gym breaks down the social barriers that can make Pisces shy. It is easier for him to get friendly with guys when they have endorphins coursing through their bodies.

The
Relationships

ARIES ☆ ARIES

Talk about putting out fire with gasoline!

The misery of being Aries is that few men can match your energy—except another Aries. If the two of you have compatible life goals, your combined energies can illuminate the world. But if not, the collision between you can send the flames splattering out to incinerate everything around you.

Though it does not look so dangerous at first.

When Aries first meets Aries, he is delighted to find someone who can take care of himself. Mr. Ram often feels that he has to walk on eggshells to spare the delicate sensibilities of those unfortunate enough to have been born under one of the other eleven signs. But with another Aries, he can just be himself, with no coddling or bullshitting.

Things happen fast. Chances are they will have sex on the first date. When they make love, these boys are all over each other with the unself-consciousness of four-year-olds wrestling to see who will be king of the hill. The Aries-Aries relationships begins (and if you are lucky, continues) in a state of innocence. Desires are stated directly, with no embarrassment, and then immediately met. There are no lies, no manipulation, and no confusion. Mutual admiration reigns—this is very important, since every Aries craves unconditional acceptance.

Since both men are so ignorant of how money works, they do not make the financial recriminations that other couples do. Aries lends money to Aries without a thought. Both have confidence that tomorrow will bring new riches and that what is lost today can be made up then. Poverty may bring down the mood, but Aries blames fate and not his lover for the lack of funds.

This relationship sometimes plays like a game of *¿Quien es mas macho?* with each partner trying to out-tough the other. Both are determined to prove to their family, straight friends, gay friends, and the world that it is the other guy who plays the woman in this relationship. Sure they know that male-female role-playing is not usually part of a gay relationship, but even so each is determined not to be pigeonholed as the femme.

And there are fights, of course. Big explosive 10,000-volt arguments. They happen so frequently and with such a lack of inhibition that witnesses always think, "This is the one that finishes them." But when each flare-up ends, it is over. And forgiveness only seems to bring the men closer together.

Until it does not.

Eternal vigilance is the price of an Aries-Aries relationship. Tact and consideration do not come naturally to this sign, so when relations are easy, an Aries drops thoughtfulness and goes on automatic pilot. Aries expects that any injury can heal and that anything broken can be fixed. It is impossible for these boys to imagine that anything can decisively separate them from each other. So just what will bring down the pair?

When one Aries becomes an obstacle to the other's dreams, it is over. He usually achieves this by attacking his partner's confidence. Because Aries is a highly competitive sign that wants to win any argument, and because the Aries-Aries couple argues a whole lot, and because Aries likes to talk first and think later, this happens all the time. Being so explosive, the fallout can affect friends, family, and others not immediately involved in the relationship.

Though Aries likes to be a lone gunslinger, when he is involved with another Aries it is important that they share a common dream. If they are working together toward the same goal, it is far less likely that some stray comment will set off a powder keg.

ARIES ☆ TAURUS

Mr. Ram and Mr. Bull are two horned—and horny—beasts.

That more or less sums up the relationship: fighting and fucking. Oh, sure, there is tenderness and love as well, but it is the two F's that this pair enjoys the most.

Live-wire Aries and stodgy Taurus have vastly different personal styles, which means that there is always something to lock horns over. Each fight has the same pattern: Aries cannot give up and Taurus cannot give in. Usually Aries starts the fight and Taurus ends it.

The conflict does not damage the relationship, since these two signs worship strength and love the opportunity to show off how much they have got. Having a lover who doubles as a sparring partner appeals to both men.

Money is a trouble area for most couples, including

Aries and Taurus. Aries believes that money was meant to be spent, right now, while you have it. Taurus believes money was meant to be consolidated. He saves and invests. Even when he does splurge, it is on things that Aries considers unimportant, because Taurus wants a home full of comfort and luxury items. Aries sees no point to this, since if you spend that much on the home, you are more likely to spend a lot of time there.

Which leads to another area of conflict—"home" means something different to each man. For Aries, it is a springboard for charging off into the world. For Taurus, it is a retreat from the chaos of the world. This is a difficult problem to resolve, since neither man is likely to articulate these feelings—they are so hardwired into his circuitry that he just assumes everyone else defines home as he does. This issue is rarely the ostensible subject of an argument, but it lurks there under the surface in many of them. Overt conflict rarely tears this couple apart—but unspoken conflict can, because these boys are oblivious to subtext, even when it is wedging them apart. Instead, Taurus might feel emotionally abandoned by a man who flees the home whenever he can, or Aries might feel imprisoned by Taurus. And neither will know why. Until the two learn to respect their differing ideas of home life, living together can be profoundly unsatisfying.

In bed, these two bring out the best in each other, though at first glance they seem incompatible. The go-for-the-gold sexuality of Aries sometimes lacks the luxuriant sensuality that comes naturally to Taurus. On the other side, the meat-and-potatoes sexuality of Taurus lacks the experimental inspiration that every Aries has. However, the specific erotic talents that each partner brings to the coupling enrich and compliment the experience of the other.

In spite of, or rather because of, their differences, the Aries-Taurus couple can be a powerful force. The drive of Aries combined with the determination and practicality of Taurus makes for maximum impact if these two men choose to also go into business together or do political work as a couple.

Yet there is a strain of selfishness in each sign—Aries is selfish in wanting to impose his will on others and Taurus is selfish in wanting to acquire possessions. The combination of their individual forms of selfishness can lead this pair to self-righteous ruthlessness. But this does not have to be so. If Aries and Taurus feel that they are working for some goal larger than themselves and if they maintain strong emotional ties to people outside of the relationship, there are few couples more caring and generous.

The Aries-Taurus partnership makes no sense to those on the outside. They just scratch their heads and say "Opposites attract." Yet those within it say *"Vive le difference"* because they know that it is their differences that give them strength.

ARIES ☆ GEMINI

Talking too loud and laughing too much *can* be the basis for a relationship.

When together, Aries and Gemini are full of outrageous fun. Theirs is a romance without angst. Friends love to go out with them as well as gossip about them since their relationship is like a carefree and hugely entertaining sitcom. They talk and argue and make up, never sticking to one topic, never keeping to one plan. They simply follow their whims and seem quite happy to do so.

Aries and Gemini appear to be in flux at every stage of their life together. Though Aries says he is after commitment, neither he nor Gemini does much toward establishing permanence. Both make passionately effusive declarations of love but seem baffled by what the next step should be. Even after they make a commitment, the relationship keeps transforming itself into new forms to meet the changing emotional needs of Aries and Gemini.

Neither man has much of an attention span, yet each can maintain an interest in the relationship. Gemini with his lightning fast mind and ever-shifting moods is a constant challenge to Aries. Aries, in turn, brings passion and energy to the detached Gemini. These two love talking to each other more than anything else. Each finds the other's mind fascinatingly unpredictable, a kind of puzzle one wants to spend a long time trying to solve.

The pair does share a restlessness. Moving, vacations, new activities—they will latch on to anything that can pull them away from old habits. Their many social commitments and their pursuit of new acquaintances are also intended to keep them from falling into a rut.

Because their life together goes through so many changes without moving in any one clear direction, outsiders might think that this couple is stuck. But owning property, living more upscale, and acquiring status are less important to these two than having an interesting time together. Some might label this as immaturity; others might call it enlightenment. Still, Aries will get frustrated at times with Gemini aimlessness, while Gemini seethes over Aries' boorish brashness, which he thinks holds them back. In truth, both of them reinforce these traits in the other, so any "progress" in lifestyle is going to come from the effort of one individual, not from the two working together.

What this pair calls physical affection, most of us would consider goofing off. And what they call sex, most of us would also consider goofing off. Aries and Gemini treat sex as recreation rather than anything heavy, so their lovemaking is giddy and varied. They often switch roles and positions, but in general Aries likes to be the pursuer and Gemini the tease. Much more attention, and much more pleasure, is taken in the preliminaries than in sexual acts themselves.

In dealing with the world, Aries and Gemini can be naive. Intensely social, they interact with many people as a couple. However, neither is suspicious by nature, so it is hard for them to judge who their real friends are. This couple is particularly prone to breakups engineered by some manipulator in their social circle. Preying on Aries' jealousy and Gemini's flirtatiousness is enough to drive the wedge. Gemini is usually the first to catch on to what is happening, but Aries is the one who works hardest to patch things up.

Even Aries and Gemini often fail to recognize how serious this relationship is. After all, love is supposed to be painful and relationships are supposed to take work. When a relationship is so much fun, how could it be anything other than casual?

Decades later they still might be asking the same question.

ARIES ☆ CANCER

Cancer is willing to let Aries be the star of the show—as long as Cancer gets to be the producer.

Because Aries so often acts as the spokesman for the couple, people might think he is the dominant partner. Even Aries might think so. But this relationship is much more complex than that. When two strong-willed men team up, the relationship is an intricate dance as each tries to press forward his agenda for what life together should be.

It takes time for this couple to really know each other, since, at the start, they hide their vulnerabilities from each other. Because neither sign likes to admit his weaknesses (especially to someone with whom he feels naturally competitive), it takes longer for this couple than for most to share painful feelings.

Oddly enough, the desire to heal hurt is another trait these two share, so sharing pain is one of the strongest bonding experiences this couple could have. When this happens, Aries and Cancer will drop some—but not all—of the competitiveness. Then the real relationship begins.

The words of each partner matter greatly to the other. To some degree Aries and Cancer each see the other as a parental figure whose approval he craves. Each ascribes great authority to the other. Cancer considers Aries savvy in the ways of the world, while Aries feels that Cancer has a great understanding of human nature.

Aries-Cancer sex can be a thrilling encounter with true otherness. Aries will find himself getting lost in Cancer as he discovers emotions that are new to him when they are skin-to-skin. Cancer experiences Aries as a megadose of espresso shot intravenously. The energy he gets from sex makes it hard to sleep afterward. Neither man is used to the kind of lovemaking he finds with this partner.

But exciting as encounters with true otherness might be in bed, they can be difficult during the day. In this relationship, the partners have opposing visions of what relationships should be. Cancer is looking for a family—not that he wants to have a house, dog, and two kids, but rather he wants to be at the center of a close network of people who love each other.

Aries thinks of family as what you escape from at age eighteen. He wants more independence within a relationship. What Cancer considers proper behavior for lovers looks to Aries like codependency.

Fortunately, this couple is more than capable of writing their own rules. However conservative they might appear, they prefer telling society how they will live to having society tell them. Though it is not easy, the process of deciding how to deal with their conflicting concepts of relationship and what compromises are acceptable is make-or-break; this is when these two each really learn who the other is.

After things get ironed out, do not expect these boys to skip a merry path to paradise. Neither man can let things rest. Both Aries and Cancer are bossy, though in different ways. Aries is always direct, so what you see is what you get—you always know when he is playing for power. With Cancer this is not so easy. He knows exactly what he wants, but his attack comes through the back door. Slyly and subtly he manipulates events so that he gets his way. It is hard to confront him, because his methods have plausible denia-bility built in. Neither is really equipped to grapple with the other's tactics, so the couple's priorities can never be fixed, but need to be constantly renegotiated. Though this may sound like a recipe for chaos, it is a recipe for a healthy rela-tionship that is unlikely to go stale.

ARIES ☆ LEO

Leo wins. But Aries may not notice.

Aries has the soul of a street fighter, so he tries. And he tries. And he tries. And he tries to end up on top. But he can never stay there long.

You see, Mr. Ram will struggle to be dominant. Mr. Lion will not struggle to be dominant. He just *is* dominant. It comes naturally to him. He may let Aries win for a time. Then he just bats him down like a pussy with a ball of yarn.

Which is fine for Aries. The Ram enjoys the fight more than the win anyhow. He also believes that he *is* the winner because he has put out so much energy.

Heterosexuals usually find this pairing less exhausting because they have specific roles for man and woman that are defined by society. Even if they choose not to follow these roles, they have a framework to build from. For a same-sex couple, everything is up for grabs, so an Aries-Leo relationship between two men can be a never-ending struggle for position that wears out the partners.

This same dynamic that makes home life tiring can make sex an ongoing and thrilling exploration of possibilities. This couple has few inhibitions and the enthusiasm of teenagers. The way they talk, you would think they invented sex.

That is another thing. This is a couple with few secrets. They should get some. Hey, you guys! The rest of us are tired of hearing the wonders of your Ram-Lion love life recounted in every detail. Your mutual affection is obvious—you do not need to convince us.

Also the ongoing soap opera that you call a relationship may be fascinating for you, but we really do not need a blow-by-blow of every argument, especially since you usually have them out in public.

Sorry. Had to vent.

If you ever lived next door to an Aries-Leo couple, you would understand. These guys are the biggest drama queens in the zodiac. They make sure you hear everything through the wall. The bouncing of the bed, the top-of-lungs accusations of infidelity, and those full-throated laughs they both have that sound like they will never stop.

Quite a theatrical duo.

After hearing a few of their fights, one would expect them to split up as quickly as they came together. But that may not be. The intensity of the fighting is matched only by the intensity of what follows. Neither the Ram nor the Lion is very good at bearing a grudge, and both love make-up sex. Of course neither apologizes for anything that was said, but in the morning they will not even remember what the fight was about. Though they will remember the insults they hurled at each other.

A double-edged sword lies between these two lovers. They understand each other. Very deeply. While this gives them a tremendous bond, it also means they can wound each other. Very deeply. Both signs will easily forgive, but if you damage an Aries' or Leo's self-esteem it is hard for the relationship to continue.

For this match to go on, the couple must move on to Stage 2. In Stage 2 the Aries and Leo see each other as an extension of the self. The lover ceases to be "other" and becomes part of one's own soul. The lover is seen as an ideal, and promoting his interests is a consuming concern. The relationship stops being an emotional bond and becomes a cause. Mr. Ram and Mr. Lion start believing they hold the key to long-lasting relationships, gay or straight.

The petty fights will still flare up. But the Aries and the Leo will see their relationship as something larger than themselves, something that ennobles them and brings out the best in each of them. That is exactly the kind of love affair that these men want.

ARIES ☆ VIRGO

It has been said that genius is 10 percent inspiration and 90 percent perspiration. If that is so, this couple is a genius, with Aries supplying the bright ideas that make Virgo sweat.

But back to the beginning . . .

It is Virgo who first feels the attraction. Aries just smells like sex to him, even before they speak. Aries likes to smell like sex and so naturally responds in kind to Virgo. When they make love, Virgo makes Aries stop looking at sex as a contest. With Virgo it becomes an act of mutual pleasure giving. And Aries makes Virgo feel more desirable and exciting than he usually does.

While the sexual attraction is undeniable, you might wonder how long a relationship can last since these two men are so different. They approach life from opposite ends. Aries starts with the big picture. He works from the top down. Virgo starts with the details. He works from the bottom up.

Can these two men, with their opposing styles, ever come together to form a stable partnership? Of course! In spite of their differences—and in spite of finding each other extremely annoying at times—Aries and Virgo have a fundamental respect for each other. So though he rolls his eyes at Virgo persnicketiness, Aries genuinely wants to be helpful to Virgo, even if it means giving up some control. Virgo looks at Aries as a wonderful guide who can teach him to think big and make his mark on the world.

The potshots these guys take at each other do not shake the trust between them. Perhaps this is because there is one important need that the two of them share, which few others understand. Each of them has a strong need to be his own man, standing apart from his mate. Others might consider their independence a sign that love is missing, but Aries and Virgo each recognizes in his partner a reflection of his own desire for autonomy. They like to think of the relationship as a meeting of two free souls drawn together by love and desire. The idea of mutual dependence is repugnant to both of them.

To keep things going long term, each man needs to be willing to break old bad habits. Aries is used to speaking before he thinks, letting loose vicious insults in the heat of the moment—this cannot go on. Virgo may be critical of one's actions, but Aries gets critical of one's very being. With Virgo, Aries has to start fighting fair. Virgo tends to use withdrawal as a technique to get what he wants. With Aries this will not work, so he needs to engage and get pushy about his own needs. It is also easy for Virgo to turn the tables and make his troubles out to be Aries' fault. When Virgo takes responsibility (rather than telling others to), Aries' loyalty will only get stronger.

Most important, both men must learn how to say, "I was wrong, I am sorry." If they take off the battle armor and show some softness, together they are genius.

Some last advice:

Credit and finances are a sore spot but they're easy to resolve. Aries often screws up with bills, while Virgo rarely does. Though he wants to be the big man taking care of the household, he would be smarter to abdicate and hand over his checkbook to Virgo, who can save him from himself.

There is always sex. Whenever difficulties arise, Aries and Virgo can always go to bed—that will usually set things right.

ARIES ☆ LIBRA

It looks as if Libra would not mind an Aries-centric relationship. But looks can be deceiving. When this pairing fails it is usually because Aries treats Libra as a doormat, then is surprised when the doormat trips him.

As a couple, Aries and Libra polarize. When they are together, each turns into a caricature of himself. Aries becomes more dogmatic and impulsive while Libra grows more dispassionate and serene. This only makes them more attractive to each other and more prone to misunderstanding—at least on Aries' part. He does not recognize that Libra's good manners are a mere tactic and that Mr. Balance will challenge him as he seeks to establish dominance.

Aries must remember that the ways in which he and Libra are the same matter more in this relationship than the ways in which they are different. The most important similarity is that they both want to be in charge, though for different reasons. Libra wants to arrange things so that there is no disharmony between himself and Aries. Aries wants to steer the relationship just to prove that he can.

With these two personalities, compromise is fairly easy— but only if each acknowledges the other's strength. Aries has the instincts of a prizefighter, trying to overpower threats immediately as they arise. Libra is like a military general, coolly anticipating his opponent's actions from a distance, never getting his own knuckles bloody. These two types of personal power complement each other, so that with a healthy respect in place, each man will find the other fixing problems he himself cannot deal with. Aries plays the heavy with those who would take advantage of Libra, and Libra smoothes over relations with those who get on Aries' bad side.

Maintaining the right public image is important to both men. They could be so poor they are living on macaroni and cheese, but god forbid that anyone see them wearing last year's fashions or driving a junker. Thus they tend to live beyond their means—but hey, at least they do not fight about it.

These signs are highly compatible in the bedroom—that is where this relationship began. Unless Libra decided he wanted to torture Aries (it happens), they were fucking practically before they met. They love to look at each other, they love to touch each other, Aries loves to smell Libra, and Libra loves to smell Aries if he's wearing cologne.

On the subject of torture, some Libras will take delight in teasing and abusing their Aries man. Though Aries plays Mr. Hard-Boiled, romance means a good deal to him, and though Libra plays Mr. Romantic, he can be quite cold-blooded when he wants to be. If he is not in love, he can pretend to be for the purpose of turning Aries into a whipping boy on whom he can take revenge for all the wrongs men have done him.

When these two come from the same cultural background, it helps in maintaining the relationship. Though the similarities between them are strong, surface differences can drive them apart, especially if they have to face a cultural gap as well. They need some common assumptions about what a relationship should be if Aries independence and Libra togetherness are to join in compromise.

This relationship often feels like it is spinning out of control, but it is very stable because underneath it all, Aries and Libra understand each other. Some friction in a relationship is necessary if the partners are to grow—in spite of what Libra thinks. This pairing has just enough friction to stimulate growth and keep things interesting.

ARIES ☆ SCORPIO

The sex would be animal, except that animals do not love. Though it might seem too athletic, acrobatic, and bizarre to be an expression of any tender feelings, Aries-Scorpio sex is always about the love they share. This does not mean the sex is whitebread. This pair can face the dark, savage side of love and give it physical expression without shame.

When the sexual connection is not there, these men are more likely to hate than respect each other. But if there is an erotic compatibility, there is also almost certainly love as well.

Aries seems to be the junior partner in this relationship— but at least he is a partner. The Scorpio trust issues are not as big an obstacle to sharing power here as they usually are. The guilelessness of Aries may seem dippy to Scorpio, but it can open him up. Even though Scorpio cannot think of Aries as being a true adult, he will put his resources and talents to use in helping Aries—something he will not do for most men. However, the pitfall is that Scorpio might be tempted to play out old patterns by restricting the exuberance of Aries, which could destroy the relationship.

While Scorpio's intuition spooks Aries, his loyalty and dedication to principle win Aries' admiration. Though their tactics differ, Aries will recognize in Scorpio a man driven by the same desire that he has to get ahead by seizing control.

Through this relationship, Aries will come to a greater self-knowledge. Still, because Scorpio does not express affection on the same hyperbolic scale as Aries, Aries might doubt his love.

When these men fight, it is a clash of the titans. The prime subject is sexual jealousy—each of these men can jump to wild conclusions about the most innocent flirting. When he is mad, Aries brings out everything he has got, splattering Scorpio with accusations, insults, screaming—the works. Scorpio is more strategic, always holding something in reserve. Arguments are best resolved with Scorpio winning, since shortly thereafter, Aries will have forgotten his grievances and bear no resentment. However, if Aries wins, Scorpio will not forget and Aries had better watch his back. Somehow, somewhere, he will pay.

The intensity of sex and fighting is so powerful with this couple that they often burn out on each other. The longest lasting Aries-Scorpio relationships have a shared goal or interest that binds them in a way that does not consume them. A child, a business, the dream of owning a home, political activity, or a common enemy—any of these can help stabilize this volatile couple. As a team, the couple can be ultra-aggressive and a tad cutthroat, but they do get results.

Because this relationship is so difficult, it changes the men within it. They bring vastly different needs and skills with them; Scorpio will be the partner most emotionally invested in the relationship, but it is up to Aries to make it work. Because he is more naturally adaptable and less judgmental, Aries is glad to accommodate those he loves. But this relationship is his loss of innocence. After learning just how unequal the energy and emotions of two people in a relationship can be, he will be much more tolerant of other individuals. Scorpio as well will be less contemptuous of those who take emotional risks.

The toughness of these two men makes it possible to weather the hard times. When this relationship works, Aries and Scorpio consider it doubly precious for the hell they went through for it. They both agree that when all is said and done hard-won love is the sweetest.

ARIES ☆ SAGITTARIUS

What would it be like if Superman hooked up with Hercules? Cosmic love, cosmic fights, cosmic rescues in the skies over Metropolis. So what if a building gets leveled—neither of these guys *meant* any harm. It takes the embarrassment of putting their super feet in their super mouths to bring them back to earth.

Aries and Sagittarius each share with the other a long-standing dream of meeting a man like himself and falling in love. A man of the same sign does not work, since then he would have his own faults staring back at him. But in this dynamic combination, each man sees an idealized version of himself, mirroring all his virtues.

When they meet, these two fire signs make a hot combination. It is like the superhero marriage described above. They shamelessly play out a grand opera of stormy love, caring nothing about the rest of the world—until something happens. It could be the appearance of an ex or an ugly exchange with family—whatever it is, it takes a publicly humiliating scene, where one or both make a big faux pas, for these two to realize how self-involved they have been.

After such an incident, they will be depressed over it for at least twenty-four hours.

As a couple these two have boundless energy and boundless confidence, but limited focus. That is why they love having the kind of argument that goes on for hours with raised voices and wild gesticulation, but ultimately resolves nothing. They need an outlet for the energy between them and you can only have sex so many times a day. Otherwise they wander quickly around, bumping into tables and children as they search for some new cause or hot fashion trend that can hold their interest.

My god, can these boys sweat! Their sex life is athletic and experimental. Goading each other on toward more outrageousness might be fun when they are out on the town, but in the bedroom it can destroy the furniture. When the lovemaking gets more mellow, it is usually because one is trying to comfort the other, not because their emotions need a more low-key expression. For the Aries-Sagittarius couple, expression of love is always full-out and wild.

What Sagittarius calls honesty can bruise the Aries ego. And Aries can let a few zingers of his own fly at Sagittarius. The guys love to throw challenges out at each other, but neither knows how to say when it is enough. So what begins as friendly teasing can escalate to nasty confrontation. Fortunately, it is easy for these men to apologize and make up. They share a belief that there is no damage that cannot be undone, and between them, it seems to be true.

It is hard for this couple to put down roots and get established in life. It is not that they necessarily lack for money, but little remains constant for them. Most Aries or Sagittarius men use their boyfriend to anchor them. The problem in this couple is that both lack interest in home and planning for the future, so while they always have fun together, they have little to show for their life together. Instead, they need to look toward career or family to provide stability. The danger is that because neither (especially Sagittarius) is very conscious of his need for stability, both might ignore it.

Because there is such a natural sympathy between Aries and Sagittarius, this coupling can lack the friction that gives purpose to most relationships. If that is the case, these two men might drift out of this relationship. If so, they are likely to remain friends.

ARIES ☆ CAPRICORN

Who is the daddy? Both Aries and Capricorn like to wield authority, so even if they are completely in love, they will always jockey for position.

But who is in charge is not always easy to identify. When you see a man walking with a dog on a leash and that dog suddenly bolts ahead, forcing the owner to run after until he can choke the dog to a halt, who is in charge? The dog who sets the pace or the man who has him by the neck?

The dog is Aries and the man is Capricorn. The lurching forward-backward motion is a dynamic played out in every area of their lives.

When they meet, it is not love at first sight, because they are not sure they can trust each other. They are more likely to see each other as a rival than a partner.

However, Aries and Capricorn are two highly sexed signs. Sexual curiosity will get the better of them. Both men doubt their attractiveness and neither is very intuitive, so Capricorn may put out tiny feelers and Aries will try to hide his attraction as they both wait for the other to make a move. Aries is less afraid of embarrassment so probably will break down first to reveal his feelings.

In bed, they are still dog and owner. Capricorn loves bringing Aries to the height of pleasure, then holding him back. Aries will try anything that might get a spontaneous response out of icy Capricorn, who likes to keep things moving more slowly. Sex is like a challenge as each competes to give a kind of pleasure that the other is not used to. Their erotic play parodies the struggle for dominance in their everyday relationship.

It is amazing how sexually compatible these boys are, since they bicker about everything else. Like the dog, Aries impulsively throws himself forward, starting projects, going places, and spending money, while Capricorn, like the owner, does nothing, goes nowhere, and spends zero until he has to. Each feels that the other is foolish for this behavior. Each is convinced that only he knows the right way to live.

Thus Aries and Capricorn each start on a campaign to change the other. The impulse is not so much to help the boyfriend as to prove who is right. Since neither can stand being criticized by the other, neither can give an inch, which can lead to open warfare. When fighting, these two bring out the absolute worst in each other. Realizing that the argument is going nowhere, Capricorn goes to his room and Aries walks out the door until they both cool off.

Though it looks as if the relationship is doomed to endless conflict, it is not. There is resolution available—through ambition. Aries and Capricorn both burn with ambition and both have a profound respect for it in others. When each realizes he has found another who understands his drive and applauds it, then they begin to look for what they can learn from each other. Aries' ambition is more naked. He sees life as an open battle in which the strongest and most talented rise. Capricorn admires the directness of Aries but believes that only through strategic planning can he build a secure place for himself in society. Though neither man is much of a team player, with Aries' energy and Capricorn's shrewdness, they can form an impressive team if they try. At the very least, they are sure to take a far more relaxed view of each other once they have found this common ground.

After the two grow secure together, they will want to formalize things. The idea of a good old-fashioned gay wedding appeals to both since no relationship seems quite legitimate to them until it is publicly acknowledged.

ARIES ☆ AQUARIUS

They can deal with the concept of relationship. It is the day-to-day of the real thing that trips them up.

Aries and Aquarius pride themselves on having an independent spirit. So while they think of themselves as a couple, they do not know how to act like one. Each tries to hang on to the "specialness" he had as a single man.

The first time they spoke, Aries and Aquarius recognized how well each played off the other. Their conversation had the momentum and intelligence that both hunger for.

Of course, while talking, Aries' mind was racing, imagining what it would be like to wrestle Aquarius to the ground then get him really really dirty. Aquarius was imagining what it would be like to have a second, more in-depth conversation. Going on a date was their compromise.

There is a tremendous energy to this pairing. Both men constantly think about the future—their own and humankind's. Anything new that might point the way excites them, whether it is a bold independent film, an innovative computer program, or an inspiring political candidate. All their focus is on tomorrow.

Unfortunately, they must live in today.

These two signs tend to skip over little things like paying rent, dental checkups, and car inspections. Neither will admit to thinking that he is above dealing with annoying practicalities, but they both do think just that. They are two men who each expect to be taken care of. Usually Aries and Aquarius will find a mature way to accommodate each other's expectations.

But not always.

Neglecting lovers is a bad habit both Aries and Aquarius frequently get into. If both men get neglectful at the same time, they can destroy the core of their relationship.

Aries finds Aquarius coolness disconcerting. The lack of overt passion seems almost evil. That is how he justifies releasing his volcanic temper, while Aquarius sits there so composed. Aquarius is embarrassed to watch his lover lose it. To think that one's emotions matter so much seems to him obscene and bestial. Thus the arguments this couple has consist of Aries screaming, yelling, and shaking with rage in an attempt to resolve things now, now, NOW, while Aquarius listens, not giving an inch, not even allowing himself to be drawn in.

After such a fight, Aries wants sex immediately, which his lover finds appalling. Mr. Ram should wait for at least twenty minutes after the end of battle before groping Mr. Waterboy. Still, it is hard to watch the clock since both men put a high value on erotic spontaneity.

The fierceness of Aries' lovemaking scares Aquarius because it makes him feel vulnerable. He responds by teaching Aries some new twists on the world's oldest pastime. Though hot Aries and cool Aquarius seem an unlikely duo, the combination of their contrasting brands of eroticism is hugely satisfying.

Though at the start Aries took the more decisive role in the relationship, when they establish a home, Aquarius comes into his own. Perhaps it is because his greater financial acumen makes it inevitable that he handles the bills. Or maybe because he is friendlier to the neighbors. Or because he is more interested in building something permanent. Whatever it is, this is one of the few Aquarius relationships where he rules the home.

Being Aquarius, though, he will never rule an especially stable home, since he (like Aries) is too busy saving the world to care much about the roof over his head.

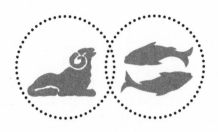

ARIES ☆ PISCES

A successful, long-lasting Aries-Pisces relationship is a fascinating thing to watch. At first you would expect the aggressive Aries to run roughshod over meek little Pisces. But over time, the two men develop a complex series of checks and balances that keep power more evenly distributed.

Neither Aries nor Pisces feels at home in the world. Each wishes that society were structured some other way that was more accommodating to his way of being. Pisces knows that he is stuck with things as they are, but Aries secretly believes that he can change the world to be as he wants it. Pisces finds this arrogance endearing.

Aries is drawn to Pisces by his depth. Because he tends to take things at face value, Aries finds Pisces' gift for seeing what lies beneath both inexplicable and irresistible. He might scoff at first when Pisces warns him away from that seeming friend who is really a secret enemy, but when time proves that Mr. Fish was right—then Aries is hooked.

Because Aries never understands the reasons behind Pisces' changes of mood, he cannot control them. Instead they control him as he runs himself ragged trying to keep Pisces happy. In doing so he takes on some of the qualities of ever-accommodating Pisces. Pisces brings out Aries' protective instincts, so instead of fighting *with* Mr. Fish (like he does with most other boyfriends), he fights *for* Mr. Fish, acting as his advocate whenever conflict arises.

Pisces himself takes care of Mr. Ram as said above, by helping him fend off hidden or subtle threats. He also starts taking on some of Aries' aggressiveness in defense of his partner. Together the couple forms an us-against-the-cruel-world cocoon. Within this cocoon they shift back and forth in the roles of protector and protected. These shifts balance power within the relationship as well.

That is when the relationship works.

There are bad Aries-Pisces relationships in which Aries is a brutal caveman and Pisces his willing doormat. These fixed roles take root when Aries and Pisces take each other for granted. However, these are two highly imaginative men who love to reinvent themselves, so there is no reason why they should get stuck in unhealthy roles.

Through sex play, this couple can resolve their relationship issues. This couple could not establish fixed sex patterns with each other even if they tried. They sample everything in the erotic smorgasbord and concoct a few new dishes of their own. The sex is best, however, when it is related to their emotional life out of bed. For example, if power issues are being addressed, resolved, and exorcised through S&M play, it will be especially hot. This does not mean that these men need to write up an agenda and post it on the headboard—the emotional material will come out on its own. It is important, however, not to immediately reject any act as too kinky or too weird, until you are sure it is not the kind of sex the two of you need at the moment.

Advice to Aries: Just because he does not say what he feels does not mean he is holding out on you. You just have to learn to read between the lines.

Advice to Pisces: Though it goes against your nature, be

sure to set clear boundaries for Aries' behavior toward you, your friends, your money, and your property. If you do not, he will take advantage without even realizing it.

TAURUS ☆ TAURUS

Taurus is no narcissist, but he does like himself. Who else has his common sense or solid values? Since the whole world is out of step except him, there is a natural attraction to his own sign.

However, because both Taurus men are slow moving and comfortable with the status quo, it may take a long time for the relationship to move beyond attraction. So they will remain friends, maybe fantasize about each other, until one man is willing to take the risk and ask for a date.

This can happen within weeks—or it might take decades. You never know with Taurus.

Their lovemaking is energetic. Have you ever been to a rodeo? You have seen how powerful a bull is as he bucks a cowboy. Now imagine one bull riding another, each bucking with all his might.

Do you get the picture of Taurus-Taurus sex?

With their shared love of music, food, nature, food, and food, this pair is never at a loss for fun things to do. Or rather, they are at a loss and like it that way. As long as they have their whole home entertainment center programmed on one remote, two plush recliners, and a stack of take-out menus to choose from, who needs excitement?

Happy as they are with each other, our two Mr. Bulls need more.

Stagnation can easily overtake this relationship. Tauruses need the jolt of energy they get from confronting behavior and attitudes different from their own. Without a strong social life, a Taurus spending most of his time with a Taurus lover degenerates into a smug slug.

A fat smug slug.

And since it is easier to jog along in a relationship that is going nowhere than to take action to end it, the stagnation cycle can go on for weeks—or decades.

The two Tauruses might not even realize that anything is wrong. They measure the success of a relationship by its peacefulness. And these boys rarely fight—with good reason. If they let loose and released anger to each other . . . Have you ever been to a bullfight? You have seen how wildly the crazed bull charges at the matador. Now imagine one bull charging at another with all his might.

Do you get the picture of a Taurus-Taurus fight?

So how can Tauruses in love ensure their relationship's health? It is often hard for gay men to stay connected to their roots. Either their families reject them or they fear their families will if they make being gay too much of an issue. However, a Taurus couple needs their friends and especially their families to feel complete. Until his boyfriend is welcomed into the family, or until he is welcomed into his boyfriend's family, Taurus thinks of the relationship as an indulgence. But family can help this couple see itself as valid.

It is also important for this pair to hook into a community of gay couples. While Tauruses need the companionship of people unlike themselves, they also need the support of their own tribe.

The most important way to ensure the relationship's health is for each Taurus to resolve that every day he will make his partner feel loved. The caresses that mean so much to this sign or the words "I love you" will do the trick. Tauruses often turn on the autopilot when dealing with their partners, but if each man allows himself to express love daily, their relationship will get better and better.

TAURUS ☆ GEMINI

While Gemini blathers on and on about some fascinating nonsense, Taurus smiles, nods, and does not hear a word. Yet both men are perfectly content because they take each other with equal doses of dismay and delight—and they would not have it any other way.

Though this couple has sex early on, they delay commitment as long as possible. Taurus is dazzled by Gemini's smooth talk and wide interests, but does not trust him. Mr. Bull fears that by giving his heart to Mr. Twin, he makes himself vulnerable to some sort of con. However, when Taurus does commit to Gemini, he will not look back.

Gemini is drawn to Taurus's steady nature, but worries

that it will become boring in time. He holds back each time Taurus wants to deepen their level of commitment. Even after throwing his lot in with Taurus, Gemini frets over whether or not he made the right decision. This is nothing personal against Taurus—Gemini is like that with most men.

Taurus wants many things from Gemini. He wants Gemini to take his mind seriously—which is hard because Gemini respects mental speed and flexibility more than the solid, logical, and literal way that Taurus thinks. He wants physical affection, but Gemini expresses his feelings with words. Gemini distrusts sex—which is the one thing in a relationship that Taurus always trusts.

Of course what Taurus wants is not necessarily what will help a relationship survive. The spontaneity of Gemini raises the energy level of Taurus and inspires him toward bolder action. Gemini makes Taurus a better man, which makes their bond strong. The ability of Taurus to anchor his lovers also helps Gemini, who can have trouble building a life for himself without another man to act as a foundation.

Not that there will not be arguments. You can be sure there will. Probably Gemini's insistence on going to some party when Taurus wants to stay home, or Gemini's premature ejaculation just when Taurus is getting started, will spark it. (Notice that Gemini starts the conflict in these examples. Taurus is pretty long-suffering and unlikely to fight without provocation.) Once the fight gets going, it is like toreador and bull. Gemini flashes the red cape, which makes Taurus lose control and start charging. It looks like sure death for Gemini, when—at the last minute—he steps nimbly out of the way. This only infuriates Taurus more, so it goes on and on, until Gemini gets tired of battling. He then delivers to Taurus a gorgeous apology, which leaves Taurus frustrated at not finishing in a show of power, but also secretly proud that he has managed to catch for himself such a brilliantly slick operator whom few other men could ever hang on to.

Sexually these men have such opposite lovemaking styles that neither can anticipate just what will happen in bed. Gemini is quick moving with active hands, while Taurus takes his time and uses his whole body to pleasure his partner. The fun they have comes from the surprises that each delivers to the other. The only thing they have in common is the directness with which they tell each other how horny they are.

Gemini stays with Taurus because he cannot figure him out. His ability to find joy in everyday life seems astonishing and his ability to stand behind what he says is unbelievably courageous in Gemini's eyes.

The awe Taurus feels for Gemini's mind is not what keeps him. It is that he knows Mr. Twin needs him and trusts him. And Taurus is a real sucker for that.

TAURUS ☆ CANCER

In a world that mocks Martha Stewart, it is hard to admit that you, like her, adore homemaking, food, and money. Will you not also be ridiculed as a shallow, heartless, self-infatuated bitch? Probably you will.

That is why Taurus and Cancer hide that side of their personalities. It is only with each other that they can let their hair down and indulge their love of material life all they want without embarrassment.

Taurus and Cancer love many of the same things, but in different ways. For example: They both love food, but Cancer enjoys a good three-course meal, while if Taurus could get away with eating nothing but desserts, he would. Cancer finds that the ritual of the meal, and the feeling of abundance that comes with it, gives him great satisfaction. The sharing of food with others is also a big part of the experience for him. The taste and texture of what he is eating matter most to Taurus, and he does not care much about the circumstances around the eating or if anyone else is there to eat with him.

There are larger personality conflicts as well. Cancer finds Taurus' stubbornness pointless and stupid while Taurus thinks that Cancer's moodiness is childish. Strangely enough, their differences bring out the best in both men. Taurus has a bad habit of taking lovers for granted, but Cancer's mood swings will not let him do that. With Cancer, the emotional laziness that mars other Taurus relationships is minimal. Cancer is an expert manipulator and Taurus seems like an easy mark for him. However, though Taurus learns slowly, he does learn, and over the long haul he will short-circuit the manipulation. Cancer finds himself being more open and direct with Taurus than he is with other men.

The reason why home, food, and money matter so much to these men is that each wants the security these things represent. Even if neither man is looking for a long-term relationship, he will be glad when one shows up because Taurus and Cancer think in the long term. The practical advantages of pooling resources with a trusted loved one is also not lost on these boys. They are both stingy, yet lovers of luxury.

There are problems when these men move in together.

They are pack rats, and within a short amount of time they will have more things than the home can hold. Neither likes to sacrifice his possessions. Cancer will probably be more flexible, but only if Taurus finds a way to make it up to him.

If the couple splits, the objects in the home become the artillery with which they do battle. Who gave who what and who paid for what are not the real issues, but they will stand in for the deeper emotional concerns that neither wants to talk about.

Still, overall this is a remarkably compatible duo. Perhaps too much so. They tend to brood in silence rather than fight when there is conflict, which makes compromise and resolution difficult. They might also turn their home into a plush, comfy cocoon that isolates them from the world. It is important for this couple's mental health to keep up outside social and emotional ties, however much they enjoy stagnating together alone at home.

Taurus and Cancer are happiest at home, turning down the lights, playing soft music in the most stereotypical romantic way. But when they make love, the communication of emotion between them is too real to be a stereotype. The lack of self-consciousness they feel with each other allows them to show their desire fully. Sexual encounters are long, slow, deep, and leave each man feeling at peace.

TAURUS ☆ LEO

These men do not want each other's attention. They *need* it. Taurus feels safe and cozy when Leo is focused on him, and Leo (though he will deny it) desperately wants the approval of Taurus. Fortunately, there is a mutual fascination, though the kind of attention these men get may not always exactly be the kind they desire.

Taurus expects Leo to nurture him. And he does—at times. However, it is hard for Leo to always be as giving as Taurus wants. When Leo expresses feelings for other friends and family members, Taurus cannot help but feel jealous. Also, Leo often finds himself rebelling against the order and clarity that Taurus represents. The constant touching and fussing makes Leo feel like Taurus's doll rather than his lover.

Frustrating as all this can be, it does give the relationship an emotional heat, which will keep it alive and lively.

Taurus and Leo do make an effective team. There are many things in life that a Leo considers beneath him, things which Taurus is happy to handle. Taurus loves being the hatchet man for Leo, talking tough to the super, negotiating with his creditors, and telling the mama Lion that her son will *not* be home for Thanksgiving. Leo will often claim credit for Taurus's efforts, which bothers Mr. Bull surprisingly little as long as he gets to bask in the reflected glow of Mr. Lion's glory.

Taurus and Leo do struggle with the roles their relationships seems to assign them. Sometimes Taurus would love for his career to come before Leo's and Leo would love it if Taurus was the one to bankroll their leisure-time activities. When they try to break out of old patterns, major battles ensue. But neither gives up easily on the idea of them remaining a couple. These men are steadfastly loyal to each other. They believe in each other's talents and believe that they can spend the rest of their lives together.

It is likely that this couple will accumulate real estate—or at least they will want to. They both fantasize about living the good life, though Taurus is more savvy about how to make the dream a reality. He will struggle to keep Leo's spending in check and argue against every shaky venture Mr. Lion proposes. (Leo is always impatient to get the big payoff ASAP.) However, for Taurus's financial strategies to work, he needs to learn tact—Leo will never give in if Taurus comes off sounding like his father.

When you are as financially ambitious as these men are, there will be setbacks. And since Taurus and Leo argued so much about how to use their resources, you might expect them to play the blame game when misfortune strikes. But they will not. Both have a remarkable ability to pick themselves up and begin again. Deep down they know that they make an excellent team, balancing out each other's flaws and enhancing their strengths.

When making love, these men have few inhibitions. Secretly, Leo envies the comfort that Taurus has in his body. Leo sometimes fears that he is not a great lover, but Taurus erases all those nagging doubts. With Taurus, Leo's stamina in bed is greater than with anyone else. Leo makes Taurus feel butch, buff, and beautiful. When Leo holds him, the love is tangible and Taurus gets an erotic charge that is rarely felt without chemical assistance.

The flip side of Taurus and Leo's intense loyalty to each other is that they stick together in this relationship long after it dies. As faults go, this is not a bad one for a couple to have.

TAURUS ☆ VIRGO

This relationship is as much a financial partnership as a romance. It has to be that way when two level-headed realists get together. Even when Taurus and Virgo are deliriously in love, they calculate the savings possible when two men share the cost of utilities, rent, etc.

Taurus was the first to feel the love tingle. Virgo just looks as good as a stick of candy to him. When Virgo speaks, it is as if he were expressing the thoughts Taurus always had but never knew he did. For his part, Virgo felt envy and admiration before attraction. He found meaning in the silence of Taurus and wished he could be as uncritical. Knowing that it is impossible for him ever to become Taurus, Virgo settled for the next best thing—loving him.

The suspicions that these two men usually have in love matters are considerably lessened in this pairing. Each finds the other echoing his inner needs rather than challenging them.

When making love, neither Taurus nor Virgo holds back. The fantasies and emotional trips that can work against pure sexual performance do not hinder them. These are highly physical men who do not impose any preconceived ideas on sex, but rather find their imaginations and feelings liberated in the act.

When this couple moves in together, they are in agreement on most household matters. Both want a degree of privacy and even in a crowded apartment complex will find a way to maintain the boundaries between themselves and their neighbors. Both men hate waste, especially of energy, so they will arrange furniture and storage for greatest efficiency. Taurus will be more concerned with the appearance of his home than Virgo, but both also want something they will enjoy looking at. Each wants systems to be in place so that they do not have to give much thought to when the garbage goes out or who does the dishes. Virgo had better stay on top of things, though, since Taurus is a notorious backslider.

There will be an ongoing disagreement about food. For Virgo, nutrition is the main function of eating. For Taurus, pleasure is. Most Virgos monitor what they eat, refusing that cream-filled dessert after dinner if lunch has already maxed out their cholesterol allowance for the day. It is hard to imagine Taurus doing the same—and even harder to imagine Virgo not giving him grief for it.

Fortunately, Taurus does not take Virgo criticism too much to heart.

Taurus's slowness to fight is a problem for the relationship, as is Virgo's blindness to the real issues at the root of their disagreements. Though Virgo tries to shake things up on a small scale, neither man is willing to instigate the big changes that any relationship needs periodically. Because this couple shies away from airing its dirty linen, family and friends who might stick their noses in, to get the partners riled up against each other, probably will not, and issues that need to be confronted will not be.

So this couple needs to develop the ability to face unpleasant truths by themselves and battle each other when necessary—if they want a long-lasting relationship.

Though Taurus is slower moving than Virgo, he usually gets further in life because his ambition is stronger. Other signs help Virgo to dream big and aim high, but Taurus is content to let Virgo stay at a lower level. This is not a problem unless the couple breaks up, in which case Virgo will feel his time with Taurus was wasted.

TAURUS ☆ LIBRA

There is something girly about this couple. They smile all the time when they are together, they love modeling their clothes for each other, and can spend hours discussing home decor. Even if neither is excessively femme otherwise, when they get together they bring out the pussy in each other.

Not that there is anything wrong with that.

When they meet, Libra is excited by the way that Taurus feels everything through his body. Ideas and emotions get translated into physical sensations, which Libra envies. Taurus responds spontaneously to the immediate stimulus, unlike

Libra, who has to think before responding. This makes Mr. Bull seem more fully alive to Mr. Balance than he himself is.

Taurus is attracted to the haplessness of Libra. Here is a man who cannot make a decision—he cannot even decide whether he enjoys something or not without turning it over and around in his head. Taurus has a natural desire to help Libra take charge of his life and his pleasures.

A mutual love of art and beauty cements the relationship. As a couple, these two prefer the decorative to the soulstirring. For them the place of art is to soothe and entertain, not to provide insight into life's meaning. Libra loves to analyze the art, music, and film that they enjoy together, but for Taurus too much talk kills the actual experience.

The favorite date activity for Taurus and Libra has nothing to do with the arts. They just like to get lazy. Lolling around, napping, and procrastinating is their idea of a real good time. Libra likes to spend his downtime drowsily reviewing possibilities for the future while Taurus prefers mindless oblivion. In spite of the different ways they relax, each man is delighted to find a partner who understands the joy of sloth as much as he does and will not criticize him for it.

At times, Libra finds Taurus too demanding. He cannot see how someone as smart as Taurus can see everything in such black-and-white terms. For Taurus, if Libra loves him, he should always be available—but Libra sometimes needs space for himself. Taurus gets annoyed with Libra's constant self-questioning. He would rather watch a dog chase its tail than listen to the running monologue of Libran self-doubt.

Still, though they can grate on each other, the two partners avoid arguments if they can at all help it—especially Libra. When Taurus goes out of control with rage, Libra finds it as terrifying as if a wild beast with blood on his lips had entered the home. For Taurus, though, it seems coldhearted the way that Libra can just walk away from a burning issue.

Loving is much more to these men's taste. Real gauze-filtered, sweet, pussy sex. Their ideas about romance are strictly traditional and edged in lace. Taurus might get a little frustrated that Libra holds back emotionally at the beginning. But in time, Taurus will teach Libra what it means to give sexually and feel love as a bodily sensation.

A sentimentally romantic relationship between two men who rarely fight—could anything be better? Well, yes. A tendency to sweep things under the rug and avoid explicit conflict has some danger. This couple will opt for denial rather than face a harsh truth. Also, both men are strong-willed, and if they do not have the outlet of an overt battle, they might use manipulation as a means to get what they want.

A little self-knowledge is all these men need to get through this. They share a strong desire to maintain their relationship and will be able to break any bad habits that threaten its health.

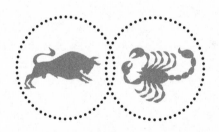

TAURUS ☆ SCORPIO

It is either love or hate. When you introduce a Taurus and a Scorpio, there is no middle ground.

If Scorpio feels an attraction, it is because Taurus is so blatantly what he is. Scorpio has an inherent distrust of others. He suspects that the men he meets are hiding something from him. But with Taurus, what you see is what you get. Here is a man Scorpio can relax his defenses with.

Taurus is agog over Scorpio's ability to penetrate to the heart of the matter. Being highly unintuitive, it seems magical to Taurus how Scorpio can just know things without being able to explain how.

It might take a while for this pair to hook up. It is Scorpio who puts the brakes on. He needs, however, to offer Taurus at least a crumb of hope or else Mr. Bull might very well give up and walk away.

For each of these men, the other seems so different as to be from another planet. If they decide to come together, it is because the merging of their differences make them feel complete in a way neither feels with any other man.

Though these men are very opposite in many ways, they do share certain obsessions. The big one is possession. Each of these men likes to think of his lover as belonging to him. This brings out their protective instincts—as well as their jealousy. Neither man will stand for sharing his lover. It has to be all or nothing.

Connected to this obsession is one with money. Both men think a good deal about money and the things one can do with it. When you have two people who are so stubborn, who not only want to control their own finances, but those of their partner as well, it is a recipe for conflict. When paired together, Taurus and Scorpio will use money as a stand-in for the deeper emotional issues they are scared to face head-on.

Fights are difficult because these men can be unbending. Taurus is more direct in stating what he wants, but usually does not see the situation in its full complexity as clearly as Scorpio does. This translates into arguments where Scorpio explains to Taurus why he is wrong and Taurus stonewalls. These arguments can go on for days.

Softer emotion gets poured into sex. For this couple, sex is never just a fun thing to do on a Saturday night. As playful as they get, eroticism is always a vehicle for them to express feelings they cannot put into words. Every stage of their emotional commitment and every mood of their partnership will be reflected in how they touch each other. As a couple they go for deep tenderness rather than shallow sentimentality.

Once Taurus and Scorpio have committed, they have very high expectations of each other. They agree that their relationship needs focus and nurturing. Neither partner is willing to take second place to anything, whether it is a job, other family, or another man. If trouble develops, Taurus is more forgiving than Scorpio, but not by much.

Advice to Taurus: The greatest gift Scorpio offers you is insight. Do not be so quick to write off his advice. Just because it was not your idea does not mean it is wrong.

Advice to Scorpio: The greatest gift Taurus offers you is laughter. He is secure enough to laugh at himself—that is one of the things you love about him! Do not be afraid to join in his laughter when he points out that you are just as ridiculous as he is.

TAURUS ☆ SAGITTARIUS

Most of us think of Sagittarius as a big-hearted, oversized kid without a dark spot on his psyche. But for Taurus, Sagittarius is a mysterious figure who is mad, bad, and dangerous to know—three qualities that are always sexy, even to Mr. Bull. The speed and spontaneity of Sagittarius seem recklessly passionate and edgy.

And Sagittarius finds Taurus's straight-shooting earthiness and clear decisiveness alluringly macho. Sagittarius needs so much from other people, but he sees in Taurus the same self-sufficiency the cowboys had riding the trail alone.

It will not take long for these men to leap into bed with each other. Their lovemaking is intensely physical and free of heavy emotional baggage. Each man has a talent for springing erotic surprises on his partner, which can keep them going as fuck buddies for a very long time.

The question is whether the relationship can go deeper.

At first, this couple makes an excellent pair of playmates. They both are hungry to enjoy life and each is glad to find someone who can match his hedonism. Taurus, though, will eventually get tired of play and want a relationship he can depend on. Sagittarius will want to feel an emotional passion as well as a physical one.

So far, so good.

But once the buddies become a couple, each man is surprised to learn who his partner *really* is. These two men face some fundamental differences in their approach to living. Let's look at money, since that is where a couple's conflicts are usually clearest. With Taurus, Sagittarius is even more generous than he is normally—which is fine by Taurus, who is like Sagittarius in his love of expensive playthings. The difference is that Taurus never pays retail and might hesitate to throw his lot in with someone so extravagant. Sagittarius cannot understand why Taurus is so miserly when he so clearly enjoys what money can buy.

Then there is how these guys see their future. When things get serious, Taurus expects that Sagittarius will leave his constant GO-GO-GO behind him and settle down. (Dream on, Taurus!) Sagittarius is horrified that Taurus would want to spend night after dull night at home watching TV.

At this stage, many Taurus-Sagittarius couples will split rather than face up to the big-time compromises necessary to go on. Often Sagittarius will promise to compromise (though he will weasel out of it later) and Taurus will drag his feet before he finally gives an inch.

That is not good enough.

Each partner must rise above himself and fully commit to working out their differences. If they do so, they can be sure that their mutual fascination and the sexual spark are not likely to ever die out.

Advice to Taurus: Giving of himself to you is in Sagittarius's nature, but if you start to make demands he will stop giving. Remember that jealousy will kill his love and only trust can keep his affection for you alive.

Advice to Sagittarius: Embarrass Taurus and he will forever shrink from your touch. There are parts of him you can never know, and if you succeed in pulling those secret parts into the light, the relationship is over.

Added Bonus: A stable, long-lasting Taurus-Sagittarius relationship brings with it wealth. Maybe not Rockefeller wealth but certainly comfortable money. Those differences in how they treat finances, and their mutual ambition to make big bucks, make for an excellent partnership. Together they check-and-balance each other to form a more effective financial strategy than either would have alone.

TAURUS ☆ CAPRICORN

Presenting a united front to the world is very important to this couple. The public fights that other couples indulge in are not for them. Neither will they indulge in excess affection. They may be a gay couple but that is no reason to marginalize themselves through undignified behavior.

Of course, these boys do have a wild side, but it is most likely to come out when they are on vacation someplace where no one knows them. As they get older, though, rather than settling down, this pair becomes more rowdy and willing to make fools of themselves.

The Taurus-Capricorn couple likes to define goals for itself, then strategize to achieve those goals, which are almost always concerned with money and career. It is harder for them to define what they want emotionally from the relationship. It is easier to put feelings on the back burner and focus on fixing up that summer house or saving to start a business.

Sex always lubricates communication and stimulates emotional honesty for this pair. In bed, they give full vent to their feelings, with an openness neither shows in everyday life. They are also more receptive. Their lovemaking is very sensual, tactile, and unashamed. Few fantasies or pre-arranged agendas enter into it. Instead, it is a time for Taurus and Capricorn to be with each other in the moment. When they face stress or when their relationship is going through a rough patch, the act of making love is the best therapy these men could have.

Taurus and Capricorn are initially brought together by their similarities. Each finds reassurance in the other's down-to-earth manner. Both go for what is sure and reliable—which in this case is each other. Taurus finds Capricorn's large-scale ambition inspiring and thrilling to behold. He feels that Mr. Goat is going places, so he wants to be along for the ride. Capricorn finds the self-sufficiency of Taurus to be staggeringly butch. Together they feel able to conquer the world—or at least own it.

If Capricorn teaches Taurus how to dream big, Taurus teaches Capricorn how to savor the little things. Capricorn might overlook the pleasure in the taste of excellent diner coffee, the smell of new-cut grass, or the warmth of a thick sweater unless Taurus forces him to take time to notice what surrounds him.

It can be hard for Capricorn to accept that he has a dependable lover who understands him. He expects hardship throughout life and the ease of this partnership gives him the jitters. He will only relax when the two of them start building something permanent that can outlive them both. For some Taurus-Capricorn pairs that will mean an investment portfolio, for others planting an orchard. And for a few others, starting a family.

Having a child in their lives is very natural for these men. Each wants to imitate and improve on the family he grew up in. That is because they feel it is not enough just to love, but that a couple must create something tangible out of their love. True, it does not have to be a child, and it might be easier for two gay men to open a bed-and-breakfast than to adopt, but however they decide to give back to the world, it is important for them to do it together as partners.

At times this couple will lock horns, but their conflicts are usually over practical matters and not fundamental incompatibilities—because these men are similar at heart. Taurus may be more lovey-dovey and Capricorn more bossy, but both talk the same language.

TAURUS ☆ AQUARIUS

Taurus is proud to be sane.

Aquarius is proud to be insane.

Could there be a conflict of personalities brewing?

Each half of this relationship thinks the other is living by values that are a tad askew.

Taurus wonders what good freedom and individuality are when you cannot take care of yourself. And Aquarius wonders why anyone would want to focus so relentlessly on the dullest practicalities of human life. Even if he acknowledges that Taurus has a deep appreciation of art and beauty, Aquarius will go on to note that this appreciation is mindless sensuality.

At times this pairing seems less like a love match and more like a contest to see who is right. Both men believe they have the answers and nothing the other can say or do will change that. They may come to a grudging respect for each other's views but they will always be bemused by them.

Of course there are things these men like about each other. Taurus loves the way that Aquarius cares about people. He finds it admirable to want to help others. He may feel that Aquarius lacks the competence needed to really make a difference, but Taurus knows that his heart is in the right place.

Aquarius envies the know-how of Taurus. So often feeling like a space alien dropped to earth, Aquarius becomes more secure with a man who seems to belong on earth. He knows that Taurus can watch out for him, even if he cannot watch out for himself.

Both men want to be part of an extended family, and each sees the other as a step toward that goal. That is why the bond they form is strong, though it may be bedeviled with personality clashes.

Aquarius usually initiates the arguments, because he feels that Taurus is out to squelch his outrageousness— which is a pretty accurate assessment of their situation. The freedom Aquarius wants overturns the order of Taurus's world.

The resolution they find comes from recognizing how much each acts out the other's secret longings. Taurus knows that he can be a stick-in-the-mud and would love to act up for once the way his lover does. And Aquarius gets exhausted from the strain of having to act like a wacky Aquarius. The stability of Taurean life has its attractions for him.

The stubbornness of each sign forbids these men from admitting how much they would like to switch places, but being together allows them to do so vicariously.

If these boys do not click in bed from the start, it will be hard for them to build a relationship. They will adapt to each other's erotic needs as the relationship progresses, but there needs to be a pretty bright spark from the outset. Taurus takes the lead sexually because he needs it more. Aquarius enjoys sex, but for Taurus it is a language with which he expresses who he is. Without sex in some form, a love relationship is impossible for Taurus. The connection Aquarius feels with his lover is more mental than physical. Over time, each of the two men in this relationship teaches his partner how to love him best. Aquarius grows more physical and Taurus more intellectual.

If these men live together, running the home will fall to Taurus—no big surprise there. The big surprise is that Taurus awakens the pack rat in Aquarius. However, he saves things for a different reason than Taurus does. Taurus keeps mementos of the past, but Aquarius keeps things for the fun they might bring in the future.

Though this is not the easiest combination for living together, there is a strong fascination between the signs that prompts many men to do their best to make it work.

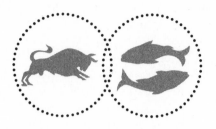

TAURUS ☆ PISCES

Too much is not enough. After all, why spend a scant hour making love when you can spend the whole night (and half the next day) in bed enjoying each other's body? Neither Taurus nor Pisces wants to miss any single possible sensation during their time together. High romance with hours of tender foreplay are absolute necessities for this couple to find satisfaction.

Taurus and Pisces love to make all pleasures linger. Long dinners, long naps, long walks at the beach. The focus for Taurus is more on the physical feeling and the focus for Pisces is more on the emotional experience. Of course, when this couple gets together, the boundary between the physical and the emotional begin to blur as it all comes together as a sensation of well-being.

A love of music unites this pair—although Pisces gets annoyed at Taurus for *always* having to sing along. Visual art also has a strong effect on this pair, so mixing a few gallery trips into their usual regimen of concerts and dance clubs can bring some welcome variety to their dates.

Taurus plans in advance what he will do for fun—he has to since it usually costs money. Pisces trusts the inspiration of the moment to lead him into something delightful. He finds it childish the way that spending cash on himself can always cheer Taurus up, even though, given the opportunity, Mr. Fish will spend far more on self-indulgence than Mr. Bull.

Their differing attitudes toward money crystallize a deeper difference in how these two men see the world. Because Taurus functions best in the cut-and-dried world of objective reality, Pisces considers his concerns trivial. It is the inner world that preoccupies Pisces, leading Taurus to question his judgment and sanity. As the relationship continues, Pisces will be less open with his esoteric concerns, but Taurus will always consider him a bit removed from reality.

These two are lucky that it is easy for them to talk about the things that separate them. Neither one is normally chatty, but with each other the things that would ordinarily be difficult to discuss are just a bit easier. So while few issues are ever completely resolved, at least Taurus and Pisces are not working at cross-purposes. In fact, a spirit of cooperation is natural to this couple, with each making up for the other's deficiencies—even if they shake their heads in disbelief while doing so.

If Taurus opens himself up to what Pisces can teach him, he will find himself becoming more tolerant of eccentricities in others. He will also grow more tolerant of himself, when his reactions to people are not what he thinks they should be. Though at first glance it seems as if Taurus is giving Pisces an education in the realities of the world, Pisces is also teaching Taurus, about the realities of interpersonal relations and the emotions they evoke.

Pisces adapts to Taurus, which is wonderfully grounding for him—and that has always been part of the attraction. Imitating Taurus's earthy practicality allows Pisces to carry within himself the excitement Mr. Bull makes him feel. Talking and being social with other friends has become more fun because of his time with Taurus.

The changes that these two men introduce into each

other's life may not last if they split. However, while they are together (which can be for a *very* long time) the transformation has a powerful impact.

GEMINI ☆ GEMINI

Meet cute, fuck fast, bye-bye.

Most Gemini-Gemini relationships follow that pattern and are over in the amount of time it takes you to read this sentence.

But a few do last longer.

Every Gemini hopes to find his twin, or at least a brother, to complete him. When he falls for another Gemini it feels like his dream has come true.

However, when Gemini meets Gemini there is likely to be a good deal of projection going on. It can go in either of two directions.

Identical Twins: These two men are similar, but each Gemini believes them to be more similar than they really are. These men overlook the things that are different about them, because they want so badly to find an identical twin.

Evil Twins: Each Gemini sees his lover as his polar opposite. He sees only differences and no similarities, as if his boyfriend were his evil twin.

The second direction is less damaging than the first, but

in either case, if the relationship is to continue, it is vital that both partners stop projecting and that each recognize the other for who he really is.

Settling for a fraternal twin as a lover rather than an identical or evil one may not appeal to the Gemini imagination, but it can still be wonderful.

The Gemini-Gemini couple talk incessantly. Their conversation forms an arabesque of topics that twine with, separate from, rejoin, and interrupt each other. Sometimes this couple stops listening to each other and goes off on parallel monologues. That is because Geminis think and talk fast, so when you put two of them together communications tend to spin out of control.

In sex as well these two men can start pushing things so fast and furious that it ends in minutes. Now, what is the point of that? In discussions, in sex, and in everything else, this pair needs to slow down, for the sake of their pleasure if nothing else.

Even when taken at a relaxed pace, Gemini-Gemini sex has the overheated atmosphere of a backseat at the drive-in. These men pop boners like pimply faced teenagers. Just like in a teen make-out session, there is a lot of grabbing, groping, giggling, and grunting. With each other, the Geminis get to treat eroticism like a dirty joke—which only gets them hotter.

A Gemini couple is slow to wake up to the reality of the love they share. They think of their relationship as a game because they are embarrassed by the bond they feel. Saying "I love you" is easy for them—admitting that they mean it is hard. So usually their hearts make the commitment before their minds are aware that it has happened.

Once Gemini and Gemini have committed, difficulties are not over yet. However much they love each other, there will be times that the two partners will feel like rivals. At least once a year they will go to some party where they seem to be competing for who can flirt with the most men and endanger the relationship most seriously. Repair work will not be hard, but these recurring dark nights of the heart reflect a lack of stability in this pairing.

For the first few years it feels as if this couple is constantly patching up its fragile bond. Then, as if by some miracle, it gets better. As is usual for these two, the heart acts in ways that the mind is unaware of. After time, the heart decides to do more than commit—it decides to trust. Consciously neither Gemini will know why they have grown more comfortable and more solid together. But they have.

GEMINI ☆ CANCER

At the start of this relationship, Gemini cannot help but feel something lacking in himself. It seems as if he is all style and no substance when compared to Cancer, who can sparkle with the best yet still feel things deeply.

Cancer would like to be as quick and adaptable as Gemini—but he feels less envy than his lover. He enjoys observing Gemini as a spectator, but is glad he is not like Mr. Twin.

Gemini and Cancer share a love of social life. They are usually the last two people at any party, the kind of couple that spends the night in the kitchen talking to anyone who comes in looking for a beer. However, Cancer will need a few nights at home, even if Gemini wants to be out every night. And it will bug Cancer that he cannot keep Gemini from going out alone.

Cancer would like to be one half of a couple and Gemini wants to be a free agent. He fears getting locked into a commitment to Cancer too soon. Cancer initially fears that Gemini is too immature to love, and his active social life away from Mr. Crab only feeds this anxiety. These fears are an expression of a larger conflict between their personalities. Cancer wants the stability of people he can depend on, while Gemini wants the excitement of instability.

Though this conflict might appear insurmountable, it is not. There is a natural tolerance for each other that makes their differences interesting challenges rather than relationship roadblocks. After a while this couple's fights (which all boil down to "You're too clingy," "No, you're too unreliable") become comforting in their own way because they are so predictable.

And they do not last long.

Everything about this relationship is subject to change. The fears come and go, there is a fight, things get worse, then they get better. Gemini and Cancer both go through emotional cycles. So the negative feelings that the other brings out are not necessarily a threat to the relationship, since they rarely settle in for a long stay.

Friends mostly see the upside of the cycle, since both Gemini and Cancer nurse their pain in private. In fact, there is much to their private lives that neither will share with anyone else. Both men love silly games, pet names, and make-believe. Their whole home life is filled with childish playfulness—especially in the bedroom.

Cancer loves warming up Gemini, who can be slow to

achieve real emotional intimacy in sex. He knows that fantasy is his best avenue to opening Gemini's heart. Gemini also brings out a directness in Cancer that other men do not. Since he is oblivious to Cancer's attempts at emotional manipulation, Mr. Crab has no choice but to openly acknowledge his needs and desires. The eroticism these two share is about communication and feeling more than physical sensation, so lovemaking can be an overpowering experience.

If this couple breaks up, it will be harder on Gemini than Cancer. Gemini will probably have abdicated responsibility for his health, finances, and home to Cancer, whose protective instincts would not let Gemini go along in the happy-go-lucky way he did before. When splitting up, it might feel to Gemini that the rug has been pulled out from under him. Cancer depends on Gemini for very little, so he will not be quite so devastated.

To sum up: The good news is that this relationship will not settle into a rut because both Gemini and Cancer are too changeable and too different from each other for that to happen. The bad news is that it will take a fair dose of mutual respect to get through the dark moods of each man and the bickering that results from them.

GEMINI ☆ LEO

Each member of this pair will always think the other is a little ditzy.

To Gemini, Leo's single-mindedness and sincerity seem supremely unsavvy. Leo thinks that all of that Gemini flitting and manipulation are distractions leading away from what really matters.

So why would a Gemini and a Leo want to spend any time with each other? It is because they fulfill deep needs for each other. And because ditzy can be cute.

For Gemini, nothing is real until it is spoken of aloud. However, though he is an entertaining speaker, Mr. Twin can have trouble finding someone willing to take part in the cross-talk. That is something Leo is always, always willing to do with a Gemini. Seeing himself as an unrecognized king, Leo loves the idea of having his own personal jester to play with—which is a role Gemini is very comfortable with. This is a talking relationship, and both men like it that way.

Except in bed. Sometimes Mr. Lion wishes that Mr. Twin would just moan like other guys instead of verbally analyzing the nuances of his pleasure. Mr. Lion will never feel like he has conquered Mr. Twin until the yammering in the sheets stops. Which will never happen. Gemini is an ongoing, frustrating, and very hot challenge to Leo's lovemaking technique.

In most other, out-of-the-bed contexts, however, Leo loves to hear Gemini talk. The Twin's words are like a marvelous window on a much wider landscape than Leo usually sees. Leos do not learn new things easily. Except with Gemini. With the Twin, Leo opens up to fresh experiences. He also meets new friends and discovers new interests. Gemini is Leo's bridge to the world. He is a kind of celestial anchorman, turning everything that is out there into small, easily digestible sound bites for Leo.

The Gemini man is better at twisting and tweaking other people's ideas than creating any original ones of his own. Whether it is an opinion about some new film or a political belief, a Gemini only knows what he thinks in response to someone else's thought. He needs a content provider. Since Leo is one of the world's foremost experts on just about everything, Gemini has lots to respond to.

In spite of all Gemini gets from this relationship (which is more than Leo does), it is the Lion that will be the first one to commit to the relationship. (Though Gemini will be the first to say, "I love you." He'll say it to Leo even before he means it.)

This couple is focused on the outside world much more than they are on each other. If they share a home, it will be more a place to receive visitors and host parties than a cozy nest for just two. This outward focus can bring energy and excitement into the relationship. Or it can dissipate the couple's intensity. The Gemini-Leo relationship has such an ease that either of the pair could take it for granted. And that means trouble.

Both these guys are outrageous flirts. Jealousy flares up from the first date on. Add to that their dizzy social schedule, which gives ample opportunity for flirting, jealousy, bad behavior, and mutual recrimination. Unless these two men make each other a conscious priority, the relationship will crack apart.

It would be stupid for this couple to pretend to be stay-at-home, lovey-dovey types. But it could not hurt to skip Sunday brunch with the boys for some quality time. Hey, its only once a week. And you can still make it to the tea dance.

GEMINI ☆ VIRGO

Irritation is next door to love.

Gemini and Virgo can really push each other's buttons—and enjoy doing so. Though this is an argumentative couple, they are also highly communicative, with very few secrets hidden from each other. They are open and honest because they have no choice.

These men observe each other, picking up on the minutiae of behavior so each can analyze the personality of his lover. They know just what makes each other tick, which is exactly what each of them finds annoying in the other. The irritation is not that they verbalize each other's faults and failings—it is that they do it so accurately.

Each partner says he wants to stand on his own, free and independent. However, Gemini would like Virgo to baby him a little and Virgo wants Gemini to tell him he is doing a good job. These are men whose personalities are full of contradictions. Others might find the ambiguities maddening, but Gemini and Virgo know how to deal with the gray areas.

Virgo is not taken in by Gemini's fancy talk. Whenever there is an evasion, an exaggeration, or an outright lie, Virgo can spot it. Strangely enough, Gemini finds that being constantly busted is liberating—the pressure to be strictly literal and the guilt over lying are gone. And even more strange, Virgo admires Gemini's ability to twist the truth, though he is proud that he himself is not deceived.

Though Virgo complains about Gemini's frequent absences, the truth is that he really does not mind having time to himself. As is usual for this couple, Gemini gets mad at Virgo's complaints because he thinks he should, not because he is really upset.

It is possible for these men to become so focused on petty issues that the larger context of their relationship gets lost. In such cases, Gemini and Virgo continue the partnership but without the deepening commitment which gives meaning to the shared lives of most couples. Neither man can tolerate stasis, so they rerun pointless (but emotionally hot) issues to provide the illusion that the relationship is going somewhere. Does it really matter that Gemini is always late and Virgo always early, since nothing they do will change this? Would it not be better to work on bringing your families together, saving to buy a co-op, or discussing where you see yourselves in five years—activities that could actually have a payoff?

If it is hard to come together, it is because of some deep differences between these signs. Gemini is carefree and Virgo is careful. Gemini thinks big and Virgo thinks small. Gemini has ideas and Virgo has savvy. A negotiation needs to happen in which the couple discovers how to let their differences complement each other rather than divide them.

It should not be hard to manage this negotiation since chances are they made a similar one in bed right at the start, with spectacular results. These men are both highly skilled in the erotic arts, though each has developed his own specialties. Rather than the sexual competition one often finds with such highly sexed men, Gemini and Virgo make a lovely and sensitive duet. They unlock the mischief in each other and bring out the naughtiness of lovemaking.

Gemini and Virgo share a love of exploration on every level. They cannot just experience the world as it is, because they always want to know why things are the way they are. This relationship is as much an intellectual partnership as a sexual one. These men realize they are far more likely to find answers to life's questions together than apart.

GEMINI ☆ LIBRA

"I am nobody's fool—least of all yours."

Either Gemini said this to Libra or Libra said it to Gemini. It does not matter, since it applies both ways. Each sees through the wit, sweet talk, and dazzle the other uses to seduce men.

But they still want each other.

Few couples talk more than this pair. Right from the start they play off each other like vaudeville comedians, setting each other up for jokes, anecdotes, and other opportunities to show off their conversational skills. It is the mental quickness and love of debate that attracts these two to each other.

It is good they have each other since when Gemini and Libra get together, they drive the rest of the world crazy.

When these two go out on a date, they make waiters go nuts with their constant questions about this, that, and the other menu item. Then they take forever to decide what to order.

Friends are baffled trying to ascertain whether this pair is a committed couple or just friends who fuck. Gemini especially revels in keeping things ambiguous. Libra may pretend to be all dewy-eyed romantic, but his actions make you think he is still on the prowl.

Then there is the bickering. Friends can never figure out if the arguments are playful, hypothetical, or deadly. Actually, these two men drive each other crazy as well with their constant second-guessing and rehashing of supposedly dead issues. Because these men do not fall for each other's bull, the points made during the arguments really hit home.

The problem is that Gemini and Libra mistake discussion for action. By examining their issues for hours on end in in-depth conversation, this pair thinks they are resolving them, when what they really need to do is change behavior. This pair is quite capable of adapting to meet each other's needs, but they do it best if it is not discussed first.

The sex life of this pair is varied and experimental. They like to keep it light and fun rather than deeply emotional, which gives them a tremendous freedom in bed. They are both as interested in the activities that surround sex as the act itself. The walk home after the date, turning on the music, the murmured words are just as erotically stimulating as the touch of naked flesh.

Gemini looks at Libra as a kind of role model. He does not want to have him just as a boyfriend, he also wants to imitate his style and character. Libra feels that Gemini is more worldly and sophisticated than he is. He loves watching how Gemini deals with people outside of the relationship and wishes he could be as comfortable facing any situation.

These men often focus too much energy outside of their partnership, which leaves them with very little to give each other. While they both enjoy parties and the gay social whirl, they need to make each other a priority. If not, sooner or later one of them will find a man who does want to focus on a relationship.

Libra is more likely to be the man who holds this couple together. To oversimplify: Gemini supplies energy and sexual excitement, while Libra supplies romance and emotional fulfillment. What Gemini gives makes staying together a desirable goal, but what Libra gives is the glue. Together these men offer each other an understanding that is difficult for them to find with anyone else. At times the relationship can feel cool, but the bond they share, even at those times, is very real.

GEMINI ☆ SCORPIO

They really ought to know better.

After all, they were brought together as much by curiosity as by passion. They dug for all the info they could get on each other, so they must have seen that each was custom-designed to frustrate and annoy the other.

Of course Gemini and Scorpio are also designed to be fascinated by each other's actions. And each of them will do whatever he can to help the other achieve his goals—even if he disapproves of them.

At the first meeting, these two men seem completely indifferent to each other. They engage in some impersonal chitchat before pumping mutual friends for the real dirt. What they hear scares them. To Gemini, Scorpio sounds like a controlling, self-righteous ass, and to Scorpio, Gemini sounds immature.

But when they meet again, each hopes to find something in the other to indicate that what he heard was wrong. Neither does, but as Gemini and Scorpio both look behind the words of the other man, they discover an appealing mystery that draws them in. These two signs love to search for answers, and someone who is a difficult puzzle to solve will keep their interest for a long while.

Neither Gemini nor Scorpio is much impressed by the smoke and mirrors that the other uses to keep lovers at an emotional distance. The schizo word games and flashy distractions that prevent most men from seeing who Gemini really is cannot blind Scorpio. The self-control of Scorpio bores Gemini. The old bullshit does not work, and each man has to find a new way of relating to his new partner.

Scorpio is the more demanding half of this couple, since he views noncompliance with his wishes as a type of disloyalty. Too bad—Gemini is constitutionally incapable of complying with anyone. He may mean to phone Scorpio when he is going to be late for dinner, but something will come up to sidetrack him—you can be sure of that.

For Gemini, dating Scorpio can feel claustrophobic. Scorpio's need to construct scenarios for them that will give him an adrenaline rush makes Gemini feel like he is a puppet trapped in another man's soap opera. Which is exactly what he is. If these two men cannot work out a way to let Gemini have his freedom, while Scorpio gets some control, they might as well give it up before either does the other serious bodily harm.

The threat of mutual abuse is real, since when these two men get together, there is a very strong desire to transgress. However, this desire is not a problem if channeled properly. Most successful Gemini-Scorpio couples limit their transgressions to the bedroom. This couple's erotic life is mischievous, naughty, and highly experimental. The curiosity that brought them together can make sex a secret exploration of the urges that neither feels he can reveal to the world at large.

At the extraordinary points in life—lease signings, crisis interventions, first dinner with the in-laws, medical emergencies, bankruptcies—this couple can be seen at its best. They thrive when staring down disaster or taking the first steps toward an uncertain future. It is the ordinary that trips them up. Gemini and Scorpio come through for each other when most couples crumble, but during the easy times, when most couples can relax, these guys have to be *more* sensitive to each other.

Mutual giving is at the heart of this relationship. The most important thing that Gemini and Scorpio can give each other is tolerance of their differences. It is okay for each of them to go on thinking the other is always wrong, as long as it is okay for him to be him.

GEMINI ☆ SAGITTARIUS

It is love on the run.

Most men think that when they find a lover, it means settling down. But when Gemini meets Sagittarius, they definitely are not settling down—they are taking off. Right off the bat, from their wham-bam-thank-you-man first encounter, their life together moves at top speed with many surprising twists and turns.

Neither man has much of an attention span, so if they do not feel a shared heat immediately, neither is likely to stick around in the hope that something can develop in time. The only factor that might delay a first date is that it is hard to find a night when they are both free.

Of course they will have already had sex before they start dating. After all, a date takes hours, but it only takes minutes for them to fuck, making it much easier to fit into these boys' on-the-go lifestyle.

Because these men are so involved with so many things, finding time to share with each other will always be tough. They both know that moving in together would solve that problem, but that means COMMITMENT, which neither man rushes into (though both Gemini and Sagittarius are thrilled to rush into anything else).

What keeps this couple together is that each man likes who he becomes with the other and sees in his partner qualities he wants to (and actually can) imitate. Gemini would love to take on some of Sagittarius's ideals, and Sagittarius wishes he could generate ideas as quickly as Gemini does. When they are together, Gemini gets a sense of purpose and sincerity from his lover. Sagittarius in turn gains a sense of tact from Gemini that escapes him when he is alone.

Both signs want freedom just as much as they want intimacy. In most relationships they will feel constricted to at least some degree. But in this pairing each member understands restlessness and the need to have some part of one's life that is separate from coupledom. No Gemini or Sagittarius will insist that his lover be home every night, because he himself will not be there.

On those rare occasions when they are together, this couple loves weekend getaways, pub crawls, progressive dinners—any activity that keeps them in motion. The films, restaurants, and clubs they go to have to be new and edgy. Holidays with family mean little to them since these two prefer to start new traditions over honoring the old ones.

Sex is the prime form of entertainment for these boys. Their lovemaking alternates between the awkward and the graceful. Nothing is consistent since Gemini and Sagittarius both dream of the ultimate fuck and are open to anything. And spontaneity counts. Settling into an erotic routine is contrary to both their natures, which can make some sessions frustratingly aimless but bring exciting new sensations into others. After that first kiss of the night, anything can happen—for good or bad.

Gemini and Sagittarius goad each other on to take big risks in life. Usually the risks pay off, though in ways no one could anticipate. Sometimes they do not. However, neither is likely to learn from his mistakes with the other reinforcing careless behavior. Though both men think a lot about the future, they have difficulty making concrete plans for a life together. Lucky for them, in the long run, the cosmos somehow, mysteriously takes care of them. It is as if being careless earns them the right to be carefree.

GEMINI ☆ CAPRICORN

Even if it is not literally true, this pairing always feels like Sugar Daddy and his Boy Toy.

Though there may be deep, sincere love, when these two get together there is a deal in place, even if they never speak of it. It goes like this: Gemini shows Capricorn a good time, teaching him how to let loose and go wild. In return Capricorn brings structure to Gemini's undisciplined life.

As long as each man fulfills his part of the deal, the relationship continues—even if love has died long ago. And in those cases where love is there but the deal is not fulfilled— it is likely that the partnership will end.

Gemini does not know why he is attracted to Capricorn, but he is. Capricorn will tell you that he sees potential in Gemini, something that he wants to get behind and inside of. (Double entendre intended.) Either man might make the first move, but Capricorn is the first to see that the initial attraction can become something more.

Yet that does not mean Capricorn is ready to move in and select a silverware pattern. Gemini and Capricorn are suspicious of each other, and need time to establish trust. Even after the relationship starts, the suspicion lingers, though both men try to hide it.

This pairing is more pragmatic than idealistic. The ideals of honesty, devotion, openness that define coupledom for most men do not mean much to these two. They are perfectly willing to live a lie, as long as it is one that works. They are even willing to tolerate a one-sided love, as long as it is one that works. In fact, both Gemini and Capricorn enjoy it when there is something askew between them that they can work together to conceal from the world.

In this relationship one of the men (usually Capricorn) has money or resources that he puts in the service of the other (usually Gemini). This causes friction since Capricorn uses money to express emotion, while Gemini sees money as a path to gratification. Capricorn thinks before he spends, but Gemini wants to get rid of his money before it gets too old. If the suspicion between the two lingers, it is because of their opposing financial philosophies.

They view sex differently as well. Lovemaking will always matter more to Capricorn. It might be fun or even meaningful to Gemini, but to Capricorn sex is central to the relationship. Yet for this couple, the differences only make their erotic pairing more exciting. The slow sensuality of Capricorn plays well off the darting, electric love that Gemini is expert in. Between the sheets, they demonstrate a deep understanding of each other that they rarely show in normal life. Neither is the lover that the other expected, but each is the lover that the other needs.

While the Gemini-Capricorn couple may sound too heartless to survive together, the bond between them is just as real as that between more mushy pairs. Just because their favorite date is going to a restaurant to make sarcastic comments about the other diners does not mean that they cannot show tenderness toward each other. Capricorn appreciates Gemini's ability to express the things he cannot. Gemini is glad to have Capricorn anchor him. Their love is based on the things they do for each other more than airy romantic nonsense—and that is okay because there is so much that they do for each other.

GEMINI ☆ AQUARIUS

Are they a couple or not?

It is hard to tell just what the nature of their relationship is and how much of a commitment Gemini and Aquarius have made to each other, since they have invented something that looks like no other partnership in the history of humankind.

Their love talk sounds more like a debate or business lunch than seduction. Displays of affection always have a self-mocking tone to them. Neither gets that upset to see his lover flirting with someone else. (Though Aquarius tries to be jealous, he cannot pull it off.)

In answer to the question that opened this section: Gemini and Aquarius are lovers without ever quite becoming a couple.

And every Gemini-Aquarius pair is not a couple in their own particular way.

It is surprising that they do not blend together better, since they have so much in common. Both are intensely social with a burning need to communicate. Often these signs do not know what they think or feel until they share it with others. When they are together the chatter never stops, as they try on different attitudes in front of each other as if each were trying on different shirts for his lover's approval.

The trouble is that once Aquarius finds something true, he will not try on anything else. But Gemini goes on experimenting with thoughts and feelings like they were so many mix-and-match accessories. Unlike Aquarius he is not searching for the truth, he is merely searching for something to hold his interest. Open-minded as Aquarius is, he will never learn to tolerate this aspect of Gemini's personality.

The main reason, however, that these two never completely merge is simple—they do not want to. Both Gemini and Aquarius love freedom and hate having their actions constricted by emotional ties. Other signs will not let them get away with being that footloose—but in this pairing each partner makes few emotional demands other than asking that his lover be available when needed. These are men who enjoy relationships but do not derive their whole sense of worth from the attention of loved ones.

However, these two men do take great pride in designing a relationship that is unique to them. Each is highly sensitive to the other's needs and able to discuss whatever conflicts they have between them. Actually, conflict resolution is their favorite leisure-time activity. If they do not have anything real to fight about on the weekend, Gemini and Aquarius will make something up, just to have something interesting to work out.

The biggest problem with their sex life is that the communication is so good and so fascinating—neither wants to shut his mouth long enough to kiss. They cannot resolve fights through sex or give emotional reassurance through lovemaking the way some couples do, but their sex life is more than satisfactory. When Gemini touches Aquarius, it is like the flame touching the firecracker. The explosion happens fast and makes a big noise. These boys are very loud, but the neighbors are not likely to complain because they do not go on for very long.

It is not quite accurate to describe the Gemini-Aquarius pairing as a relationship. It would be better to use the plural and call it relationship*s*. Periodically (and that could mean once every two years or once every hour, depending on the specific pair) they need to rip apart what they have together and rebuild it from scratch. Their partnership is self-renewing and changes to meet the evolving needs of Gemini and Aquarius. So while the relationship may look passionless and structureless to the rest of us, there is something very healthy about it that we all can learn from.

GEMINI ☆ PISCES

Pisces believes that there are some things that should remain unspoken.

To which Gemini asks, "Why?"

That in a nutshell is the difference between how Gemini and Pisces are wired.

Gemini has an overpowering need to express what he experiences. He often does not know what he thinks or feels until he speaks. Even when he does ponder silently, he tends to do it in the form of an imaginary dialog within himself.

Pisces on the other hand believes that some things are destroyed when shared. He prefers to feel his feelings without broadcasting them. With a high tolerance for ambiguity, Pisces has little need to resolve the questions about this relationship that drive Gemini up the wall.

When it comes time to decide where these two are going as a couple, the discussion usually turns into a monologue by Gemini with Pisces nodding and smiling. Pisces believes that things will go where they will go, no matter what actions he and his boyfriend take. Gemini's dissection of the minutiae of emotions seems hopelessly naive and pointless to Mr. Fish.

And he is right.

This couple's relationship goes through many changes, most of which they could never anticipate. Nor do they need to. It is easy for Gemini and Pisces to make new beginnings with each other whenever necessary, because each responds effectively to whatever is thrown at them. For these partners, making it work is the bottom line. They can compromise on almost anything, even abandon any ideal they hold, if it means hanging on to someone they love.

Pisces is an enigma to Gemini. He knows that this is one man he can never fully understand—though he will certainly try. Gemini considers Pisces very wise and desperately wants his approval. The trouble is that Pisces rarely gives it in the overt way that Gemini wants.

Pisces, on the other hand, finds Gemini to be perfectly understandable. There is something familiar about him that Pisces finds comforting—Gemini feels like home.

When they are together, little arguments frequently flare up. Little erotic moments also flare up. Every relationship has its ups and downs, but in a Gemini-Pisces pairing they come and go with dizzying speed. Both men have mercurial temperaments and hair-trigger emotions. Strangely enough, they each enjoy having a lover who is equally changeable.

However, each partner does need time apart to recharge his emotional batteries. For Pisces that will be time alone, and for Gemini time with friends. It is important, though, that this couple be sure to have some focused time with each other. Though it is easy for Gemini and Pisces to grow together, it is equally easy for them to grow apart unless they check in and try to pay attention to who the other is becoming.

The sexual potential of this pairing is great as long as Gemini does not try to run the show. He should understand that what happens between them in bed is one of those Pisces-unspoken-mystery type things. Analyzing it or manipulating it too much will kill it. If Gemini can give over to Pisces, the combination of Mr. Fish's imagination with his technique promises ecstasy on both a physical and an emotional level.

Honesty with each other is difficult for this pair. Perhaps that is why neither takes what the other says at face value. Their conversations are filled with smooth evasions that reveal everything to the partner, who is reading between the lines. Yet neither one resents the other for the evasion or the inference. These men may be vastly dissimilar in how they approach life, yet they accept each other without judgment.

CANCER ☆ CANCER

There is always some regret in a Cancer's life, something that he wishes he would have done differently. When Cancer hooks up with Cancer, it is an opportunity to make up for past mistakes and set the future right.

Even when one of the Cancers recognizes that fate is offering him the chance to correct past wrongs, he is slow to seize the opportunity. Cancer is a back-door man, so he likes to sneak up on things. This sign likes to let the other guy make the first move, so that he does not have to risk rejection.

Now imagine two of them, each waiting for the other to make his pitch. Eventually they will date, but it may take a while for them to work up the balls to ask.

Once they do go out, both Cancers will find that there is a great deal of good in this pairing. Each is a moody man who needs the soothing touch that only another moody man can give.

Two men born under Cancer have the ability to heal each other. Their mothers were the emotionally dominant figures that psychiatry used to say caused homosexuality in their sons. Though the boys might say that their mothers were lovely and loving, in truth they probably have quite a few psychic scars from their rearing by these women. The two Cancers are willing and, more important, able to do the re-parenting needed to erase those scars.

Of course, the influence of Mom will always be present to some extent. That is why these men want so badly to find some socially acceptable way to be gay—they want their moms to be proud. They might try to be part of the radical fringe, but they will never go all the way.

Part of the excitement of sex for these two is the game-playing that surrounds it. The challenge is to find new ways to seduce or trick one's partner into erotic submission. Things get especially hot during the full moon, which acts as an aphrodisiac to all Cancers. They cannot sleep anyway on that night so they might as well do something to occupy the time. It is affection more than acrobatics that excites the Cancer lover, so even a hand caress can bring Mr. Crab to a climax if there is honest love behind it.

Both Cancers are obsessed with food and money. They need to know that there is enough of both for each partner. If there is not, the impact is felt in other aspects of the relationship. The most dramatic example is in bed. If two Cancer men discuss their dismal financial situation some evening, it is unlikely that either will be able to get it up that night. A disastrous dinner could have the same effect. Not to mention the arguments and mutual recriminations that will follow when their moneys are in a bad way.

Keeping finances separate is one strategy to ensure continued emotional health for the Cancer-Cancer couple. Each man will feel more secure if his own money is his alone. Opening a joint checking account is a bigger commitment for this couple than any gay wedding could be. It is best to wait until a strong trust and commitment have already been established before opening one.

The main pitfall this couple faces is that they can get so wrapped up in each other and the little world they create together, that they never leave the house. Separated from the rest of the community, the pair will reinforce all their worst traits.

However, by staying connected to others, Cancer and Cancer will find the emotional stimulation they need to grow. And by coming to recognize himself reflected in his partner, each man will gain the insight that will make that growth meaningful.

CANCER ☆ LEO

Think of Leo as the sun.

Think of Cancer as the moon.

Consciously or unconsciously, the sun and moon divide all between them. The sun rules what is public and out in the open and known. The moon rules what is emotional, private, hidden, and sexual.

The sun seems to be more powerful than the moon. That is, until an eclipse. Then the moon blots out the sun's glory, turning day into night. The event reveals unknown energies so strong that they blind anyone who looks at it.

Kind of like a Cancer-Leo breakup.

Early on the pair are drawn together by their differences. The boldness of Mr. Lion is invigorating for Mr. Crab, whose nature is more cautious. The deep empathy and concern for others that defines Cancer is a fascinating mystery for Leo, who can only understand the world through his own experience.

In the next stage things get harder because each sign lives in a different world. A Crab crawls sideways through a half-lit world of memory and unspoken feelings. A Lion pounces into a sunny world where everything is just what it looks like. Cancer and Leo do not really conflict. They just do not understand each other's world.

Each sign has a very strong but very separate energy. To introduce yet another metaphor, the two are like PC and Mac. Translation and sharing is possible. The two can work harmoniously for years, each using its individual strengths when needed. But then one day some minor glitch—a misplaced comma, a stray piece of code—exposes the fundamental differences between how these two are wired. And that difference can destroy everything. This coupling will not end over some big issue, but over some minor incident that shows how differently these men think and sets up a chain reaction that makes going on impossible.

Leo may resent the hold the past has on Cancer. He might be upset to know by some stray mention that he reminds Cancer of some love from long ago, since Leo wants to be a unique original. Mr. Lion will start screaming for his lover to open up more to what is happening now. Then Cancer will retreat from the big, blunt, and reckless Leo. Mr. Crab will freeze out all of Mr. Lion's warmth. The cause of the breakup is something that seems small, but leaves a path of devastation behind by the time it is finished.

What you want to know is how to avoid this. Here are four steps toward a lasting Cancer-Leo relationship.

1. Love each other. Without love, and that means *real, true, unconditional love,* this pair has no hope. The relationship will only survive if it is of supreme importance to

both partners. Does the volatility excite you or drain you? The answer to that question will tell you if there is love.

2. Love is not enough. Respect is more important. Go back to the sun/moon metaphor at the beginning. The two can co-exist as long as they stick to their own corners of the sky. The moment one tries to step into the other's territory—eclipse. Mutual understanding is probably out of the question, but mutual recognition of the forces driving each of you is vital.

3. Each partner needs other outlets. Together you temper each other's nature. You each need a place apart from the other where undiluted Cancer and unfettered Leo impulses can be acted out and relished.

4. Enjoy your differences. Find delight in your individual peculiarities. You have been reading about what problems your differences can create. Throw away this book and for-get all that. If you have read this section and still look at your lover as a treasure, rather than a bomb ready to explode, then it was meant to be.

CANCER ☆ VIRGO

They just seem too nice to be for real. In public they are so polite and deferential to each other, it is hard to imagine any arguments between them. Each seems to be completely avail-able emotionally to the other.

Have we found the perfect couple?

No. When something seems too good to be real, it usually is. The Cancer-Virgo couple faces the same ups and downs that everyone else does, but they do not broadcast their difficulties.

Cancer and Virgo come to the relationship with expectations that seem diametrically opposed. Cancer equates love with dependence and Virgo feels exploited if he does not have independence within the relationship. A visual image for their dynamic is Cancer trying to lean on Virgo as he edges away. These are two signs that love to complain—with each other they find a lot to love.

If this couple does tend to bicker, it is only because their line of communication is so open. Cancer and Virgo would really like to help one another, but do not always know how. Cancer thinks that adding to Virgo's already tall pile of guilt will somehow give him the confidence he lacks, while Virgo thinks that making Cancer feel incompetent to live will motivate him to become more self-sufficient.

Note to Cancer and Virgo: You are both wrong.

It is funny how these two men act as unpaid therapists to their friends, effectively resolving their emotional ills, yet they cannot do the same for each other. Maybe it is being in love that makes the difference.

Being so security minded, when they move in together these men treat their home as a fortress. Then instead of feeling imprisoned they actually feel more free. Cancer, who chronically feels unappreciated, finds Virgo's criticism of his homemaking skills reassuring. It may be negative attention, but it shows that someone actually notices what he does. Virgo feels safe with Cancer. Though he may not like the in-your-face intimacy they share that much, he likes knowing that Cancer would never do anything to hurt him.

A major benefit of this pairing is that when together, the

Cancer-Virgo couple is extremely social, which is a wonderful change since both tend to isolate when single.

As time goes on, Virgo will be keen to improve on their quality of life though Cancer is content to let things go on status quo. This is the number one reason they argue. They are pretty much in agreement about money matters, but when Virgo reads an article on how to improve one's diet or gets on a kick to throw away old junk, long-suffering Cancer flies into a rage. In the end, though, no one has to win or lose the argument since compromise is easy for these two men.

A bizarre thing happens when this couple fights. Each man is likely to accuse the other of being controlling. Each will say that the other is prone to dark moods and needless worrying that make him impossible to be around. But even more bizarre—both men will be right! Talk about compatibility!

When Cancer and Virgo make love, it is disgustingly healthy and wholesome. Together they agree that exciting sex is the god-given right of any two people in love. Both are willing to do almost anything to please the other, yet their love never degenerates into empty acrobatics or desperate thrill-seeking. Rather it is emotionally full acrobatics and delightful thrill-seeking.

Even if this couple decides to split, the relationship will not be over. Cancer and Virgo have a way of popping back into each other's life at unexpected moments.

CANCER ☆ LIBRA

These two are so into their little couple act that you would swear they were lesbians. Or rather heterosexuals, since their cutsey-pie cooing is beneath the dignity of our sapphic sisters.

Neither Cancer nor Libra is an impulsive sign, but when they meet they leap at each other with surprising speed. Both have been frustrated in the past by men who were ambivalent about relationships, and are overjoyed to find another gay man who dreams of white veils and orange blossom.

Even if Cancer and Libra do not immediately start planning a gay wedding, they do like everyone to know that they are a couple. And they like to show everyone just how a couple is supposed to act. Cancer knows that the picture-perfect coupledom that they present to the world is not the real relationship, though Libra believes in it wholeheartedly.

Talking about their frustrations and anger is difficult for them, because both men are afraid of direct confrontation with a loved one. Mind games and passive-aggressive behavior are their preferred ways to let loved ones know when they have transgressed. Finding better ways to express negative emotion is essential to this relationship's health.

Cancer and Libra have the ability to help each other navigate through their emotions. Cancer has no problem in facing the darker feelings we all carry around. He can help Libra overcome his fear of conflict, anger, and hatred. Libra can return the favor by demonstrating to Cancer how to be more direct in expressing his emotional needs.

Libra does need to watch out for Cancer's pessimism. Naturally slow to take action, Libra will grind to a halt when Cancer points out all the dire consequences he is sure his lover will face. In his own mind, Cancer may believe he is merely counterbalancing Libra's naïveté, but the truth is that he is manipulating Libra into doing what Cancer himself wants.

The Cancer-Libra couple love to collaborate on erotic fantasies that speak to the emotional core of their relationship. The buildup to sex is as important as the act itself. Prior to any foreplay they will set the mood using the music, scents, food, and clothing they reserve for their special times together. Anyone else would laugh at their over-the-top scene setting, but they approach it with high seriousness, since it is what gives them the security to express deeply felt emotion in their lovemaking.

When Cancer and Libra move in together (which will probably be on their second date) they need lots of closet space—not for themselves but for the gazillion tchotchkes they will accumulate. Together they decide that they must have some fabulous tag sale treasure. But after a few months, Libra will tire of it, though Cancer cannot bear the thought of letting it go. If they do not have a closet to toss it into, the two of them face an hours-long discussion of what to do with the damn thing.

Cancer and Libra work hard to deserve each other. Nothing makes either of them sadder than a look of disappointment in his lover's eye. There are power struggles ahead for this pair since each has strong life goals that he is unwilling to sacrifice. However, there is a respect for each other's emotions and desires that makes it possible for them to bend a little, even when full-scale compromise is impossible.

Advice to Cancer: It is not fair to be angry at a man for not taking care of you the way you want him to. Grow up.

Advice to Libra: Stop with the comparisons! He is who he is, and if that is not good enough for you, give him his freedom. It is not right to keep him hanging.

CANCER ☆ SCORPIO

It is not what it looks like.

The calm surface of this relationship conceals an ongoing, silent power struggle between Cancer and Scorpio. Both know what is going on even though they choose not to discuss it. Rather than creating bitterness, the fierceness of the struggle only increases the respect these two men have for each other.

Right from the start, even though Cancer and Scorpio had no problem talking, the real communication was silent. No one had to test the waters with mildly suggestive comments to see if the other would be receptive to a come-on. They both knew. Thus they were able to discuss politics and current films, since there was no question a date would happen.

At every stage of the relationship, for as long as it continues, in battle and in love, subtext will count infinitely more than any surface communications.

Each of them is more easily hurt than he will admit, so both are happy to find a lover who understands him. Protective of themselves and of those they love, Cancer and Scorpio see the relationship as a cocoon promising safety in a nasty world.

Unfortunately, neither is willing to surrender control of his life to his cocoon-mate. They have always admired each other's strength, though neither expected to find himself pitted against it. Cancer and Scorpio are tolerant of any personality flaws they find in each other, but they will ruthlessly use them in their battles.

So why do they stay together?

It is the subtext. These men live for the half-hidden and the subliminal. Not trusting anything overt, it is hard for them to trust men who wear their heart on their sleeve and say exactly what they mean. With each other, in a relationship filled with silent but clear communication, each feels he has finally found a man who speaks his language.

Normally Cancer and Scorpio are signs that jealously guard their secrets, but in this relationship they reveal a great many of them. True, not as many as the other would wish, but still more than they do to most other men.

Sexually, these men seek a perfect merging of two into one. They want to be inside each other, figuratively as well as literally. Their lovemaking is a long, slow, almost religious ritual in which each touch carries great meaning. There is no empty pillow talk after, but rather a still appreciation of their communion.

In spite of the power struggle, Scorpio shows such steadfast loyalty that Cancer gains the confidence to take greater emotional risks outside of the relationship. His sense of connection to others, which was always intense, grows even more so.

Scorpio should be careful not to get overly critical of Cancer's money management. This is the one arena in which the power struggle becomes vocalized. Since there is a fundamental agreement between the two on financial goals ("Get enough to cushion against any bad turn of fortune"), this conflict could be easily resolved if deeper emotional issues did not get in the way.

Though they are sympathetic to each other's touchiness, these two get all-out bitchy about everyone else. When they get together, it is as if they think that by tearing others down they can build themselves up. Showing love and concern for others can be tricky for Cancer and Scorpio when they are single, but it is even harder when they form a couple. But if they do not make the effort to show some warmth, that cozy little cocoon can become a prison cell cutting them off from the rest of humanity.

CANCER ☆ SAGITTARIUS

This is the kind of relationship that inspires country-western songs—if you look at it from Cancer's point of view. Long-suffering Mr. Crab keeps dinner warm, waiting for the return of that rambling Mr. Horseyman who just does not know how to return love.

But things are not that simple.

Sagittarius sees the relationship as a kind of sex farce in which sincere Mr. Horseyman has his world turned inside out when the groundlessly jealous Mr. Crab misinterprets situations—such as an innocent hug with some boy in a bikini who was merely expressing his gratitude for directions to the beach.

Each sees himself as wronged by an unfeeling or unthinking partner. This is because, though it is easy for this couple to love each other, understanding between them is much more difficult.

Cancer pines for a home and security, while Sagittarius longs for the freedom of wide open spaces and the excitement of living on the edge. These two were drawn together by their common need to share good times with good friends. At first, their differences were fascinating, but as their relationship progresses, Cancer and Sagittarius need to find ways to accommodate each other while staying true to themselves.

Sagittarius has got to learn to watch his mouth around Cancer. He may be permanently unembarrassed, but Cancer is permanently embarrassed. The verbal faux pas sends Mr. Crab either into tears or withdrawal mode. Though the actual content of the comments is small potatoes and Cancer recovers quickly, this is not a healthy pattern for a relationship. It is the petty things that erode the foundations of love.

The differences in the way they treat money cause tremendous conflict. Cancer squirrels away anything he can, and when he does buy, he wants the product to be something of lasting value. Sagittarius feels weighed down when he has too much money. He spends money on things that do not last, just on a whim. Each man's stomach turns when he witnesses how the other handles finances.

Neither Cancer nor Sagittarius will listen when the other tells him what to do. Each prides himself on being the master of his own fate, so they get prickly at any interference. Sagittarius likes to follow his desires on his own and is willing to give Cancer a similar freedom. However, Cancer wants to set not only his own direction but that of Sagittarius as well. Any fights on this issue can be squarely blamed on Cancer's attempts to control his lover.

There are a few meeting points for this pair. One is their love of nature. While their tastes in film and music may differ, plop the two on a hiking trail in the middle of nowhere and they will ooh and ahh in unison at every single bird and bush they come across.

Cancer and Sagittarius both love telling jokes and laughing. Though this may seem like a minor consideration, if a couple laughs at the same things it is a sign that they have a good shot at a long future together.

Sex for this couple breaks boundaries. Cancer inspires Sagittarius to use his body to express what he feels inside. Sagittarius in turn inspires Cancer to dream big—in bed and out. Together, they make each other believe that a great love, the kind Dante and Shakespeare wrote about, is possible.

If they are lucky, they find that possibility in each other. If they are not lucky, they leave this relationship with faith that a great romance might be just around the corner.

CANCER ☆ CAPRICORN

Being gay can be embarrassing, what with having to explain "He is my lover, not my brother" to clueless B&B owners and "I do not have a wife, my domestic partner is a man" to the insurance rep. The Cancer-Capricorn couple handles these situations with magnificent aplomb, since they appear to be the kind of solid couple banks jump all over themselves to give mortgages to.

Few gay couples feel as comfortable living in a heterosexual world as this one does. Perhaps it is because both partners have a fundamental respect for the norms of society. Cancer and Capricorn look to tradition as a guide to living their lives.

The seriousness of this pair can freeze into a mask of self-righteousness. Even if it does not, friends often think of them as parental figures. Which makes sense, since when Cancer finds himself alone with Capricorn, they talk about others in their circle as if they were children. They do not mean to be condescending, but in their eyes they are the only ones who act like grown-ups.

This is part of the attraction. Usually a guy looks for a lover he can let his hair down with, but when Cancer meets Capricorn each finds a partner he can put his hair up with.

They both think this is dandy, since uptightness is part of their natures.

Cancer enters this relationship expecting that Capricorn will take care of him. He admires Mr. Goat's confidence in handling money and wants to see it used for his benefit.

Capricorn thinks that Cancer should do some of his feeling for him. Because it is hard for him to express emotion, Capricorn views Cancer's ability to tap into the emotions of others as a grand opportunity to get off the hook for wading through grief, fear, anxiety, and other unpleasantness.

Because of these preconceptions of what life together will be like, Cancer and Capricorn pressure each other into assuming overly defined roles. However, since each takes his own obligations in the relationship so seriously, the pressure is no greater than that they put on themselves.

Neither man is good at all-out frontal assault. Cancer takes an indirect approach and Capricorn goes slow. This means that this couple uses a soft sell when negotiating with co-op boards or persuading a sister to invite the boyfriend to Thanksgiving dinner. By not being confrontational, the Cancer-Capricorn couple can break down the homophobia of persons who resist the rhetoric of the activists.

For fun, this pair will tell you they love to go antiquing. And they do, but they love bargain hunting at the mall just as much. No one is stingier than these two men, though they are embarrassed to admit it. The antiquing that they talk of is more likely visiting tag sales where they mercilessly pressure some grandma to part with her heirlooms for pennies.

Going out for a date, Cancer and Capricorn always opt for the tried and true in their choice of film, music, or whatever. Both feel better buying tickets for something labeled as "classic" than for something labeled as "hip."

Still, these boys are not total fuddy-duddy sticks-in-the-mud. They know how to have fun, though their fun usually has a purposeful side. Even their jokes tend to be ironic, carrying a deeper meaning and resonance.

The erotic pleasure they share is great. Both feel obliged to do all they can to please the other. While this makes sex into a kind of work, it is work they enjoy. Their lovemaking is slow and sensuous. They savor it as the well-deserved reward for maintaining a successful relationship. When they get kinky, Cancer and Capricorn like role-play with an S&M edge.

CANCER ☆ AQUARIUS

When Cancer loves a man, he just wants to eat him up. But Aquarius is like a habanero pepper. You *can* eat him, but you should not, since his burn will make every inch of your digestive tract pay.

Aquarius cannot be consumed by Cancer the way most men are. Others might fight and go for heavy drama as they resist Mr. Crab's demands, yet they know he will ultimately win. But Aquarius does not know that. He also fights Cancer more effectively than anyone else. Rather than criticizing the manipulation or manipulating back, Aquarius acts oblivious, which renders Cancer powerless.

The resistance may be passive, but it stings like the pepper since the passivity is focused and pointed.

Aquarius is also resistant to the affection showered on him. He loves that Cancer loves him, but gets embarrassed by the displays. He also gets embarrassed by heated arguments. Whenever emotion, positive or negative, is shown, Aquarius tries to talk Cancer out of feeling it. He is afraid of being overpowered by Mr. Crab's tidal waves of emotion.

Because he values openness, the natural secretiveness of Cancer pushes Aquarius's buttons. But it also intrigues him. Cancer finds the unashamed honesty of Aquarius shockingly naive in someone so sophisticated. The attraction results from differences between these two men that each finds so incomprehensible that he can spend a lifetime trying to figure out his partner.

Moving in together only deepens the differences and the fascination. Their opposing approaches to home life can be summed up as follows: For Cancer, the home is his world. For Aquarius, the world is his home. You can foresee what scenarios will follow—Aquarius stays out late, Cancer is uninterested in Aquarius's friends, etc. etc. etc. The arguments are so repetitive that neither pays much attention to them after a while.

Still, this is not a relationship that falls into a rut. Consistency is not the hobgoblin of Cancer or Aquarius. Moods change all the time. Cancer's operate on more predictable cycles than Aquarius's, and the mutual effort to synch up their emotional energy is what gives this combo its heat.

Cancer mellows out the rough edges of Aquarius's sexuality, but there is still a dangerous edge to their eroticism. It is hard for them to admit that they play at sadomasochism, not because of shame, but because they do not want their sexuality put into a neat category. The thrill for them is finding unique forms of sexual and emotional expression. Label it and they lose interest. In and out of the sheets, Aquarius shows his love through giving Cancer delightful surprises.

The ability to separate his sex life from the rest of the relationship is an Aquarius trait utterly at odds with Cancer, for whom sex is an integral part of all his interaction. While this might not affect their satisfaction while making love, it can cause misunderstandings before and after unless communication is good.

While Aquarius is willing to put all he has at Cancer's disposal, Cancer should beware of taking this for granted. He might assume that Aquarius is signaling submissiveness, though this is unlikely. Explicit questions and explicit expressions of gratitude are hard for Cancer, but necessary here.

Cancer likes to read into the words and actions of others, but this is a bad idea with Aquarius. He is disturbed when Cancer infers things about his thoughts and feelings—especially if the inferences are right. Aquarius thinks that Cancer is being controlling in these cases, illogical as that seems.

The Cancer-Aquarius relationship takes work, but can be enormously stimulating if the couple is committed to each other. As a casual fling, it is a disaster; as a lifelong love, it can work very well.

CANCER ☆ PISCES

Not everyone who drinks is an alcoholic.

Not every Cancer-Pisces relationship is addictive—but the possibility is always there.

These two signs want an escape from the normal pressures of life. If they cannot escape in a healthy way, they will turn to drugs, drink—or each other. If this relationship turns addictive, the couple cuts itself off from the world and believes that only they can understand each other. When this happens, Cancer and Pisces lose all sense of themselves as individuals.

In other words, they live out their ideal of what love is.

In a healthy Cancer-Pisces relationship, there will also be a deep empathy between the two men. They are almost able to experience what each other feels, because there is a constant line of mental telepathy between them. The psychic communication is their strength, but it can also be their downfall. If they come to depend on the unspoken more than the explicit, Cancer and Pisces are reinforcing each other's worst personality flaws and opening the door to addiction.

Fortunately, for most Cancer-Pisces pairs there is enough conflict to save them from themselves. This is one partnership where anger and resentment are positive forces. Most of the conflict revolves around Cancer's pushiness and Pisces' flakiness.

Cancer likes money. Or rather he likes the security he thinks he can buy with it. Pisces does not have the same trust that a cushy savings account can insulate him from harm. Money feels dirty to him, so he avoids thinking about it. A lover without a portfolio, or at least a wallet full of coupons when he goes to the supermarket, is seen by Cancer as a threat to the security he has tried so hard to build.

Thus Cancer will set out to teach Pisces the right way to live. And it will work. Under Cancer's direction, Pisces will become more responsible and savvy. But he will also feel that he has lost an important part of himself—his anti-materialist, spiritual side. Sooner or later he will rebel.

The squabbles explode and subside, since Cancer and

Pisces know how to keep them in perspective. Neither sign will ever forget their arguments, but both will forgive after a time.

Sex is the one place where a healthy Cancer-Pisces couple acts out addictive behavior. Their telepathic abilities make it possible for them to merge and become one in a way others only dream of. The sex is more psychic than physical. Their souls merge as well as their bodies. While they make love, the rest of the world simply does not exist.

This does not mean their sex life is all hunky-dory. Both men are prone to dark moods, which turn them into emotional sponges, sucking up their partner's energy while giving nothing back. Pisces can usually see when such a mood is coming up for Cancer, but Cancer gets blindsided because he can never tell when Pisces will turn sour. And sex is not the only thing that goes bad during these periods. Nothing will go right in any part of the relationship.

And then it will get better, just as suddenly and mysteriously as it went bad. In an addictive relationship, both partners get drawn into the darkness of the one. In a healthy relationship, the unaffected person knows that the depression will pass eventually. He is there to help, but does not feel obligated to join in the gloomfest himself.

When Cancer and Pisces are supportive of each other but maintain their independence, few relationships are better. The main difficulty they face is that both think love means sacrificing their individuality, which is ultimately damaging to both of them.

LEO ☆ LEO

Understanding your partner can be a real advantage.

It can also be a real disadvantage.

When Leo meets Leo, he has found someone who can really get inside where he is coming from. The kind of understanding that Leo finds here is like heaven—until it turns against him.

More than other signs, Leo is attracted to itself. *Quelle surprise!* It is a thrill to not have to supply all the sparkle and star power in a relationship. However, it is hard to turn off that charisma juice. That is why the problems start.

No one outside the Leo-Leo relationship can really figure it out. The two seem to be in a never-ending struggle for dominance. They each try to out-charm, out-style, and out-speak each other. The rest of us are exhausted just watching. Leo would like to turn down the 5-million-megawatt personality, but he cannot. Thus this pairing tends to burn itself out.

Remember Sean Penn and Madonna? That was the Leo-Leo relationship played out in the tabloids. The relationship came from out of nowhere, moved with an intense speed, then ended bitterly. And through it all, no one quite understood the attraction. Each partner found their judgment clouded by the other at each stage of the relationship and did things that they really should not have. (Their icky lovey stuff at the start and mutual public recriminations at the end made both look bad. And let us not even mention *Shanghai Surprise*.)

Lions can sniff out each other's vulnerable spots. They can use this knowledge against each other when they want to wound. In a Leo-Leo pair, each man brings out the best qualities of the sign in his partner. And he brings out the worst as well. The petty jealousies and imagined slights are small provocation. But the ugly insults give this couple's battles a momentum and pain all out of proportion to the initial cause of the fighting. (Note to friends of this couple: Stay out of the way when there is a fight. You can be certain that if they do make up, they will blame anyone but themselves. If you are around, they could very well decide to punish *you* for their disharmony.)

Of course, the bloodletting is all part of the game. No astrological pair can beat this couple for the hydraulic power of its make-up sex. Sex is the glue that holds two Leos together. The moment their sex life together goes south, so will the relationship. Sure, Leo loyalty can hold the pair together for a time, but when Leo competitiveness comes into play again, it will be hard to stay together without the lure of make-up sex.

So how does the exceptional Leo-Leo couple manage to stay together? With great delicacy. If the relationship lasts, it becomes an intricate dance. Since both men need to be a dominant force in the relationship, it takes careful balancing for both to be satisfied. Usually they will somehow arrange a zone of dominance for each partner. Each man is allowed to dominate in some aspect of the couple's life. The other graciously bows out of that zone. If this sounds hard, it is. Leos are generous to their lovers, but they are not always sensitive to their needs. Remaining sensitive to each other's zone of dominance takes great effort.

It makes you wonder: If Madonna had stayed out of film, might the relationship have lasted? Probably not. The fact that both partners were in show business made the intricate dance nearly impossible. Their areas of dominance overlapped far too much.

For ordinary Leos with careers more separate, a relationship is a little easier to maintain—though it will never be simple.

LEO ☆ VIRGO

It looks so uncomplicated.

At last, Virgo has found his hero, and Leo has found his doormat.

Then reality sets in, so each man discovers he had the other one pegged wrong.

Virgo comes to Leo after a string of disappointments with weak, unimaginative, dull men. Rarely have his standards even come close to being met. Leo looks like a man who could do it.

Leo fantasizes about finding a man who will love only him and give him service with a smile in and out of the bedroom. Since Virgo is good at acting impressed, Leo thinks he has found his willing slave.

The weird thing is that each lover can go on for a while

playing the role the other has assigned him. But eventually something has got to give, since neither is completely what he appears to be.

Instead, he is something better.

The last thing Virgo needs is a hero. What he really needs is to learn tolerance by loving an imperfect man. Leo's ability to live with his mistakes and his optimism about life will help Virgo learn how to tolerate his own shortcomings as well.

Leo might think he wants someone submissive, but sooner or later he would lose respect for such a man. Virgo is willing to provide support to those he cares about, but he is too independent to be totally subservient. He gives Leo the dose of common sense so often lacking in his grandiose schemes.

Though the relationship improves after the disillusionment, that period is trying and could end everything if it were not for the spectacular sex. When this couple is together, their appetites and abilities increase exponentially. They just cannot give or get enough. There will be a tendency to reenact the dominance-submission of the early relationship in the bedroom, but both men are too imaginative to play those games exclusively.

Virgo is confident about few things except for his erotic skills. He does need to curb the criticism of Leo's techniques, since Mr. Lion will be intimidated by Virgo's lovemaking, even if he will not admit it. Cutting Mr. Lion down to size is appropriate everywhere except the bedroom. Remember this, Virgo: Zip your lip, and you will get ample reward.

For this relationship to last, both men need to be dedicated to it. A sure sign of their commitment is moving in together. Neither one takes this decision lightly, since each prizes the life he has apart from his lover. But each recognizes that at a certain point they must build a life together or split.

If they move in together, Leo and Virgo will once again

fill defined roles in the relationship. The difference from before is that these roles are self-selected and they are chosen from the instinct to protect the other, not to perpetuate some fantasy.

So Virgo will deal with the practicalities, like making reservations, paying bills, and contracting car repairs. He does this because he knows how crazy these tasks make Leo (who also does them less skillfully), not because he is trying to be the perfect Geisha boy.

In return, Leo goads Virgo to take more risks and helps him pursue large goals. It may sound as if Virgo does the dirty work and Leo merely pontificates from his sofa. In a bad Leo-Virgo relationship that is what happens. But Virgo has a real craving for inspiration that few can fulfill. Leo can. Moreover, he takes the task seriously and genuinely wants Virgo to become all he can be.

So who is getting the better end of the deal? It is hard to say.

LEO ☆ LIBRA

Listen to this couple talk. You will notice how Libra constantly uses the pronouns "us" and "we." Leo emphatically does not use those words (unless it is in the sense of the royal "we"). However happy this pair is together, their relationship means something quite different to each of them.

Libra sees Leo's superior attitude as fundamentally unfair to the rest of the world. Leo finds Libra's slow deliberation and diplomacy to be huge wastes of energy. Leo wants the relationship to be a coming together of two separate and not-quite-equal people. Libra wants to merge with another to form a new harmonious entity. Somehow it all works out, mostly because of Libra's deviousness and Leo's gullibility.

The initial attraction is shallow. Each of these men wants to be seen with the other. Neither Leo nor Libra likes to admit that he responds to social pressure, but they both do to a great extent. So while they might claim they are looking for love or for a hot time in the sheets, both will be satisfied with an unloving dud if he is a good trophy to show off at parties. At least for a time.

If this couple has a sexual spark, it is of a very particular kind. These men like to look at each other. Sex for them does not begin and end in bed. It starts when they first meet for dinner, watching each other approach from opposite ends of the block. If they like what they see, the game has already started. Both are expert flirts and love the preliminaries as much as the act. The afterglow and admiring of the other man's butt as he gets out of bed—these are as memorable as the orgasm itself for a Libra and a Leo.

Libra thinks "If he looks right, then he is right." Leo makes a big effort to look right. Leo loves attention and Libra loves accommodating the men he is with. The sexual ease these two share can actually be a problem, since Leo loves taming the difficult man.

If the couple decides to get serious, there is a strong foundation for a relationship. Both Mr. Lion and Mr. Balance have a strong concern for the well-being of others. This concern shows itself in the easy comfort of their dinner parties, participation in walkathons, and political activity.

In addition to sharing a social idealism, the pair also shares an aesthetic idealism. They like pretty things. Painting, music, film, and the other arts are not pure entertainment to these men. Their taste is a big part of who they think they are.

However, even what Leo and Libra share means something very different to each of them. Leo believes that he is one of those rare people who can make a difference to others. Libra views those in trouble or discomfort as peers, so his altruism has a different flavor.

Leo feels that his taste should be a guide to others and he may try to impose it on his scaly friend. The things he likes are the only things that are good. Period. Libra's taste is more wide ranging. Libra enjoys sharing what he likes with others, but is also genuinely interested in their tastes. Learning what gives them pleasure is a way of getting to know others.

Leo might not even notice their conflicts since Libra is so expert at defusing them and twisting events so that the scales come out on top. Libra is every bit as determined to get his way as Leo, but is more subtle in his tactics. Libra convinces Leo that he is the alpha in the relationship while it is actually Libra himself who sets the agenda and makes all the plans. But hey, if it works, who can criticize Libra for manipulating the relationship this way?

Leo is for commitment in a long-term relationship. Libra says he is for commitment. He may even think he is for commitment. But what he is really for is falling in love—even if he already has a boyfriend. Leo is a notoriously jealous sign. In this relationship, his jealousy is completely justified. In fact, it can be a good thing. Leo jealousy can force Libra to really measure the good thing he has against his fantasy of life with some new pretty face.

LEO ☆ SCORPIO

Since neither partner is ever wrong, this is a perfectly harmonious relationship about which nothing needs to be written.

Well, actually, neither partner will *admit* being wrong, which is a different matter. Compromise and apology are difficult for this couple, which makes progress and forgiveness equally hard.

However, this same stubbornness ensures a steadfastness in their commitment to each other, which makes them stick out the tough times when other lovers would call it quits.

When Leo meets Scorpio, they circle each other warily before anyone makes a move. Neither wants to blow it all by being too aggressive, too soon. The basic respect for each other that is obvious within minutes of meeting will last for the entire length of the relationship.

Good old-fashioned passion drives this relationship. Leo and Scorpio find each other maddening, frustrating, and thrilling. Almost against their will they find themselves drawn together. These men are innately aggressive, so conflict only heightens the erotic excitement they feel together.

Their methods of battle differ greatly, though they share a ruthlessness in seeking control of the relationship.

Scorpio goes for covert action (which Leo thinks is sneaky and dishonest), while Leo takes a more open approach (which Scorpio thinks is kind of lunkheaded). Thus their arguments consist of Leo sputtering in rage while Scorpio stares at him in stony silence. The outcome is decided in the following days when Scorpio, without fanfare, takes some action to get his own way which renders the whole argument moot.

The private fights remain private. Leo and Scorpio maintain a unified front before their friends and family. They may even work to make it look like Leo is in charge. There is no point to this since everyone knows that Scorpio is in the driver's seat. (Bill and Hillary Clinton are Leo and Scorpio. Guess which is which.)

Leo and Scorpio trust each other. Their fights will not change that. Leo will give up center stage and Scorpio will forgive—things they do not do easily—for the sake of that trust. Much as each of them claims to want the other to change his ways, Leo and Scorpio can do little to alter each other's behavior. Nor do they really want to. The stability of each partner's personality is the source of the trust that holds this couple together.

The predictability of his lover's response in bed is both a comfort and a challenge to each of these men. The familiarity brings a warmth to erotic play. However, each man will also find it exciting to experiment in the hopes of provoking a new response. Leo is more willing to try new kinks than Scorpio, though the new kinks Scorpio suggests usually get a bigger and splashier response.

Though both Leo and Scorpio can get insanely jealous, chances are that it will be unfounded. Both parties will stick to whatever agreement they make about sexual matters, be it strict monogamy, open relationship, or whatever. A sense of honor and loyalty are traits Leo and Scorpio share.

Note to Leo: Scorpio's everyday behavior over the long run speaks louder than his words. Give up on getting that grand declaration of love—Scorpio's deepest feelings are the ones he never speaks of. You like to have all the answers laid out in front of you. That will not happen here.

Note to Scorpio: You wanted a real man and now you got him. You probably thought he was a pushover, but Leo matches you in willpower. He plays an important role in your development as a person, because he teaches you generosity.

LEO ☆ SAGITTARIUS

Let the good times roll!

This is the sort of fun-loving, larger-than-life couple who wake the neighbors by screaming with laughter at two in the morning. They are always daring and double-daring each other to commit some fresh outrage against normalcy.

Energy runs high in Leo-Sagittarius pairing. Each has a tremendous hunger for all life has to offer, so when you put them together they become insatiable. Often couples like this break up early on, due to burnout. After all, you cannot live that high without eventually hitting a low.

Because both Leo and Sagittarius are visionary dreamers rather than practical doers, it can be hard to get down to the serious business of building a life together. Thus many Leo-

Sagittarius pairs prefer to keep it casual and stay fuck buddies rather than becoming lovers.

It is possible, however, for a Leo and Sagittarius to have a committed long-lasting relationship—if they both really want love and are not merely out for a good time. (Though they will get plenty of that too.)

When the giddiness dies down, there is some real personality clash between these two men. Sagittarius's brutally frank comments offend Leo, who would prefer dishonest flattery to honest criticism. Leo's bossy, know-it-all attitude brings out the rebel in Sagittarius. Each partner wants to tell the other how to act and how to be, while the other wants no part of it. Each man feels that his lover is childish in his behavior.

Their arguments are volcanic, with dishes thrown and knives brandished. But when the fight is over, it will be forgotten in minutes. Leo and Sagittarius would love to hold a grudge against each other, but, alas, they cannot. No sooner have they vented than their minds turn to fun instead of vengeance.

The bed burns when they go at it. The initial attraction between Leo and Sagittarius was purely physical and that excitement will not fade. Okay, they do need to keep adding to the repertoire to prevent Sagittarius from getting bored, but it is the specific acts he finds dull, never his Leo lover.

Because of the high-octane action it will see, the Leo-Sagittarius couple needs to make sure that their bed is strongly built.

Financial woes plague this couple since they cannot live within a budget. Though they forgive each other their extravagances, they might need outside help in managing their money. They will resist this suggestion—until their credit card payments balloon to epic proportions. Leo and Sagittarius have many hopes for the future but few concrete plans, so they are always taken by surprise when reality catches up to them.

Leo is the more grounded, traditional, levelheaded of this pair. Which is not saying much. He is forced into the role of anchor when he would rather be the free spirit.

Sagittarius has the role of challenging Leo on his self-righteous, self-involved crap. Of course, Sagittarius can be just as full of it as Leo, so he brings a sympathy to this role—though not a sensitivity. No matter how much he loves Leo, Sagittarius just cannot be tactful with him.

Though they can be combative and confrontational with each other, Leo and Sagittarius share a generosity of spirit. Each wants to get his own way, but not at the expense of hurting another. The main hazard they face in this relationship is not deep pain, but rather overstimulation and exhaustion. Leo and Sagittarius simply wear each other out.

LEO ☆ CAPRICORN

This pairing is like the relationship of a manager and a star.

Capricorn makes it happen.

Leo takes the bow.

And they both like it that way.

Capricorn looks for ambition in a lover, which Leo has in abundance. Capricorn might stalk Leo for a while, waiting for the right moment to pounce. If Leo makes the first move, he will do it more quickly. Either way, the attraction will be more rawly sexual for Capricorn and more emotional for Leo.

Mr. Lion unleashes something new in Mr. Goat's sexuality. While Mr. Goat is always a deeply sensual lover, comfortable with his body, Mr. Lion brings out in his lover a boldness that breaks through any lingering hang-ups. With Leo, sex play, positions, kinks—it's all up for grabs. When Leo sees Capricorn's delight in exploring new sexual avenues, he cannot help but respond. This is the sexual role that Leo wants so badly and so rarely finds: With Capricorn he is the muse of sex.

Leo is the star. He lives a life that Capricorn only fantasizes about. His quick thinking and ease of action are thrilling to Capricorn, who cannot take a single step without hesitating first to consider consequences. Leo trusts Capricorn. He cannot help it; Capricorn is his ideal manager. It is the most natural thing in the world for Mr. Lion to tell Mr. Goat all his secrets and to entrust him with his money. Many Capricorns find themselves acting as bookkeeper or financial adviser (or wallet in hard times) to their Leo lovers.

Separately these two are nice people. Together they make an ambitious and ruthless team. The combination of Capricorn cynicism and Leo righteousness means they will slit your throat and tell you all is for the best as you lie bleeding in the gutter.

Of course this relationship is not all Billy-the-Kid-meets-Dracula. It is just that each man realizes that he has found the partner that could put his greatest ambitions within reach. After that realization, the rest of the world does not matter. Think of Jackie and Aristotle Onasis, the most famous Leo-Capricorn couple. When the rest of the world derided the marriage as opportunism, they just got on their yacht and shut everyone out. With Leo-Capricorn, if you are not for them, you are not worth noticing.

The reason is that this couple is intensely for each other. And they need to be. The pressure of achievement is strong for each, and they both desperately want encouragement. This they will give to each other.

There are two key battlegrounds in this relationship: money and family.

Watch them on a shopping trip. Notice how each one eggs the other on to buy more and more upscale clothing and housewares. Oh, how these boys love their little status symbols. There is some competitiveness that comes out in Capricorn's snipes at Leo's love of Versace and Leo's reply that Capricorn's Brooks Brothers suits are drab mass-produced crap. On more mundane spending matters, these two men differ to a much greater degree. To put it simply: Leo overspends and Capricorn is a Scrooge. Both will spend to impress without a second thought, but send them to the corner for milk and an argument is sure to ensue over whether the vitamin-enriched brand is worth the extra ten cents.

Family is a sensitive point for both men. Each has an emotionally hot relationship with his father. The desire for and fear of surpassing his father's achievements is just part of the mishmash of conflicting emotions boiling in each one's psyche. Negative comments about Dad (and the family in general) hurt tremendously in this relationship.

Capricorn and Leo both need to be fathers themselves. This does not necessarily mean raising a child (though that is a possibility). Rather, these are men who have a strong drive to make something that will outlive them. It can be a business, an artwork, or just a circle of friends who have benefited from their company. Because this relationship plays to their individual strengths, it is one that is likely to have the lasting impact both partners want.

LEO ☆ AQUARIUS

When an attraction forms between Leo and Aquarius, they are stuck with it. It is irreversible. They can choose whether or not to act on it, but in either case they *must* deal with it.

It is just there.

It can be an uncomfortable attraction, because each man exposes uncomfortable truths about the other. Leo's generosity makes Aquarius face his lack of empathy. Aquarius's social consciousness shows up Leo's selfish motives. Each would rather deny what the other's presence flings in his face.

Leo and Aquarius are both highly social animals, so their dates take them to parties, picnics, and fund-raisers more than secluded getaways. However, they cannot seem to prevent themselves from embarrassing each other at these events. Leo is shocked to discover that a gay man could possibly have as little fashion sense as Aquarius. The bizarre nonsequiturs that pepper his conversation do not help either. Aquarius finds Leo's air of entitlement and obvious social climbing to be arrogant and gauche.

Yet each of them chooses to overlook these shortcomings—Leo through a sense of noblesse oblige and Aquarius because he thinks it wrong to impose his standards on others.

Although the two members of this couple often take similar actions, they usually do so for different reasons. Both will stop at an accident scene to offer aid. Leo does this because he identifies with the victims, and Aquarius does it on general principle. Through such events, each half of this couple comes to understand himself better. They already know *what* they do; through this relationship Leo and Aquarius learn *why*.

The heat of Leo and the coolness of Aquarius are obstacles for each other at every stage. Leo loves to treat his lover as the most lovely soul on earth. He showers his partner with attention and gifts, but Aquarius finds his attentions a smidgen overblown. His protestations of love are more modest (if there are any at all). Leo wants to be treated like a king, but Aquarius treats his lover as a very good friend. When Leo tries to put his frustrations on the table, Aquarius misreads the emotional issues, which only adds fuel to Leo's ire.

There are no easy resolutions to the clashes between these lovers. Fortunately, they have the imagination and the tenacity to work out their differences, even if it takes a lot of time. Once something finally is resolved, it is settled in both their eyes, so they can go on without the poison of resentment infecting the relationship.

Finding ways to erotically surprise his partner becomes an obsession for each man, but Aquarius has a greater talent for this. He provides the sexual pyrotechnic, while Leo provides the heart. Aquarius introduces new kinks, new toys, and new techniques into their lovemaking, but it is Leo who figures out how to use them most effectively. Leo shows his lover how to turn a novel physical sensation into an intimate emotional expression.

Though each man is sure to fulfill his promises to the other, Aquarius makes fewer than Leo does. Most of the time, this is not a big issue. Until the relationship gets serious. When things get to the point where Leo wants this partnership to move to the next level, Aquarius will weasel out of commitment. Leo will press the point, which Aquarius will interpret as a lack of respect.

Leo needs to relax and give Aquarius time. And Aquarius needs to get off his high horse. Each man needs to remind himself that their love is rooted in mutual challenges as much as mutual support. Only if they recognize and embrace their differences will their love last.

LEO ☆ PISCES

Even the most butch Pisces likes to play the damsel in distress. And Leo is a knight in shining armor waiting to happen. After a long day of fighting dragons, there is nothing Leo loves more than collecting the accolades. Which works out fine, since piling on flattery is a Pisces talent.

Thus we have two men who each fulfill roles in the other's fantasy. The question is: Can this couple survive in the real world?

At first meeting, on some level, Leo and Pisces recognize that their deepest fantasies mesh perfectly—so they cannot wait to hop into bed to see how it all plays out. Even Pisces, who usually hesitates and stops and hesitates again before doing anything, is willing to take strong, aggressive action to bag the Leo.

Naturally the lovemaking is wonderful. These men are

die-hard romantics who often feel ashamed to be as unabashedly sentimental with other lovers as they can be freely with each other. But their eroticism is not all tender. Their long first night will include murmurs, moans of surrender, and shouts of conquest. Together Leo and Pisces act out an idea of sex they have had since they were small boys sneaking peaks at the guys in fitness magazines. Like all the best things this couple shares, their sex life is based on fantasy.

When the boys come back down to earth, they will find that they have a good foundation for a relationship. Leo provides the emotional security that Pisces needs. He gives Pisces a sense of structure and permanence that Mr. Fish has trouble building for himself. Pisces brings the gifts of insight, humility, and acceptance to Leo. With Pisces, Leo feels less pressure to always be on top.

However, it is possible for the relationship to tilt out of balance. When Leo starts treating Pisces as his personal slave, when Pisces depends on Leo to tell him what to do, and when they treat their life together as an improvised soap opera rather than a union for the purpose of maintaining love and support—then the relationship is in danger of toppling. Unfortunately both partners genuinely enjoy being in the out-of-balance version, so they might not recognize how wrong the situation is.

The indecision of Pisces will make Leo crazy if the two of them set up housekeeping together. Mr. Lion will be tempted to dictate all household decisions rather than endure the agony of watching Mr. Fish hem and haw. The problem is that Pisces *wants* to give up control—which would weaken the very real strength they have as a couple. For example, if Leo takes over the finances because he is better organized, he will suffer without Pisces' input. Leo overspends anytime he can, but Pisces is shrewd about where to cut corners and where not to. Whether it is with an electrical contractor or with the lady at the tag sale, Pisces can haggle. This is a couple whose strengths compliment each other, but because they like to have rigidly defined roles in this relationship, Leo and Pisces often do not let that happen.

By being flexible, this couple ensures themselves of a good life together. Their relationship is rooted in imagination. Unless they allow themselves to invent and reinvent the terms of their bond, Leo and Pisces will watch everything they build wither away. But if they remain open to new possibilities, the relationship will nurture them both for years and years.

VIRGO ☆ VIRGO

Since Virgos spend so much time scrubbing, scouring, and showering, they do not have much time to hit the watering holes to meet boys. Chances are the Virgo-Virgo couple met at the supermarket in the detergent aisle, where they made small talk about the relative virtues of bleach and bleach alternative.

Virgos have a reputation for being anal because they are about most things—though not about sex. Well, yes, sexually they actually can be anal. Or oral. Or anything. Even the most unimaginative Virgo has an extremely active imagination when it comes to Subject X. The sign is well known (and well loved) for its sexual engineering skills. No position is beyond Virgo's capabilities, so when you get two of them together the possibilities are endless.

The sexual happiness of this couple is pretty much a given. It is in other areas that problems exist. Not that the two Virgos mind. Rather than raising children, gay Virgo-Virgo couples raise problems. They nurture them from the time they are little annoyances, help them as they become difficulties, and see them through to the time when they blow up into full-grown problems. This couple loves its problems. The two of them feel that working on a problem, or even just worrying about one, constitutes showing commitment and affection to their lover.

This might not be so terrible, were it not for the way that the Virgo-Virgo couple tries to solve problems. The two Mr. Virgins avoid the bother of long-term resolution, preferring instead short-term peace. Thus they deal with the immediate need by mortgaging the future.

But one day the note will come due.

With interest.

So the smart Virgo-Virgo pair tries to get at the root of conflict, discomfort, disharmony—the problems they share—even though it goes against their instincts.

Also it will help the relationship (and their lives in general) if these men learn how to have fun—normal fun like other people have. Too often a heavy critique session or a hot night at the Laundromat substitutes for the mindless good times that Virgos need as much as anyone. Just because your boyfriend loves hearing his faults enumerated while he presses and folds does not mean you have to do it. How about dinner and a movie instead?

One hazard of having two Virgos in one relationship is that their focus becomes too narrow. When Virgo is with a man of another sign, he is forced to look at life from another point of view. With another Virgo, both men could become preoccupied with senseless minutiae, thinking that since his lover is similarly preoccupied, such mundane things matter.

Another hazard is that they could become locked in a blame cycle. While Virgo usually plays Mr. Nice, he can become Mr. Nasty when he thinks he is in the right and his lover is wrong.

Both hazards are minimized when Virgo and Virgo make an effort to take the long view. A bit of perspective and a sense of humor will do wonders.

Being in love with a man of the same sign is usually harder than being in love with one of another sign. But just as sharing one's life with a person of the same sex has unique rewards even though it is more difficult, so it is with sharing one's life with someone of the same sign. Virgo is frequently misunderstood. Only another man who has the same impulses and agenda can understand what Virgo goes through. That understanding is just one of the unique rewards.

VIRGO ☆ LIBRA

"Excuse my reach, but I could not help but notice your rather large erection. Would you mind terribly if I might have a try at bringing you to orgasm?"

Sometimes the Virgo-Libra couple is so polite to each

other that it is hard to imagine how they have sex. Do they murmur "Thank you" and "You're welcome" during each thrust? Maybe some do. The good manners these lovers show to each other reflect the mutual respect and well-defined boundaries in this relationship.

Their lovemaking is more softly contented than recklessly passionate. Virgo, in the beginning at least, is intimidated by Libra's looks. In his head, Mr. Virgin worries about how he can hang on to such a beauty, but his body knows exactly what to do. Libra holds back (in the beginning at least) since he is intimidated by Virgo's erotic prowess.

When ground rules are established, Virgo and Libra stop being intimidated. After a few encounters, the pair can relax together in a warm sexual glow of delight in each other's body.

Libra is more of a romantic than Virgo, but even he understands the need for independence within a relation-ship. However, he will deny this understanding in social settings, since there Libra wants to be seen as half of a cou-ple. The self-sufficiency that Virgo likes to assert in front of others embarrasses Libra. This is the prime conflict of this relationship.

Virgo cannot help but criticize his Libra lover, which stings because, in spite of what you may have heard in other astrology books, Libra is the biggest perfectionist in the zodiac. He hates having his shortcomings noticed by anyone, let alone his lover. Virgo's complaints usually boil down to Libra's lack of savvy, common sense, and stick-to-it-iveness. The Libran response is to rationalize and make excuses, which, surprisingly, Virgo is willing to accept. In part, this is because Virgo has no patience for talk. He worries that if challenged, Libra would spout more empty hot air, so it is better to let things lie.

Still, these two men are highly motivated to improve

their relationship, even if talking about their problems is ineffective. Because both men are so observant, they learn—and teach—better through example than words. Sure, Virgo will miss the point sometimes and Libra will deceive himself for a while, but eventually they will figure out how to increase their bliss.

When they move in together, Libra will do the decorating and Virgo the cleaning. All the big plans for travel, purchases, and retirement planning will come from Mr. Balance, though he will get too distracted to bring them to fruition. That is where Mr. Virgin leaps in to save the day by implementing and improving what his lover began.

Virgo feels less exploited with Libra than he does with other men, because, though Libra usually takes the lead, he regards Virgo as an equal partner and not a mere follower.

Some personality traits will continue to annoy these lovers till their dying day. Virgo will never understand the indecisiveness of Libra, who will always find Virgo shortsighted and harsh. But these annoyances will not fossilize into bitterness. Instead, they will remain the pet peeves of two men who love each other very much.

The boundaries and respectful politeness, which may seem silly to the rest of us, are what allow Virgo and Libra to be such tolerant lovers.

VIRGO ☆ SCORPIO

Hot, dark, and obsessive sex is the basis for this relationship. It did not happen quickly or easily, but when they finally did come together it was sexual on a profound level.

At first it looked as if Virgo and Scorpio were going to be friends and not lovers. They talked so easily about so many things and obviously enjoyed picking each other's brain on this and that. And even when the sexual attraction became obvious, neither seemed to be in that big a hurry to consummate it.

But when they did—BAM!!!!

The erotic tension between Virgo and Scorpio marries the sacred to the profane. It is dirty, sordid, nasty sex of a deeply emotional nature. The first night will be memorable, even if both partners hold something in reserve. Neither will want to let go of the sensations he experienced, so there will be a second and third time. Each time each man gives a little more and a little more, until they get hooked on each other like addicts.

Mom may have said that good sex was not a good basis for a relationship, but Virgo and Scorpio are the exception to that rule.

There are other advantages to this pairing that have nothing to do with body contact. Both men are comfortable in this relationship just being who they are. Virgo is not frightened of Scorpio's intensity and Scorpio is unfazed by Virgo's criticism. They easily accept each other, flaws and all. Perhaps this is because these are two signs that look for imperfection in themselves and others without flinching.

The nosiness of these two signs can cause some discomfort in this relationship. As is usual for these two, the conflict usually does not erupt into flaming angry battle, but rather into cold withdrawal and passive-aggressive behavior. Being shrewd amateur psychologists, Virgo and Scorpio are each expert at getting under the other's skin while appearing innocent. However, since Scorpio is the more suspicious and more psychic of the two, Virgo is less likely to get away with score settling.

The couple's psychological skills also pay off when Virgo and Scorpio want to offer mutual support. Each of them places much faith in self-awareness, Virgo so he can eliminate the parts of himself he does not like and Scorpio so he can know where he is vulnerable. Dinner conversation can sound like psychoanalysis, which would be obnoxious if the pair were not so accurate about each other's makeup. The sad part is that neither man knows quite what to do with what he hears.

Neither Virgo nor Scorpio likes to face the unexpected, so they will arrange their lives to leave as little to chance as possible. Holiday schedules, budgets, meals, and everything else are planned out in as much detail as possible. Yet the Virgo-Scorpio couple needs to have a spark of spontaneity somewhere other than the bedroom or they will stagnate. Finding a shared interest that is completely unproductive and provides only fun will help them to deal with this concern.

Their social circle is also freaked by the eerie way that the Virgo-Scorpio pair seems to know every last piece of gossip days before anyone else. Even astrologers cannot explain how the couple does this, though a hidden network of sur-veillance cameras is as good a guess as any.

Friends often think that this partnership is emotionless, an arrangement rather than a love match. They are very wrong. Virgo and Scorpio find a tenderness in each other hidden from the world at large. Both men have known what it is like to be outcast, but both need to belong. And they do—to each other.

VIRGO ☆ SAGITTARIUS

Some relationships are prisons. Any Virgo or Sagittarius can tell you that. But when they fall in love together, both of them make a conscious decision to live free or die. Of course, each man means he himself will be free, not necessarily that his partner will be.

Sagittarius does not want to be tied down in any way, by any kind of domestic responsibility. Yet somehow the rent has got to be paid and he needs to eat a balanced diet. Even though Sagittarius holds off on making a commitment, right from the start he looks at Virgo as a parental figure who can keep him from screwing up his life.

It's like living with Mom, except that he does not have to answer to Virgo for anything he does not want to. Or even live with him. That is freedom.

And Virgo is glad to rescue Sagittarius from himself—under certain conditions. As long as Sagittarius will be fully loyal and ever ready to come running when called, Virgo will feel free.

But these are conditions Sagittarius is constitutionally incapable of fulfilling.

Early in this relationship an impasse is reached when each partner realizes that his dreams of perfect freedom are not going to come true. Because neither man is well equipped to respond to his lover's disappointment, many Virgo-Sagittarius couples split at this point—though that does not have to happen.

Virgo and Sagittarius tend to either look up to or look down on each other. Neither view works. Both harbor romantic fantasies in which one lover swoops in to save the other from danger, when for them the down-to-earth love of two equals is a much better model to imitate.

When they look at each other as equals, Virgo and Sagittarius find that there is much they share. Both partners feel responsible for their fellow man. They do not want to help others, they *need* to. Both are fearless about making necessary changes in their lives. Even their faults (such as Virgo's need to loudly criticize and Sagittarius's tactlessness) bear a family resemblance.

They will also find that their differences are surprisingly complementary. The Virgo attention to detail meshes perfectly with the Sagittarius concern for the big picture.

Of course, there are some real conflicts as well. Virgo finds Sagittarius excess a bit excessive. He also feels Mr. Horseyman's exaggerations to be borderline lies and his impulsiveness to be juvenile. Tolerant Sagittarius cannot stand Virgo's judgmental side. The fussiness bothers him too. He cannot see why Virgo has so much trouble enjoying life. Both partners look at the other's concerns as trivial. Virgo thinks it is frivolous for Sagittarius to think globally when there is laundry to be done; Sagittarius believes that Virgo is running away from life's big questions by burying himself in the mundane.

However, none of these differences are deal-breakers.

The place where this couple goes to make things right is—you guessed it—under the covers. Their erotic life is no-holds-barred and near compulsive. The question they ask is: How low can you go? The only limit on what they will try is Virgo's embarrassment when Sagittarius tells his friends the next day. If Mr. Horseyman can keep his pie-hole shut, Mr. Virgin might have a few surprises for him.

The challenges do not end for this pair, which is just what keeps them together. Both are easily bored, so they could never stay long in a static relationship. What will ensure longevity is if both Virgo and Sagittarius focus on the ways in which they are similar, rather than harping on the differences.

VIRGO ☆ CAPRICORN

You only get out of a relationship what you put into it—or so Virgo and Capricorn would say. Few couples come together in such fundamental agreement about what one should expect from a lover.

That the joys of love bring with them responsibility is an

easy concept for straights to get, since their type of fucking makes babies, plus they have a little institution called marriage. Though AIDS has darkened the picture for gay men, most of us still see love as a free ride.

Not so for gay Virgos and Capricorns. They feel a profound sense of duty toward those they love. For these men, serious relationships are the only ones they really enjoy. One-night stands might be fun, but, in their minds, such frivolous hookups only exist to fill the gaps between longer relationships.

When Virgo and Capricorn meet, it does not take long for each of these guys to register that the other is also looking for Mr. Right-till-death-do-us-part. However, neither is arrogant enough to immediately think he is the one to fit the bill—that will take at least ten minutes. Even then neither will risk making a move until he sees some clear signal that the other is receptive.

Their dating is great fun since Virgo and Capricorn know exactly how to show each other a good time—by living the high life and hunting for bargains. Going to fancy restaurants in underwear from K-mart. That just about sums up the partnership. Virgo and Capricorn do tend to overplan their weekends, which leaves little open space for spontaneity. Both men have a fear of time slipping away, and unfortunately they reinforce this fear in each other.

Capricorn takes on upgrading Virgo as a project, teaching him how designer labels have a better fit and longer durability, how people judge you on the car you drive, and how quality leisure time improves your productivity. Virgo returns the favor by eliminating stress for Capricorn by showing him step-saving household procedures. The two of them enjoy this part of the relationship better than their dates.

Expressing themselves physically is natural for Virgo and

Capricorn, so sex is comfortable in this pairing. Both men like to be composed when dealing with the world, but in bed they let it all hang out. Here each man sees his lover as he really is. Here each man is accepted. The latent masochism of Virgo can connect to the latent sadism of Capricorn with no one feeling any shame whatsoever.

Before this relationship moves into the heavy commitment stage, these men will probably sit down to discuss what they expect out of life and each other. Virgo and Capricorn will find—if they did not know already—that they look at things in a similar way. They believe what happens between them should remain private, that financial security eases emotional stress, and that work gives life meaning. Capricorn thinks more of distant goals in the far future, but Virgo is willing to follow his lead in that area.

Though this couple sometimes feels socially awkward about being gay, they should consider a public commitment ceremony—and invite lots of straight relatives. Receiving toasters and waffle irons from distant cousins will give them a sense of validation they can only partly get from the gay community.

And their gay wedding will be so hyper-traditional and mega-meaningful that it will make any straight newlyweds attending feel grossly inadequate.

VIRGO ☆ AQUARIUS

"What were you thinking?" is a refrain heard frequently in the Virgo-Aquarius relationship—because these men genuinely have a hard time understanding what goes on in each other's head.

It takes a bit of prodding to bring this couple together. Yet there is a natural fascination between Virgo and Aquarius based on their differences. One trait they share is a profound curiosity that leads them to want to study each other—from a distance. Some interested friend or a twist of fate is needed to force them into close enough proximity to actually talk. If they see each other for the first time at a bar or party with no third-party introduction, they will stick to opposite sides of the room just stealing glances.

The attraction on both sides is weirdness. The two signs vacillate, unable to decide whether the other is cute or icky, smart or dumb. The trouble with vacillation is that it keeps you thinking about someone for a very long time, which is why there is an obsessive quality to this pairing.

At first, each lover thinks he sees something of himself in the other one. They are both mistaken. The Virgo restraint is not the cool rationality that Aquarius hoped for. And the calm front Aquarius displays in overheated situations does not come from tact, consideration, and manners. It is mere indifference. However, by the time this couple figures out what they have misread, the two of them are already hooked.

Since Virgo likes to put things together and Aquarius likes to pull things apart, this couple generates much energy but accomplishes little because each cancels the other out. They are the original vicious circle. Whenever Virgo has a dinner reservation or theater tickets or travel plans, it all unravels due to some wrench Aquarius throws in. On the other hand, the crazy spontaneous weekends that Aquarius loves are ruined when Virgo organizes a schedule of events without telling him.

The deeper Virgo's love is, the more disturbed he gets over Aquarian behavior. Why is it so hard for Mr. Waterboy to make a simple apology? Why do birthdays, anniversaries, or even the time he is supposed to show up for a date seem so difficult for him to remember? When the chips are down and Virgo needs help, why is Aquarius so afraid to get his hands dirty?

Aquarius has issues with Virgo too, but they all come down to one thing: Aquarius does not want to be judged. When Virgo holds him to a standard or tells him what to do, his emotions freeze. For both men, articulating what annoys them is the first step to resolution.

The erotic is erratic in the Virgo-Aquarius relationship. Sex happens on an irregular schedule, which can make it a delightful surprise or an inconvenient task depending on just when things pop up. Heavy kink and off-the-wall fetish action are the language of love in this pairing. The defined structure of that kind of sex liberates a twisted spontaneity for the two men.

Hard as it is for these boys to get inside each other's head, there is much that these two men admire in the way each other thinks. Virgo wants to imitate the detached and tolerant attitude of Aquarius. Aquarius, in turn, is blown away by the sharply analytical Virgo mind. However, they need to acknowledge that it takes more than a mental affinity to make a relationship. Neither Virgo nor Aquarius likes to discuss his emotional life—but they both need to. This relationship can last for a long time, but it needs bright-burning emotional fuel to sustain it.

VIRGO ☆ PISCES

"After you."

"No, after you."

The Deference Championship is *on*! Who will be more self-abasing—Virgo or Pisces? Each will show his strength by trying to lift the other up onto a pedestal.

Then in the Victimhood Finals once again Virgo will meet Pisces as they attempt to knock each other off the pedestal using only underhanded means such as sarcasm, emotional blackmail, and passive-aggressive withdrawal.

Who will win each of these two events? Read on, then make your prediction.

Virgo and Pisces have many of the same relationship issues, though they deal with them in different ways. The biggest shared issue is how to be truly giving with another person without losing the core of one's identity. For these signs, this conflict is present in any relationship, though usually as an inner drama played within the psyche of Virgo or Pisces. When the two are lovers, they act it out, with Pisces giving too much and Virgo holding too tightly his independence.

Now can you guess who will win which competition? Still, you have to admit they give each other a run for his money. However, with a little self-awareness, if the combatants are willing, both events can be canceled.

Both Virgo and Pisces are masters of rechanneling their inconvenient emotions. The difference is that Pisces knows he is acting out unexpressed anger when he spills coffee on Virgo's suit. Virgo, however, has no idea that he "accidentally" dented Pisces' car door because Mr. Fish spent the afternoon over at his ex's apartment. These two men are natural reactors, sensitive to any emotional energy thrown their way. But they are not naturally expressive, so their feelings become known through indirect means.

One of the Virgo-Pisces couple's favorite indirect means of emotional expression is—SEX. When these boys are between the sheets, everything they think and feel about each other comes out. If one of them is angry or resentful, the session will be a dud. If, however, both are feeling love, it will be a short vacation in paradise. Their best times together will be achingly slow, achingly subtle, and achingly tender. The extreme sensitivity to the feelings of others that can paralyze Virgo and Pisces in other activities heightens the eroticism they share.

The intangibility of Pisces drives Virgo wild—in a good way. Try as he might, Virgo finds that the essence of this lover is impossible to pin down. He is a mystery wrapped in an enigma served with a side order of improbability. It is easy for Virgo to figure out most men, but he adores the challenge that Pisces brings.

The intense practicality of Virgo frightens his lover, but

it intrigues him as well. Pisces spends his whole life feeling like a stranger in a strange land. Virgo is intensely at home in the world, and Pisces finds comfort and security in that. Pisces does not trust easily, nor does he enjoy asking for help, so when he asks Virgo for help on his tax return, Virgo should think of it as his way of saying, "I am so glad you are you."

For this relationship to go long-term, two things must happen:

First, the pair must learn to laugh—at themselves. It is easy for the two men to make everything that they go through seem so *meaningful* that they suck the life out of it. Eventually they can become so emotionally exhausted by the relationship that they will run at the sight of each other. Lighten up!

Second, both Virgo and Pisces have to give up keeping secrets. They hid stuff from their past when they first met, which was okay. However, they must reveal more for their level of commitment to increase.

LIBRA ☆ LIBRA

This couple believes in the kind of love that the divas sing of. Barbra, Celine, Whitney, and Aretha all get it right according to these guys. Though bound to fall short, being only human, Libra aspires to the ain't-no-mountain-high-enough, wind-beneath-my-wings, crazy-for-being-so-lonely, stop-in-the-name-of kind of love.

Because Libras are known for hesitation and procrastinating, you might expect that when Libras meet the pace would slow down exponentially. *Au contraire!* Double the Libra, and the relationship moves double-time.

Libra is usually good at hiding his slutty side from everyone but another Libra. The two Mr. Balances hop into bed at a shameless speed and tell themselves it is true love at last. And it may become that, though it is not yet.

When Libras get together, they try to top each other's romantic declarations. This leads to *Luv Inflation*—gross overstatements intended to gain reciprocal affection greater than actually exists. In English: Any Libra should take his Libra lover's professions of undying love and firm commitment with a grain of salt. What he feels is actually two notches below what his words say.

Libra-Libra dates sound like episodes of an irreverent talk show. Whatever activity they do, they will talk. And the talk will be clever and sharply analytical of nothing in particular. Like expert comics, Libra #1 sets up Libra #2 to show off his wit, and vice versa. Often there are mock fights and a few serious debates just to vary the program.

Their conversations resolve little and open more questions than they answer. That is why the Libras enjoy them so much. Any actual disagreement or dissatisfaction will not be talked of until it reaches critical mass. These guys hate to fight. It ruins their image of the kind of couple they are. Some divas may sing songs of anger like "Respect," "You Keep Me Hanging On," or even (gulp) "I Will Survive," but the two Mr. Balances skip those tracks.

The sex between them can also be insubstantial. They view it as a game shared by buddies rather than a means of emotional expression. True they may screw in the red lightbulb and buy the edible briefs—but they do that for its own sake. Setting the mood and assembling the props is just as interesting as the lovemaking. Romance is what they are after, not raw animal passion.

It can be difficult for the Libras to make decisions as a couple. The moment one has a plan, the other will point out the flaw so they can go around in circles for a long time before deciding to summer in Provincetown or to paint the kitchen mauve. They can also become afraid to take individual action when needed, pointlessly checking and rechecking with the other for his approval.

Just because the relationship runs smoothly does not mean it is a good one. But the Libras think so. With a fervor bordering on the evangelical, they will self-righteously elevate themselves to the role of ideal gay couple. "Look at how considerate we are of each other. Look how we never do anything alone!" they shout.

And you cannot deny that the Libras are very polite to each other. But is it love?

In time, the politeness will wear off as this couple runs into real trouble. Their prefitted world will collapse—and that is the beginning of love. Neither man likes to face the world on its own terms until he is forced to. When that happens, Libra is more than equipped to deal with reality. When forced to deal with his lover's real problems as the fairy-tale illusion dissolves, the Libran heart is capable of sincere deep love.

So there can be love between Libras—but it comes later than they think it does.

LIBRA ☆ SCORPIO

Libra should just give up.

After being busted by Scorpio for cleaning up messy reality (in plain English: LYING) so many times, he should learn his lesson. But the nature of Libra is to pretty up ugly facts—and the nature of Scorpio is to ugly up pretty ones. Sometimes it feels as if these boys were living in two separate worlds, so it is a wonder that they ever get together.

The biggest obstacle to this relationship is that Scorpio sees through Libra. The good manners and deceit that make up his extraordinary charm have no effect on Scorpio. Libras want to control how others see them, so when a Scorpio looks behind the mask, most Libras will run away. And with their distaste for dishonesty, most Scorpios will fly from someone whose social mask bears such minimal resemblance to the real person inside.

If they both stay, it is because the sexual electricity between them is powerful.

Libra at first finds Scorpio cold, because he does not talk about his feelings. Scorpio finds Libra cold, because he *does* talk about his feelings. Libra is an idealist who thinks that one's emotions should match one's thoughts. But Scorpio is well aware of the heart's irrationality and can help his lover to recognize what is really happening inside. To return the favor, Libra can help Scorpio in articulating the complexities of his inner life to others.

Though both men claim to want the same things from a relationship, they actually do not. Libra says he wants a life-long, passionate, romantic, damn-the-rest-of-the-world kind of union just like Scorpio. However, the reality of such a partnership would be too claustrophobic for him. Unless Mr. Balance moderates his inflated rhetoric, he could lose Mr. Scorpion's trust.

Scorpio can be a trial for Libra as well. The jealousy, the judgment, and the secrets are not fair. Libra may be a flirt, but Scorpio ought to wait until he has a real reason before he throws a fit. It is pointless for Scorpio to criticize Libra—he will not change and Scorpio knew what he was getting before he started dating. Scorpio's secrets are merely a way to retain power, which will not work since, like it or not, Libra is steering this ship (even if it takes him forever to decide which direction to go).

The sexual demands that Scorpio makes on Libra exhaust him. Usually Libra likes to keep it light, but Scorpio likes to keep it heavy—nothing less than juggernaut sex will do. Libra enjoys recreational lovemaking, which Scorpio considers blasphemy against the sacredness of sex. Though he is willing to go more vanilla than usual for Libra's sake, Scorpio is still likely to push for something deeper and longer than his lover is used to.

The wimpiness of Libra astounds Scorpio. He wonders how someone so indecisive and so nicey-nice can accomplish anything. Yet when he sees how effective Libra can be at getting good tables, negotiating with creditors, and bowing out of holiday dinners, Scorpio will come to regard Libra as his personal stealth bomb, to be deployed at those times when a direct assault would be ineffective. Scorpio will offer his services to his lover for those instances when aggression is called for—but Libra will rarely use him. Still, in time, Libra will come to depend on Scorpio's advice and wisdom.

Opposite as they seem, Libra and Scorpio have much going for them as a couple. The intensity of their sexual attraction is not likely to fade, while their ability to learn from each other and appreciate each other's talents will only increase.

LIBRA ☆ SAGITTARIUS

When the good boy meets the bad boy, it is a sexy combination. Libra has been coloring inside the lines his whole life, while Sagittarius has been scribbling on the walls and getting away with it.

Part of the attraction between these two is getting to see what it is like to live life differently—to play by the rules or to write your own.

Yet Libra was never as squeaky clean as he appears. The only reason why he behaves so well is that he is afraid of getting caught. With Sagittarian support, the white lies grow darker in shade and trivial mischief becomes minor crime. Neither man would do anything that could hurt someone, but Libra might start stealing flowers from his neighbor and parking in the handicapped space.

Sagittarius changes as well. Libra's well-aimed under-the-table kicks prevent him from making his usual social blunders. In trying to please his boyfriend by acting more normal, Sagittarius learns that tact and diplomacy are not synonyms for fake.

What Libra and Sagittarius have in common is a love of people and a desire to do good. Though they might find each other's choices in life questionable, each man can be certain that his lover's motivation is always the highest.

It is easy for this couple to talk. And talk. And talk. Both are suckers for gossip, especially if they get a chance to second-guess their friends' actions. Libra and Sagittarius consider themselves experts on interpersonal relations, and they love to dissect human behavior.

Deepening their level of commitment is bound to cause conflict. Libra and Sagittarius have different ideas about what commitment is—even about what love is. Because there is such open communication between them, the issue is not insurmountable. After a prolonged debate, the two will come to some sort of understanding, and the compromises that each was willing to make can only make his partner love him more.

The two men will always have some petty annoyances between them. Libra cannot stand that Sagittarius does not keep him updated. Mr. Balance wants to know everything that Mr. Horseyman did that day and what he plans for the next. The shrug he gets when he asks for info bugs the hell out of Libra.

Libra is never ready to go when Sagittarius is. And even when he is he still holds Sagittarius up with his dithering— he cannot walk down the street without looking in every store window and stopping at the fruit stand to see if clementines are in season yet. Sagittarius is just as prone to distraction as Libra is, but somehow it does not slow him up.

It will take some practice for the two men to synch up

their sexual timing. Once they do, good clean sex will be good clean fun. Sagittarius will probably adjust the most by slowing himself down. The impulsiveness of his erotic energy is heightened in a tantric way by the need to restrain himself with Libra. Their lovemaking is divinely decadent and sensuously shameless. Libra and Sagittarius are in love with love, but they are head-over-heels for sex. Pleasure, their own or another's, is a strong motivation for both men in every aspect of life—most particularly this one.

The Libra-Sagittarius couple faces a few challenges, but they also have many advantages for building a permanent relationship. The biggest one is that any problem can be discussed and resolved. Each man introduces the other to a new circle of friends, exciting unfamiliar ideas, thrilling emotions, and a different way of treating life.

So what if Libra gets too bossy or Sagittarius too messy— are these men not giving each other the important things?

LIBRA ☆ CAPRICORN

Capricorn is like the strict parent and Libra is like the conniving teen who plots and manipulates to get his own way. They reenact this family dynamic (which at least one of them grew up with) because it feels comfy and familiar—even if it is unhealthy.

But nobody sees that side of the relationship. For all the world Libra and Capricorn are a politically correct, non-threatening gay couple. Family, friends, and coworkers think of this pair as an ideal match. After all, they do not fight in public, do not shove their social agenda down anyone's throat, and do not embarrass anyone with overenthusiastic public displays of attention.

Behind closed doors it is a different story.

There this relationship is a battle for domination, with Libra ever attempting to pull one over and Capricorn asserting his will with an iron fist. For these men, it is heaven. Being in love, neither cares much who wins, but they love the struggle and machinations. The battle supplies the emotional heat that makes this partnership so energizing for these normally reserved men. It cements their bond.

Libra and Capricorn each feels that he is the one carrying the relationship. Libra thinks that he saves Capricorn from his own gloom and isolation. According to Capricorn, his boyfriend would be condemned to a life of superficial socializing and pointless procrastination without him. In truth, they do much to improve each other's life, but if this really were a lopsided relationship, neither would stay in it.

The competitive nature of both men might make you expect each to try for top position in bed. Sexually, however, they are a cooperative duo. Each man has his particular erotic talents, though it takes time for them to be revealed. Libra and Capricorn are slow to commit sexually to each other, so their first encounters leave something to be desired. But all good things come (in buckets) to him who waits. Libra's dirty chatter and lazy dexterity give just the slow buildup his partner needs to get from warm to hot! hot! hot! The pounding physicality and sensual abandon of a properly worked-up Capricorn can overwhelm Libra. But who says overwhelming is a bad thing? As Libra gets used to the

Capricorn experience, he will start looking forward to that mad, stimulating rush.

Libra and Capricorn share a liking for the high life and high culture. Where they are seen matters to both of them, so dating is as much about the people around them as what passes between them.

Since these men are commitment junkies, they both will want at some point to either get serious or split. Though Libra is usually the one to hesitate when making a decision, Capricorn is the holdout in this case.

If they get serious, then the tone of the relationship will change. Both men will shift their focus from what goes on between them as individuals to what goes on between them as a couple and the world. Their partnership is not something that needs protection from the cruel world—just from the foolish actions of its two members. Neither partner has any scruples about doing anything that might preserve their union. Each will lie to Grandma and hide his infidelities if he thinks it can hold them together.

And the other would never blame him for doing so.

Keeping the relationship going and keeping up with the Joneses can become so important to this pair that they ignore personal happiness. Too often the Libra-Capricorn couple thinks they are doing fine because everyone else says they are. Introspection and honest communication should keep this problem from getting out of hand.

LIBRA ☆ AQUARIUS

The things that Aquarius likes best about himself are the very things that make Libra froth at the mouth. What Aquarius calls determined, unique, and visionary, Libra calls pigheaded, oddball, and unrealistic.

The labels they apply to traits matter to Libra and Aquarius. For them it is almost like magic—the word becomes the thing. So the negative words make the traits negative, while positive words have the opposite effect. For this reason their arguments are as much about defining terms as about the issues themselves.

This couple's fights tend to focus on abstract concerns rather than the nitty-gritty specifics. So instead of screaming at Aquarius for getting mud on his sofa, Libra will cite that event as part of a pattern of inconsiderate behavior that needs reforming. Neither man much likes bloody and heated battles, so they use abstraction to lower the emotional temperature. Of course this does not always work, so it can get hot, with biting Libran sarcasm slamming into Aquarian mania. The resolution usually involves an elaborate compromise on Libra's part or a stony silence from Aquarius.

It is important to distinguish arguments from the debates that are this couple's favorite leisure-time activity.

Questions about full-term abortion or the leadership of the Klan—anything with no direct bearing on their lives—can keep this pair chattering for hours.

While not effusively empathetic toward each other, Libra and Aquarius both understand where the other comes from. There is a strong mutual admiration between them. Libra has an especially high regard for Aquarian tolerance and Aquarius feels the same about Libran impartiality—most of the time. When Mr. Waterboy tolerates actions that are too bizarre or Mr. Balance is impartial toward the enemies of Aquarius, the admiration ceases.

When they finally get to it, their lovemaking sparkles. Their minds have to meet before their bodies do, so Libra and Aquarius will spend a good deal of time talking about sex and sharing fantasies before they get to it. Libra would be more comfortable if Aquarius could be more romantic and less experimental, but that does not necessarily mean the sex would be better. Aquarius's greatest erotic talent is for challenging his lovers into finding a wider range of sensual pleasures.

Libra worries that Aquarius is not fully committed to having a lover. And with good reason. Fearing that he will lose control of the relationship, Aquarius withholds those signs of affection that his boyfriend craves. He will tell Libra how much he values their friendship, knowing that Libra wants to hear "I love you." It is the rules that Libra wants to impose on their partnership that spook Aquarius so much. If Mr. Balance lets Mr. Waterboy take a greater role in setting the ground rules, his level of commitment will also be greater.

These lovers run in different social circles. Libra will try to draw his partner into a closer association with his friends, but Aquarius will try to keep his buddies to himself. This will cause tension and misunderstanding, until they start making new friends together as a couple.

Though these signs are usually considered extremely compatible, they need to be careful about the terms of their compatibility. Both prefer to avoid strong feeling rather than display it. If they have joined together to sidestep their emotions, the relationship can last forever but kill their souls. If they use their mutual understanding to nurture free expression of emotions, the relationship can last forever and heal their souls.

The choice belongs to Libra and Aquarius.

LIBRA ☆ PISCES

Their theme song is the old Culture Club hit that goes "Do you really want to hurt me? Do you really want to make me cry?" Libra and Pisces are after tenderness and gentility. They want a refuge from the harsh world. Together they hope to build a fantasy they can live in.

Libra and Pisces both are given to imagining what their ideal lover would be like. When they meet, they start to picture what life with each other would be like. Though a lot is going on in their heads, it can be hard for these signs to approach each other—but when it happens they are ready.

The outlook seems positive since they seem to be so much alike. However, some of the similarities work against the relationship.

Neither Libra nor Pisces has the juice to initiate emotional engagement. These signs are both natural reactors. But what is there for them to react to? Too often this partnership meanders, since neither man has the energy to move it on to the next level.

Libra and Pisces use diplomacy and indirect means to get what they want, rather than openly asking. They are also willing to shade the truth or outright lie when necessary. All of this places a layer of mistrust over their communications.

There are also differences between Libra and Pisces as significant as the similarities.

The biggest difference between them is how they deal with emotion. If someone is going to bring sorrow to Libra, he will run the other way. If someone is going to make Pisces cry, he just cries. For Libra, emotions are obstacles to be avoided. He seeks tenderness as an escape from harshness. For Pisces, emotions are the meat of life. He seeks tenderness for its own sake. Though Pisces is very self-protective, he is not motivated by fear to the extent that Libra is.

Another difference is that Libra wants to define the relationship. Even if legal marriage is not possible for gay men, Libra wants some sort of understanding of what lovers owe each other. Pisces does not want any part of this. He likes to keep relationships as fluid as possible.

The Libra-Pisces couple will find their attraction to each other a flickering one—sometimes burning bright and other times shrinking to a tiny glow. The eroticism they share is a dithering one. Rather than beginning with foreplay then moving into action focused on orgasm, their lovemaking makes detours. Foreplay can come in the middle, role-play can interrupt at any time—Oops! Forgot all about coming. Each man is so sensitive to the moment-to-moment response of his partner that the larger arc of the experience gets lost.

Libra and Pisces want to give to each other and would

want to even if they were just friends. They will work tire-
lessly on one another's behalf and offer any resources that
they have. Unfortunately what they are able to give is not
always what is needed. However, if Libra and Pisces each
looks closely at his lover, rather than make assumptions about
what he is like, they will be able to give genuine service.

This pairing only works if both Libra and Pisces are
highly motivated to make it work. Unfortunately, their partnership has an erratic energy level which makes sustained
effort difficult. A heavier burden of responsibility for keeping it going falls on Libra's shoulders at first, but as the relationship continues the burden will become more equal.

SCORPIO ☆ SCORPIO

No one gets under a Scorpio's skin like another Scorpio.

These boys were wary of each other at first—and with
good reason. It is true that Scorpios like a challenge, but not
this much of a challenge. Though equal partnership may be
most people's ideal for a relationship, Scorpio likes to be just
a little bit more than equal to his lover.

Others consider it an advantage to have a lover of the
same sign, who will bring an extra understanding and sympathy to the relationship. Not Scorpio. He does not want to
be understood and does not need sympathy.

The only advantage he sees in having a same-sign lover is that another Scorpio would be one of the few men to have the emotional stamina to love with the intensity that he wants.

Of course, certain ground rules need to be established. No Scorpio will get into a relationship where another man will have power over him. There needs to be a tacit truce before the first date—though this truce may be canceled at any moment.

Between Scorpios there is an understanding, a kind of professional courtesy, or in this case an astrological courtesy. The underhanded power games they play with other signs will not be part of this relationship. Here it is aboveboard power games only. Often men feel that Scorpio speaks in a secret code not understandable by ordinary mortals, which is basically true. Another Scorpio will have the ability to unscramble the encryption.

Scorpio is more giving with another man of the same sign. Money and forgiveness, two things Scorpio does not part with lightly, will be available to both partners in this pairing.

Sex with another Scorpio is an expression of whatever emotion is going on in the relationship. It can be sweet or bitter, tender or angry. At times it might feel like an erotic competition to see who can take the experience to the next level. Both men see sexuality as central to the partnership, even when they are not having sex so often. (Yes, even a Scorpio-Scorpio couple will have dry spells.) Sex is sacred for this couple. Usually they will choose strict monogamy and keep what they do private. If they go for kink, it will probably be domination-submission scenarios and not dress-up or fetish.

Jealousy might cause conflict at any stage of this relationship. When a Scorpio wants a man, he wants him for himself alone. Double the Scorpios and you double the jealousy. Even when he has no real suspicion, Scorpio might pretend to go into a possessive rage just to keep things interesting.

As if things were not interesting enough.

Emotions run high in this pairing. The Scorpios love their shared intensity, while they hate the claustrophobia of being with a man from whom they have no secrets. Add to this their delightful talent for needling lovers just where they are most sensitive. So pressure builds to the point that home life (if the boys move in together) has the overheated feel of a trashy soap opera, though with the surface restraint of an Ingmar Bergman film.

It can be quite a bitch's brew at times, yet neither man is likely to go screaming into the night. Though they are closet romantics, Scorpio men are also wise about how emotions operate. They understand that no love is perfect and that all relationships hit rough spots. This couple will honor the commitment made to each other and will not just toss away their life together—without a VERY powerful reason.

SCORPIO ☆ SAGITTARIUS

At last! Scorpio meets someone who can give him an effective stickectomy (i.e., the removal of that pole up his butt). Of course, Scorpio will try to hang on to that stick with all the strength his buns possess. That is his nature. And Sagittarius enjoys the challenge. That is his.

Sagittarius is sunnier than a Shirley Temple movie. He goes through life expecting the best and trusting everyone. Scorpio on the other hand is as suspicious as film noir. He can guess where the bodies are hidden, because he knows that the world stinks and no one is innocent.

These boys share a love of danger. They like to drive themselves to the brink, thinking that in extremis they reveal to themselves who they really are. And both of them want to know.

In fact, they want to know everything. The word "curiosity" is not strong enough to describe Scorpio and Sagittarius's shared hunger to ferret out the answers to life questions. Both men know that there is more to the universe than what we see. However, their searches take them in opposite directions. Sagittarius looks to the external world and to a higher power. Scorpio looks within himself.

Because these men are oriented differently (Scorpio inward, Sagittarius outward), some friction is inevitable. For Scorpio the things that are precious are the things that are private. For Sagittarius the things that are precious are the things he shares with the entire world. Thus Sagittarius feels compelled to tell everyone what he loves about Scorpio, including the cute little potbelly, the funny face he makes during orgasm, and his silly habit of alphabetizing the spice rack. Scorpio considers such talk to be a betrayal of their love.

Being a freedom loving kind of guy, Sagittarius is horrified by the rules and restrictions Scorpio places on him in an attempt to preserve privacy. This combination unites a man who cannot live by another's rules with a man who seeks control over his lover. Unfortunately for both men, the very traits they find so frustrating are the same ones that are so fascinating.

What saves their partnership from becoming a checkmate is honesty. Scorpio can recognize the truth and Sagittarius can speak it. That is enough to heal all wounds. There will still be game-playing—Scorpio goes silent or acts out dramas of revenge while Sagittarius shows off how tough he is. But the bottom line is that neither man is afraid to acknowledge what is really happening between them at any given time.

One of the benefits of honesty is a fantastic sex life. There is no need for fantasy or role-play or any kind of pretending—though they might enjoy it on occasion—because these men act from a sincere passion. Nothing is fake. Sagittarius might complain that they do not make love often enough, but he will admit that when they do, it is well worth the wait. Sagittarius releases a pure physical joy that Scorpio has kept locked up, while Scorpio brings an emotional joy to Sagittarius, which he had not suspected was possible.

If these men decide to live together (or rather when Sagittarius gives in to Scorpio's requests that they live together), they will start using money as a weapon against each other to play out the freedom vs. control theme that has been the soundtrack of this relationship since Day One. Sagittarius will overspend and Scorpio will tighten the purse strings. But the battle is less vehement than it was because the stickectomy is almost complete. Scorpio has loosened up a little and in the process Sagittarius has grown up some.

SCORPIO ☆ CAPRICORN

They are not lovers—they are coconspirators.

Neither Scorpio nor Capricorn communicates easily, except with each other. As partners in crime they have to trust each other and be forthcoming—their safety depends on it.

The trust between these two notoriously suspicious signs was there at the start. With delicate hesitancy they chatted about nothing important while mentally undressing each other. They each knew what the other was thinking. In fact, each knew that the other knew what he was thinking. But in spite of this, no one did anything embarrassing or untoward—that was the basis for the trust. (Scorpio and Capricorn hate messy public displays of spontaneous feeling.)

Besides their raw physical attraction (which would never be enough for them), intensely ambitious Scorpio and Capricorn are drawn together by that fire in their bellies. These are men who want to matter. Early on they recognize that as a team they can better claw their way up, and they will encourage each other to take focused, ruthless action to do so.

Scorpio and Capricorn are control freaks, but somehow they join together in a spirit of cooperation. These men rarely shy away from conflict if it means the chance of coming out on top, but with each other they try to keep the peace—better to hang together than to hang separately. They communicate well but know when to shut up. Capricorn will not pry into things that Scorpio wants to keep buried. Scorpio *will* unearth Capricorn's secrets, but never shame him by letting him know that he has. Even money, which causes misery to so many couples, will not do so here. These lovers are both stingy, and they appreciate stinginess in others.

When Scorpio and Capricorn do argue, they can make the most cutting, mean-spirited comments to each other in the calmest of tones. Not nice, but at least they are talking. When their rage at each other is at its most intense, they go silent. They do not even acknowledge their lover's existence. This anger is a cold one that can chill the hottest day to a subarctic temperature.

Fortunately their bed play is as hot as their fights are cold. Though neither Scorpio nor Capricorn would choose a mate on sexual chemistry alone, without some major ya-yas between them, there can be no relationship. Maybe they do act repressed most of the time—yet behind closed doors the boys are intergalactic mega-sluts with voracious, insatiable appetites. High-gear eroticism is a powerful emotional outlet for both men, and each is determined to make the most of it. The seriousness that can spoil the fun on dates makes sex more meaningful and satisfying.

Ultimately both lovers want a commitment. They cannot do halfhearted or casual relationships over a long period of time. Being so cynical and pessimistic, Scorpio and Capricorn do not expect a perfect romance to happen by itself. They know that they have to work hard to build a worthwhile relationship, and they recognize that there are many factors that pose a danger to love. If anxiety about these dangers overtakes desire, either one of these lovers might choose to isolate himself rather than risk a broken heart.

However, if Scorpio and Capricorn want true love, loyalty, and a strong life partner, they can find them within each other.

Advice to Scorpio: He may not be as sensitive as you might like, but at least he is for real. It is time you hooked up with a lover who has more respect for you than fear of you.

Advice to Capricorn: Yes, he is too intrusive. And petty. And demanding. But since you can see through his manipulation, what harm is there in all that?

SCORPIO ☆ AQUARIUS

This is a nervous romance.

Two men, with little in common other than a mile-wide streak of stubbornness and an inability to color inside the lines, come together to frighten the bejesus out of each other between sudden, uncontrollable attacks of sexual passion.

If that isn't love . . .

The attraction between Scorpio and Aquarius is a strong one, though they probably wish it was not. This is one hot couple with hot issues because they see everything from opposite points of view.

Aquarius has trouble acknowledging his dark side, while Scorpio acknowledges nothing but. Aquarius feels that he is being propelled into the future; Scorpio feels that he is being exiled from the past. Aquarius considers personal relationships trivial compared to the fate of mankind. Scorpio (you guessed it) thinks the fate of mankind is unimportant without strong personal relationships between individuals to make it worthwhile.

None of this would be a stumbling block if these two boys could take maybe thirty seconds a day to try looking at things from their lover's point of view.

That, however, would be more compromise than they could handle.

Thus there is an edge of friction running through this pairing that gives it a tense energy. It is always exciting, but not always pleasant.

Mutual attraction without mutual understanding at the start means that this is a learning relationship. Much of what drives the partnership forward and builds commitment is a curiosity about each other. Scorpio and Aquarius stick around so as not to miss another exciting episode.

Though he may have a good number of secrets himself, Aquarius demands that his lover tell him all. As if Scorpio would. Scorpio, on the other hand, is too shrewd to directly ask Aquarius to spill his beans. Instead, Scorpio plays amateur private eye and launches a covert investigation.

Aquarius may feel smothered by the constant barrage of emotional stimulation he gets from Scorpio. Alone time is necessary for Mr. Waterboy's mental health, though it can be misunderstood by Mr. Scorpion as stemming from a lack of love. This is not a problem since he interprets most of Aquarius's actions as stemming from a lack of love.

The clash of desires makes for a sexually explosive combination. Often there are fireworks, but sometimes there are duds. The passion is spontaneous, so they just cannot predict where their lovemaking will go. Aquarius lends a cool hand and edgy imagination to Scorpio's deeply felt, slow-burning erotic style. Aquarius appreciates Scorpio's enthusiasm for the new positions and techniques he introduces, while Scorpio is thrilled by the new emotions that these experiences bring up.

If this couple decides to live together, they should look for a new place rather than just going into an apartment one of them already has. Turf is sure to become an issue, so it is best to start out in a neutral space. Once they have spent a week together, each of them will have a list of annoyances with the other. The good news is that there will not be anything new to add to the list ever. The bad news is that the annoyances on the list now will never decrease—they will all be there as long as these two are together.

It is not all bad, though. When Scorpio and Aquarius move in together, they gain appreciation for each other's talents. Aquarius will proclaim from the rooftop how grateful he is for Scorpio's gift for finding lost keys. And Scorpio will tell all his friends that he could never hook up his computer or program the VCR without Aquarius's help.

What they will not tell anyone is how much more interesting and sometimes even fun life is because this man is around. What they will not tell anyone is how much love they share.

SCORPIO ☆ PISCES

They are looking to find *somewhere*—as in "Somewhere a place for us" or "Somewhere over the rainbow." The Scorpio-Pisces couple knows it exists since they have seen it in their imagination.

You see, these boys get confused. It is hard for them to tell the difference between what is real and what they want to be real. Some would call that faith and others foolishness. The fantasies Scorpio and Pisces share have more meaning to them than the mundane realities they face in the street.

Both men are used to being misunderstood by boyfriends who cannot get into their head. But in this combination each has a boyfriend who can. From their first meeting, Scorpio and Pisces have been on the same telepathic wavelength. Each knows what the other is thinking and feeling. Each almost seems to know what it is like to be the other.

When the communication is deepest, the pair is completely quiet. If you have the uncanny connection that Scorpio has with Pisces, you start to trust silence more than words. Spoken conversation is not just unnecessary, it is a distraction from something far more intriguing.

Drugs and alcohol give the Scorpio-Pisces couple easy access to the *somewhere* they seek. Either man might be susceptible to abuse on his own, but when you put them together, then add in the availability of substances in the gay world, the temptation is huge. The two men might support each other reaching for a high or in maintaining sobriety. Either way they will do it as a couple and not alone.

Though united in so many ways, Scorpio and Pisces have different coping styles. Scorpio is strong. He is the white-knuckle king and likes to stand alone. Pisces might be strong, though he avoids threats before he ever has to use his strength. He prefers evasion to confrontation. At first, both men are mystified how the other can get by coping in the manner that he does. Eventually, both men start imitating each other's tactics, Scorpio to a limited extent, Pisces more wholeheartedly.

The Scorpio-Pisces couple fights through implication. Using indirect and passive-aggressive means, they jab at each other's weaknesses (which they discover using their telepathic sense). The pain they cause is no less sharp because it was inflicted in a subtle or underhanded way. ("Ooooops! Pardon me, I really did not mean to drop that dagger through your heart.")

The same accurate intuition that allows the Scorpio-Pisces couple to hurt each other effectively also allows them to love each other effectively. They know what hurts, they know what gives pleasure. The stimulation they want from sex is emotional as much as it is physical. Scorpio and Pisces have few inhibitions and no preconceptions, so their love-making is both wild and tender, raw and meaningful.

In spite of the profound insight these signs have into each other, there will always be pockets of distrust. Usually, the distrust centers around Pisces' inability to stick to a plan and Scorpio's need to dictate the terms of the relationship. It comes out when Pisces goes off budget, forgets to clean the oven, or forgets a promise. It also comes out when Scorpio talks down to Pisces, goes behind his back, or withholds information. It is hard to resolve trust issues since this pair does not talk much about significant matters. The explicit reassurance that needs to be given may not be. Instead, Scorpio and Pisces send waves of affection and concern to each other, which feels nice but heals nothing.

Still, this couple is emotionally in synch, which gives the relationship a resilience. If they want to stay together and are willing to talk more, there is no issue they cannot work through.

SAGITTARIUS ☆ SAGITTARIUS

What do you expect to happen when one walking hard-on meets another? The Sagittarius motto: Fuck first, think later.

Someone more cynical might think that the Sagittarian belief in love at first sight is merely a tactic to alleviate the guilt of casual sex. (And it is a bit much when Sagittarius claims to have found love at first sight four times in one weekend.) Yet when Sagittarius falls in love with another Sagittarius, in every case it truly is at first sight.

In one night these men can move from being total strangers to timid suitors to passionate lovers to regretful exes. The difficulty they face is pacing themselves. It is like running downhill—the trick is to make yourself move at a moderate pace when momentum wants to speed you out of control.

Words fly out of their mouths when they are with each other. They also fly in one ear and out the other. Fighting is fast and furious, ending as abruptly as it started. And there are no lingering resentments after. The battle may be bitter, with name calling, accusations, and gratuitous physical intimidation. But at the end, the Sagittarian talent for forgiveness comes to the fore. There is no need for either man to apologize—absolution will come anyway. Then the make-up sex.

Like the fighting, Sagittarius-on-Sagittarius sex sparks up out of nowhere, rages with a pounding fury, then ends in a mess that is easily cleaned up.

But it is more fun than fighting.

Each man will spur the other on to push his body to its erotic limits, because both understand that sexual love should transcend the physical by surpassing it. So if one of them gave his lover two orgasms yesterday, he will want to give at least four today—with more cum. Too much is never enough for the Sagittarius-Sagittarius couple.

Of course by going for the ultimate, these boys may miss out on the smaller joys of intimacy. They need to remind each other that sex is not about setting records.

Every interaction between these two plays like grand opera. They date in loud voices, they have sex screaming, and they argue like banshees. It is hard for them to hold back anything they feel. In fact, it is hard for them not to exaggerate everything they feel.

Kindness and generosity toward each other will be easy for these two men. Respect and restraint toward each other will be harder, but much more important. Just because fights are quickly resolved does not mean one should go on picking them. Too often self-righteousness can lead one Sagittarius to belittle another unnecessarily.

No man can be right all the time. But Sagittarius would like to be. Both of them would like to be. This means that each half of this partnership is a constant reminder to the other that he is sometimes wrong. If they can get past that, the rest of the relationship should be smooth sailing.

Moving in together is a big step for these men—and not only because they are too disorganized to move efficiently. After a lifetime of playing Lone Ranger, neither wants to admit how much he needs Tonto. Chances are they will try to deny that they are making a commitment and rationalize that they are just trying to cut expenses by becoming roommates.

However, their friends know the truth. The two Mr. Horseymans cannot share every private detail about their love with the entire world, then expect us to be taken in by such a transparent falsehood.

That is one thing to be said about a Sagittarius man—he is a terrible liar. And the two of them together are even worse at it.

SAGITTARIUS ☆ CAPRICORN

Capricorn sets the rules for Sagittarius to ignore.

Mr. Horseyman is happy, because if there were no rules to flout, he would have nothing to do all day.

Mr. Goat is happy, because he gets to roll his eyes, which is his favorite form of exercise.

The biggest challenge they face is to take each other seriously.

The first thing they noticed about each other was how differently they use their bodies. When Capricorn saw Sagittarius darting around, he was drawn to his speed and energy. Even when he is standing still, Sagittarius seems ready to spring into action at a moment's notice. For Sagittarius, it was the solid power and self-containment of Capricorn that drew his eye. Here was a man sensual enough to luxuriate in the moment rather than sprint through it.

Needless to say, this had implications when they finally made love a few hours later. Sagittarius pops wood first, but his partner's eroticism will make its deeper impact felt later. The languor of Capricorn sexuality as well as his just plain delight in Sagittarius's body transform Mr. Horseyman's erotic style. Though a passionate lover, he has often felt that his physical expression did not live up to the emotions he had inside. Sex became rushed. But now, Capricorn gives him confidence, so he can stop and smell the jockstraps. In return he dares Capricorn to imagine greater pleasures— then to let himself experience them.

If they decide to form a relationship, the differences between these two men need to be considered. Sagittarius sees the glass as half-full and Capricorn asks why he did not throw it in the dishwasher. Footloose Sagittarius thinks that surefooted Capricorn is too careful. Mr. Goat moves so slowly that to his lover he looks stuck. Capricorn finds Sagittarius too scattered, unfocused, and immature. Though he admires the tireless energy of Mr. Horseyman, he feels it is wasted, since there is no payoff. Capricorn wants answers, but Sagittarius keeps opening up more questions.

Humor can form the bridge between them. So, though they need to learn to take each other seriously, dates that make them laugh, such as going to the latest Hollywood comedy or playing miniature golf, are better than gallery openings or classical concerts.

From the outside, the dynamic of this couple is not always clear. It might seem as if Sagittarius is the boss, ordering his lover around. In truth, Capricorn wears the pants because he thinks of them as a couple. For Sagittarius, even after he has made a commitment and blown his savings on a too-ostentatious gay wedding, they will always be two individuals joined together, and *not* a couple. Thus he can only make plans for himself (and not for himself and Capricorn).

Paradoxically, Mr. Relationship (Capricorn) is less inclined to combine finances than Mr. Individualism (Sagittarius). Sagittarius does not gain any respect from Capricorn for this generosity, because Capricorn thinks it is another example of his lover's carelessness.

Their attitudes about money reflect a deeper difference between them. For Sagittarius, we live in a world of plenty with enough money, food, and love for everyone. Capricorn believes this is a world of scarcity. Give up too much and you will be left with nothing.

The differences between Sagittarius and Capricorn make for a manic-depressive household, should they move in together. But they ought to consider it, since they give each other a healing balance—if neither maims the other one first. When they learn how to bring to the relationship the same enjoyment of differences that they have when they make love, they will have a relationship that gives them all the security and all the freedom they could ever want.

SAGITTARIUS ☆ AQUARIUS

They treat each other with such tolerance and respect you would think they were already exes.

Valuing freedom themselves, both Sagittarius and Aquarius give their lovers plenty of space. Neither thinks it is right to place restrictions on someone he cares about. (That does not mean that neither will—it just means that they will feel bad about it.)

The Sagittarius-Aquarius relationship can feel like a ménage à trois, with the general public as the third party. These boys met in public, like to date at big community events, and involve their friends in all the intimate details of their love that might better be kept private. It is hard not to gossip about them when they do all their fighting and making up right in front of you.

With all the freedom this couple gives each other, what could they have to fight about? In spite of many similarities, each has personality traits that misalign with his partner: Sagittarius finds Aquarius too cold and inflexible; Aquarius finds Sagittarius too unstable and histrionic. The arguments will arise when Aquarius is unresponsive or when Sagittarius is impulsive.

Strangely, though, the brutal tactlessness of Sagittarius does not bother Aquarius much. It is not that he is thick-skinned, but rather fair-minded enough to accept the comments as data to be evaluated. However, when Sagittarius accuses his boyfriend of lying—even if it is true—Aquarius flies into a rage. Honesty is such an important ideal for him that he cannot come anywhere close to objectivity on it.

Rages might also arise when Aquarius gives unwelcome advice, or when Sagittarius demands his lover's attention.

Even when one of them loses his temper completely, there are no obvious consequences—or so they think. This is supposed to be the Teflon Relationship—strong, durable, and nothing sticks. No bitterness. No resentment. Just bury the issue and move on.

Until it pops up again in a different form.

Sagittarius and Aquarius are willing to glide along without the self-examination necessary to resolve their core issues. As long as they are there for all the openings and get invited to all the new parties, they think they are having a successful relationship. When they become willing to turn the brilliant powers of analysis (which they use in looking at everyone else) back onto themselves, then the partnership can become as strong in reality as it is in their imagination.

Fortunately, the Sagittarius-Aquarius couple can discuss anything. Also, their friends are a valuable resource, providing a reality check on their issues.

Their shared sexuality is based on breaking taboos. The boys dare each other to show how far he is willing to go, and each is willing to try anything once—but only once. Their motto is: If we did it before, it is done. They get wind of every erotic fad that comes out of New York or San Francisco months ahead of other gay couples. To other men, their forays into the sexual smorgasbord sounds delish, but to Sagittarius and especially Aquarius, the constant restless search for new thrills can be exhausting if it is an escape from true intimacy, which it often is for this couple.

Physical intimacy is easy. Emotional intimacy is harder. The pillow talk after sex is where Sagittarius and Aquarius are most willing to open up to each other. If they use that time well, they can get off the erotic merry-go-round and start building a life together.

SAGITTARIUS ☆ PISCES

Risk.

Few men understand the concept. Sagittarius and Pisces do. They are constantly attaching their hopes to one solitary, unstable, unlikely chance. Even though most of their risks fail, a few succeed spectacularly, so overall they come out ahead.

Not that they care. They just love the roller-coaster ride of expectation. They are hope junkies.

Both men are willing to hazard everything because they believe in destiny. For Sagittarius it is the belief that life has a plan for him and is just waiting for him to seize an opportunity. For Pisces it is the idea that none of his actions will have any effect on the final outcome.

The love they share is a risk. It makes no sense. From their first dates the differences between them are glaring. Sagittarius is an active optimist, Pisces a lazy pessimist. Sagittarius tries always to tell the truth, Pisces tries never to.

The personal style of Sagittarius is loud and rough, that of Pisces is reticent and refined.

However, Sagittarius and Pisces are willing to go against common sense (because neither has much) trying to make this relationship work.

And sometimes they succeed.

The main advantage they have is that they balance each other's energy level. Sagittarius is like an amphetamine to Pisces, who is like a tranquilizer to him. They also look at situations with greater objectivity when they are together.

Each man is extremely responsive and adaptable, which can weaken the core of their relationship. Unless one or both has something in his life that gives him stability, this pair could drift aimlessly, reacting to what destiny throws them but never taking charge of where the relationship is going. In such a case, Sagittarius and Pisces will change enough to convince themselves that they are helping each other grow. But these changes will lack the direction of true growth.

It is possible for Sagittarius and Pisces to benefit from this relationship. Both men are spiritual seekers, though each follows his own path apart from any organized religion. If they unite their individual quests into one, this can result in stability and a genuine progress toward enlightenment for each of them.

Now to move from the sacred to the profane.

When a Sagittarius and a Pisces make love, they are bold, bad, and beautiful. They have no restraint and no inhibitions. At times this couple treats sex as an endurance test, but that is only because neither can find a way to bring the event to a close. Sagittarius tends to initiate and Pisces to respond—but if Mr. Horseyman wants Mr. Fish to take the lead, he will. In fact, with Sagittarius, Pisces will do anything that is asked of him. But when Sagittarius has no particular erotic agenda, the session could end up without a satisfying climax.

The deference Pisces shows in bed could carry over into daily life, which might spell the end of the relationship—depending on how his lover responds. If Sagittarius uses Pisces' submission as a cue for self-aggrandizement and starts taking advantage (which does often happen), then Mr. Fish will withdraw, come up with an escape plan, and hit the road. The ego of Sagittarius and the self-pity of Pisces are their Achilles' heels. Each weakness plays into and exacerbates the other.

Either partner might use these weaknesses to sabotage the relationship because he is ambivalent about committing to his lover. If, however, they are both willing to take the risk of commitment, things still might not work out—or then again they just might.

These boys' risks do pay off often enough for it to be worth taking a shot.

CAPRICORN ☆ CAPRICORN

Sometimes it feels like there are no grown-ups in the gay community. Go to any gay bar and you will find no one there other than a mixed bag of whiny and giddy babies, who probably do not vote, cannot balance a checkbook, and forget to call home on Mother's Day.

Or that is how it looks to Capricorn.

Sure, he may put on a frivolous persona to fit in with his gay brethren, but when one Capricorn falls for another they both sober up. They play courtship like it was chess. They do not rush into dating with the headlong passion of adolescents. This is a mature attraction—sure, each might want to rip the other's clothes off with his teeth, but they will act with calm deliberation, waiting patiently for that moment when defenses come down. Then—*whoosh!*—no sign moves faster.

After they become a couple, these two men see little point in maintaining much of a social life. However, neither will curtail his involvement with work or family, which might also cut into boyfriend time. Capricorn will not criticize Capricorn for this neglect, since he feels it is a positive trait.

If the two Mr. Goats get serious, they will crave recognition for their union from their families and from the world at large. Yet they dislike causing uncomfortable scenes, so if they are not already well out of the closet, it will be hard for them to press for recognition. However, they will never feel legitimate until Grandpa invites them both to visit, and the boss invites them both to the office Christmas party.

Living with a lover is an important goal for both of them, so they will make it happen as soon as possible. The security of sharing a home moves their love to the next level. The only danger is that once a Capricorn has his lover at home, he sometimes takes him for granted. The situation is even worse when you have two Capricorns doing it.

Neither can take the other for granted in bed. There, all the Capricorn possessiveness comes out. Each man wants to physically have his way with the other, so they jockey for position and greatly enjoy doing so. The two Capricorns are passionate though conservative—except for a taste for nasty kink. They like their lovemaking to alternate between the cruel and the cuddly.

Outside of kink eroticism, these boys show nothing but respect and consideration for each other. They can trust each other to keep conflicts and anguish private. The unfortunate part of this is that for the sake of keeping up a good front, they prevent each other from seeking help and support. Some secrets cannot heal until they are shared, in spite of what Capricorn thinks.

When two Capricorns hole up together and isolate themselves, they feed each other's dark side. Resentment, fear, and anxiety dominate their home. Because neither has the emotional resources to pull his lover out of depression, connection to family, friends, and the community is essential, though it goes against their nature to seek the help of others in facing emotional crises.

Capricorns measure the success of a relationship by its longevity. And there is longevity in this relationship. Over time, the Capricorn-Capricorn couple drops its pretensions and learns to have fun. They tend to think that anything worthwhile takes work. Which may be true. But after a while the momentum of this relationship does the work for them. Then Capricorn can lie back and bask in the love of Capricorn as both laugh at all the crazy, childish nonsense surrounding them.

CAPRICORN ☆ AQUARIUS

Capricorn often wonders if it is better to have a solid, dependable boyfriend, or one who is loony tunes but exciting.

He never expects to find the two possibilities in one man, until he meets Aquarius. This boy is organized and lives according to principle, but might at any moment pack up a U-Haul and move to British Columbia. He is sure about everything, except for his direction in life. The 180-degree turns that Aquarius takes seem impossibly brave and unspeakably foolish (a *trés* sexy combination) to Capricorn, who would never deviate from his set course.

Aquarius is drawn to Capricorn's cynicism. The single-mindedness of the sign also fascinates Aquarius, who cannot keep a single thought going for more than a minute.

Their mating dance is done in public since both men are fixated on what others think. However, Capricorn wants to maintain a composed public face, while Aquarius wants to astonish and delight. Mr. Goat's attempts at fitting in or winning admiration will be continually thwarted by Mr. Waterboy's outrageous antics.

Capricorn feels like he is dating Kramer from *Seinfeld*. He enters the relationship hoping that he can change Aquarius. The lectures on when it is acceptable to wear shorts, the money management tutorials, and the introductions to a better sort of people are part of an ongoing campaign doomed to failure. Aquarius will never fit neatly into Capricorn's world.

Aquarius also wants to change Capricorn, but he is more successful. He uses guerrilla tactics to shake Mr. Goat's judgmental attitudes. Surprise visits to Capricorn's home with riffraff, spontaneous agitprop at family gatherings, and nonchalant guilt trips do the trick.

At times their relationship seems oddly at arm's length. Neither man thinks of himself as passionate, so emotional displays are embarrassing. Aquarius especially is afraid to obligate himself by showing his feelings. His attitude is that though he might love Capricorn today, there is no guarantee that he will tomorrow—so by keeping quiet he spares his lover disappointment in case things do not work out. Capricorn is accepting of this reticence, feeling no resentment for it, as long as Aquarius treats him with respect.

Capricorn is more sexual than Aquarius, but Aquarius has a freer imagination. Capricorn can teach Aquarius about the possibilities of his own body, while Aquarius teaches Capricorn how to use sex to transcend the limits of the body. Mr. Goat would better appreciate the experience if Mr. Waterboy would talk less and fuck more, but for this couple sex is just one aspect of the relationship—and not the whole enchilada. They see any erotic incompatibility as a fixable problem, not an insoluble impasse. For added fun, the boys go for toys. Any play that includes props raises the heat— but be careful with the stun gun.

Coming out as a couple is difficult for Capricorn and Aquarius. For Capricorn the issue is tied to family concerns, while for Aquarius it is about something more abstract. However, when they are together, they feed a paranoia in each other, portraying themselves as the gay couple under attack. This role does not always represent the reality of their situation.

If he ever actually commits, Aquarius is glad to have Capricorn act out Aquarius's dark side. The materialism and the suspicion that he hates to admit to are openly displayed by Capricorn. He in turn becomes the outlet for the rebellious spirit that periodically rises up in Capricorn.

And is that not what a couple should be? Two persons expressing parts of themselves that neither can express on his own.

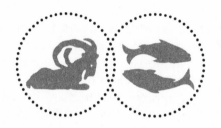

CAPRICORN ☆ PISCES

The best boyfriend is one you do not have to talk to.

Capricorn and Pisces talk to each other more than they do most men—not because they *have to* but because they *want to.*

It is remarkable how much these two are in tune with each other's needs and can fulfill them without being asked. It is lucky since a direct statement of what he wants is impossible for either. Capricorn and Pisces hesitate to ask for anything unless they are sure the answer will be yes.

They prefer to hint at their interest in dating or to joke about it, so that they can back out if it looks like a rejection is coming. Since they do enjoy talking with each other they do not want to louse up the possibility of friendship if sexual interest is not reciprocated.

Even after they form a relationship, Capricorn and Pisces will avoid any aggression toward each other. Just as they hung back instead of making their sexual attraction known, they will hang back rather than make their anger known. This couple fights rarely. Their conflict comes out in little actions—Pisces loses a gift Capricorn gave him, Capricorn stays at work so long that he misses a date. It is like a chess game, civilized on the surface but bloody beneath. Nothing is spoken yet everything is communicated.

The conflicts are surprisingly few anyway, since the two are in agreement on the basic issues. Both Capricorn and Pisces want safety. For Pisces this means emotional stability, and for Capricorn material stability. In practice, the two things are almost the same since Capricorn substitutes the material for the emotional and Pisces substitutes the emotional for the material.

While dating, Capricorn will fear getting sucked into the chaos of procrastination, evasion, and self-destructiveness that he thinks Pisces lives in. Pisces is scared that Capricorn's controlling nature will squeeze all pleasure out of life. Of course the same qualities that so appall the two men also intrigue them. Ambivalence is a powerful fuel for energizing relationships. These two signs are especially aware of how mixed feelings can guarantee a tighter bond than unambiguous ones.

Without a second thought, Capricorn provides Pisces with the protection that he craves, because Capricorn is grateful to have a lover who can read his emotions, even when he is uncomfortable about expressing them openly. A division of labor (Capricorn handling practicalities and Pisces handling emotional concerns) is established early in the relationship. In time the division becomes less strict, though Capricorn will always consider Pisces irresponsible and Pisces will always be aghast at Capricorn's insensitivity.

However, in bed Pisces loves Capricorn's rough edges.

Pisces loves men who know what they want and are uninhibited about getting it. And face it, Capricorn is a pig—he loves sex, loves bodies, loves sweat, loves cum. He has got what it takes to make Pisces feel desired in an animal way. Both men enjoy pampering and being pampered. They can easily spend the whole weekend in bed (except for trips to the phone to order in Chinese).

These men are excellent candidates to become live-in lovers. They both thrive in a secure home setting. There is a danger that they can start to use each other as household conveniences rather than lovers. To circumvent this they need to avoid idle conversation and bring more substance into their talks. Because there has been so much subconscious communication, they have probably neglected the conscious.

After they move in together, they cannot neglect it anymore.

AQUARIUS ☆ AQUARIUS

"I never knew that you liked me in *that* way."

That dim-witted line is usually heard the morning following the first night of the Aquarius-Aquarius couple. Until their throbbing erections are pressed against each other, these guys have no clue as to the sexual undercurrent of their friendship.

Of course, if circumstances had never made this discovery possible, it is not as if these boys would have wasted their lives pining for each other. They are glad that their feelings are reciprocated and the relationship is happening, but the friendship would have been enough.

In fact, the sexualization of it somehow makes them feel dirty.

The sexuality of Aquarius-Aquarius is cool. Encounters happen either after an excruciatingly slow buildup or with an impulsive suddenness. Their taste for experimentation might lead the Aquarius-Aquarius couple toward sex with multiple partners or in public places. The erotic choices they make provide them with greater or lesser pleasure, but they have little impact on the direction of the relationship. Their sex life exists in its own separate little bubble, apart from other aspects of their life.

Though this sign is known for tolerance, it can be downright intolerant to other Aquarians. Each one wants to be the special one, standing apart from the herd. That means you want your boyfriend to be part of the herd, since two men standing apart lack the distinction of one such man.

One of these two lovers will make the sacrifice. He will tone down his own eccentricity to emotionally invest in that of his lover.

In spite of the sacrifice, this will be a difficult relationship to maintain. The wild independence of Aquarius guarantees a lack of agreement on most of this couple's plans. In fairness, they can work out compromises—but neither wants to devote all his energy into fixing a relationship.

Here again, one lover *might* make the sacrifice by making his will subservient to his lover's—but this is a lot harder for him than giving up his eccentricity.

When the two Mr. Waterboys set up a household together, they will find it hard to be confronted by the same face across the bed each morning. Often one of them will get so sick of the other's problems that he switches off. Arguments become ice storms, turning the home into a barren, desolate place. Because each Aquarius thinks of himself as easygoing, all problems become the partner's fault.

To prevent this, the couple needs to come clean about what terms they are willing to commit under—sort of what the straight community would describe as a pre-nup. They can do this without fear of scaring each other off, since every Aquarius knows that no love is truly unconditional. Unless the expectations are made explicit, neither lover can honor them.

The hard part is that this discussion depends on a kind of self-disclosure that Aquarius, with all his openness, finds difficult. These men would be much happier discussing in the abstract what a good relationship should be, rather than getting down to specifics about what they want their particular relationship to be. Still, when they finally can bring themselves to have this conversation, the two Aquarians will be fair and honest with each other.

The relationship that two Aquarius men build might look passionless—but they do not care, since they did not design it to please anyone other than themselves. Even so, this relationship will not live up to their ideals (no relationship could).

Yet the two will stick with it. And they will make it work if at all possible.

They just do not like to think of themselves as quitters.

AQUARIUS ☆ PISCES

When two misunderstood men find each other, the result should be bliss.

It would be, expect they do not understand each other.

Aquarius and Pisces may be mystified by each other's unpredictability, but at least each allows his lover room to be as weird as he wants.

They noticed their differences at first meeting. Pisces revolved around Aquarius like a satellite, following his conversational lead and acting in an accommodating manner. He had to accept Aquarius as a given, since this man was not about to twist himself into knots for the sake of some guy, however cute.

When the electricity started, it was sudden. These men take emotional leaps like a needle skipping on a vinyl record. One moment, they were talking about the weather, the next they skipped directly to the kiss track, passing right over the steady acceleration of desire that usually proceeds a first kiss.

These leaps become a standard part of how this relationship operates. When the leaps move this couple forward into greater intimacy, it is obviously a good thing. However, the leaps can be backward as well. Aquarius will balk at some of Pisces' emotional demands and lower the intensity a few notches. Pisces as well might pull back when he experiences a blast of Aquarian coldness.

The pixilation of the relationship is one reason why these men hesitate to commit to coupledom. Another is that they both hate to make promises. Aquarius also considers Pisces a bad relationship risk after he catches him in a few fibs. Mr. Waterboy can be as self-serving as he wants but will not stand for any smudging of "truth." Pisces, however, feels he has to shade things a bit since he does not have the tools to confront his lover's rigidity head on.

Secrets are an issue here. Pisces has them. Aquarius claims not to. Pisces likes a lover with secrets, since he enjoys probing under the surface. But with Aquarius, what you see is what you get. As an example, the irrational streak in his makeup that Aquarius denies is obvious to even the casual observer. On the other side, Aquarius takes his lover's secrets as a personal affront. Prying is not much better in his view. Even Pisces' delight in gossip and analyzing the actions of friends is offensive to Aquarius.

In the erotic arena, these boys either have it or they do not. And some nights they can go from having it to not and back in the course of a few hours. They might want to ensure greater consistency through the use of drugs, but for these men especially the long-term results are disastrous. What both men seek in sex is transcendence. Aquarius wants to transcend the limits of the body; Pisces wants to transcend by using his body as an emotional instrument. Though it sounds slightly out of synch, their needs can work together—even more smoothly than other aspects of the relationship—as long as Aquarius stops dictating like he was *The Joy of Gay Sex* brought to life.

Should it all work out and these two decide to live together, new concerns will arise. Pisces needs domestic calm and Aquarius needs domestic stimulation. Thus Mr.

Waterboy (consciously or not) might find himself stirring up his lover's pond. His hope is that Mr. Fish can let loose some stimulating chaos for Mr. Waterboy to clean up.

Organized anarchy of this kind works for Aquarius, but makes Pisces more nuts than he usually is. Then he withdraws. And withdraws. And withdraws, until Aquarius notices—which can take a very long time.

These lovers need to abandon their reticence about discussing emotional issues if they want to share their lives. If they do, that will be the first step toward real understanding.

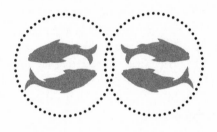

PISCES ☆ PISCES

Even in this age of special edition DVDs, the Pisces-Pisces couple snuggles under the covers to watch the yearly broadcast of *The Wizard of Oz* just like they did as kids. Back then, just like Dorothy, they dreamed of a place over the rainbow.

But unlike Dorothy, these boys do want to live in Kansas.

The Pisces-Pisces couple spends quite a few dates revisiting old escapes with each other—old movies, favorite drinks, clubs they used to frequent. They each recognize that when you see what a man has built his fantasies out of, then you know him thoroughly.

In this relationship, who these men imagine themselves to be inside is more important than what they actually do.

Face it, when a Pisces is involved with another Pisces, they spend a lot of time on the sofa with some beers vegging out. They do nothing. Even working up a good argument is too much bother. The two Mr. Fish could probably muster up some irritability or petty bickering in a pinch. But what these boys do best is get hurt, followed by withdrawal and sleep.

The challenges to one's complacency that are the meat of most relationships are nonexistent. (Unless one of the Pisces decides to pretend he is a Virgo or some other sign. They do that at times.) Instead, they reinforce each other's complacency and laziness.

Yet, like twins, two Pisces will develop their own secret language, untranslatable by ordinary folk. Through this language, they communicate the complex inner dramas they have been carrying around inside since they were born. What makes this relationship special is that nothing needs to be made clear or explained—it all just is.

This couple goes on dates as if they were undercover assignments. It is true that gay men often are timid about broadcasting their relationships to the straight world, but even the two Pisces' brethren are unaware that their relationship is a romantic one.

Though Pisces men are known for lying, they do not do it to each other. Because they cannot. Each knows exactly when the other is spilling an untruth, so why bother?

The erotic imagination of Pisces expands when another Pisces is in the picture. Sexual impulses bounce from one to the other easily because both men really know how to feel desire. The kinks that they are afraid to show with other less sensitive men fill their nights with smooth, fleshy pleasures. Speaking that Pisces-twin language brings fantasy to life when the boys make love.

The only danger is that the fantasy love play can be confused with reality—especially when Pisces-Pisces get rough with each other. They *must* agree on a safe word, since they will protect each other everywhere but in bed.

When these two move in together, they will want to take care of each other. Not smart. Pisces needs a man to kick his butt, not an enabler. If they do fall into the pattern of mutual coddling, shared depression and agoraphobia is certain to follow.

But enabling is one of those things Pisces does best, so this is a tough temptation to resist. Only by engaging more with practicalities, whether as important as paying bills or as trivial as making colorful seasonal floral arrangements, can the Pisces-Pisces live-in couple avoid the slough of despond.

Other lovers present a challenge to Pisces far greater than the one he gets from those sharing the same sign. That means that in this relationship it is up to the individual Pisces to challenge himself.